## Praise for *Building a Web 2.0 Portal with ASP.NET 3.5*

"Omar and his collaborators have applied their awesome talents and a huge amount of time to crafting what might be the most advanced web site yet that's based on ASP.NET and Ajax. In this book, Omar distills everything he's learned from his experience, going in-depth into design goals, architecture, and implementation, including many pitfalls that he teaches you how to avoid. If you're serious about creating a high-performance, modern, Ajax-based ASP.NET web site, *Building a Web 2.0 Portal with ASP.NET 3.5* is for you."

— Mike Pope, Microsoft User Education, Microsoft Corporation

"An outstanding overview of the technologies, techniques, and best practices involved in working with today's most popular web application model. Highly recommended for any web developer who wants to stay relevant."

—Craig Wills, Training Manager, Infusion

# Building a Web 2.0 Portal
# with ASP.NET 3.5

# Other Microsoft .NET resources from O'Reilly

| | | |
|---|---|---|
| **Related titles** | C# 3.0 Cookbook™ | Programming ASP.NET |
| | C# 3.0 Design Patterns | Programming ASP.NET AJAX |
| | C# 3.0 in a Nutshell | Programming C# 3.0 |
| | Learning ASP.NET 2.0 with AJAX | Programming .NET 3.5 |

**.NET Books Resource Center**  *dotnet.oreilly.com* is a complete catalog of O'Reilly's books on .NET and related technologies, including sample chapters and code examples.

*ONDotnet.com* provides independent coverage of fundamental, interoperable, and emerging Microsoft .NET programming and web services technologies.

**Conferences**  O'Reilly brings diverse innovators together to nurture the ideas that spark revolutionary industries. We specialize in documenting the latest tools and systems, translating the innovator's knowledge into useful skills for those in the trenches. Visit *conferences.oreilly.com* for our upcoming events.

Safari Bookshelf (*safari.oreilly.com*) is the premier online reference library for programmers and IT professionals. Conduct searches across more than 1,000 books. Subscribers can zero in on answers to time-critical questions in a matter of seconds. Read the books on your Bookshelf from cover to cover or simply flip to the page you need. Try it today for free.

# Building a Web 2.0 Portal
# with ASP.NET 3.5

*Omar AL Zabir*

O'REILLY®

Beijing · Cambridge · Farnham · Köln · Paris · Sebastopol · Taipei · Tokyo

**Building a Web 2.0 Portal with ASP.NET 3.5**
by Omar AL Zabir

Published by O'Reilly Media, Inc., 1005 Gravenstein Highway North, Sebastopol, CA 95472.

O'Reilly books may be purchased for educational, business, or sales promotional use. Online editions are also available for most titles (*safari.oreilly.com*). For more information, contact our corporate/institutional sales department: (800) 998-9938 or *corporate@oreilly.com*.

**Editor:** John Osborn
**Production Editor:** Laurel R.T. Ruma
**Copyeditor:** Laurel R.T. Ruma
**Proofreader:** Mary Brady

**Indexer:** John Bickelhaupt
**Cover Designer:** Karen Montgomery
**Interior Designer:** David Futato
**Illustrators:** Robert Romano and Lesley Borash

**Printing History:**

December 2007:     First Edition.

 This book uses RepKover™, a durable and flexible lay-flat binding.

ISBN-13: 978-0-596-51050-3

# Table of Contents

# Preface

Web 2.0 Ajax portals are among the most successful web applications of the Web 2.0 generation. iGoogle and Pageflakes are the pioneers in this market and were among the first to show Ajax's potential. Portal sites give users a personal homepage with one-stop access to information and entertainment from all over the Web, as well as dashboards that deliver powerful content aggregation for enterprises. A Web 2.0 portal can be used as a content repository just like a SharePoint or DotNetNuke site. Because they draw on Ajax to deliver rich, client-side interactivity, Web 2.0 portals improve usability and provide faster performance compared to non-Ajax web sites. Also, because portals are commonly composed of widgets (small plug-and-play type applications), there's no limit to how much functionality you can provide, simply by adding more and more widgets. Their use also keeps the core architecture of the portal clean and simple because widgets are developed and maintained independently. DotNetNuke is a great example of a widget-powered portal concept that has created a new era in highly decoupled enterprise web applications.

This book takes a fresh new look at portal solutions using the latest cutting-edge technologies from Microsoft. In developing personal, educational, community, and enterprise portals, I have had to deal with many interesting design, development, scalability, performance, and production challenges. In this book, I have tried to show solutions to some of these challenges by building an open source Web 2.0 Portal prototype, and then walk you through through the design and architectural challenges, advanced Ajax concepts, performance optimization techniques, and server-side scalability challenges involved. The prototype also shows you practical implementation of the cutting-edge *.NET 3.0 and 3.5* frameworks, including *LINQ* and the *Windows Workflow Foundation*. Moreover, it explores Ajax web site details, browser performance and compatibility challenges, security challenges, and *ASP.NET AJAX* framework advantages and shortcomings.

The project is available at *www.dropthings.com*. Dropthings is an open source example of what can be done with the new technologies from Microsoft. It is intended for educational purposes only. Although it does not come close to real web portal (like Pageflakes) in terms of its feature set, performance, security, and scalability, it does a good job of showing you how to put together several new technologies in a working web application.

## Who This Book Is for

This book is primarily for ASP.NET 2.0 or 3.5 developers who have already developed one or more web applications and have a good grip on JavaScript and ASP.NET 2.0. The reader is also expected to have basic understanding of ASP.NET AJAX. This information is available in numerous publications, including several from O'Reilly that are listed in the Roadmap page for this book.

Intermediate developers, looking for ways to gain insight into web development challenges and learn how a successful production web site is built and run, will greatly benefit from this book. Advanced developers will learn how to build a rock solid web application that can withstand millions of hits every day around the clock, survive sudden scalability demands, prevent hack attempts and denial of service attacks, deploy and run a web site on a distributed cluster environment utilizing Content Delivery Networks (CDN), face real-life production challenges, and much more.

## How This Book Is Organized

This book first describes what an Ajax web portal (aka a Web 2.0 portal) is and how it can be useful as a model for personal web sites, corporate intranets, or a mass consumer web application. Then it walks you through the architectural challenges of such an application and provides a step-by-step guide to solving design issues. It explains what a widget is and how widget architecture can create a highly decoupled web application that allows the addition of an infinite number of features to a web site.

It following chapters, you'll find step-by-step guides for developing several components of the web project using ASP.NET 2.0/3.5 and ASP.NET AJAX 1.0, the business layer in Workflow Foundation, and the data access layer using LINQ to SQL. Once the basic foundation is up, it goes deep into difficult challenges like first-time visit performance, browser compatibility and memory leaks, advanced caching techniques, putting too much content and functionality on a single page and so on. It then goes into some real-life Ajax and ASP.NET 2.0/3.5 challenges that I have solved in building high-volume commercial portals.

I have also sprinkled a number of real-life war stories throughout the book that highlight some of the real-life problems I have encountered in building portals like Dropthings. You'll find them, not surprisingly, wherever you encounter the heading, "Real-Life."

Finally, it presents some hard-to-solve scalability and security challenges of Ajax portals and 13 production disasters that are common to web applications that reach millions of users all over the world.

Here's a chapter-by-chapter summary:

Chapter 1, *Introducing Web Portals and Dropthings.com*
Introduces you to the attributes of a web portal and to the applications that you will learn to build throughout the book. Chapter 1 also shows you how ASP.NET AJAX and .NET 3.5 are used in the product.

Chapter 2, *Architecting the Web Portal and Widgets*
Gives you an architectural overview of Dropthings.com. It also explains the widget architecture and how to build highly decoupled web applications using widgets. It touches on some performance and security challenges of Ajax web sites.

Chapter 3, *Building the Web Layer Using ASP.NET AJAX*
Gives a detailed explanation on how the web application is built, starting from the homepage and the widgets. It shows how the drag-and-drop functionality is provided using ASP.NET AJAX 1.0, how a real widget is built, and how ASP.NET 3.5 is used to build the server-side part of the web layer.

Chapter 4, *Building the Data and Business Layers Using .NET 3.5*
Shows how LINQ is used to build the data access later and .NET 3.0 is used to build the business layer by extensively using Workflow Foundation.

Chapter 5, *Building Client-Side Widgets*
Shows how to build widgets using JavaScript for faster performance and better caching. It shows how a content bridge or proxy service is built that allows widgets to fetch content from external sources.

Chapter 6, *Optimizing ASP.NET AJAX*
Goes deep into Ajax-enabled principles for making sites faster, more cache friendly, and scalable. It talks about browser specific challenges and many under-the-hood techniques to get maximum performance out of the Ajax framework.

Chapter 7, *Creating Asynchronous, Transactional, Cache-Friendly Web Services*
Shows you how to build a custom web service call handler for Ajax calls in order to overcome some shortcomings in ASP.NET AJAX 1.0 and enable your web services to become asynchronous, transactional, and more cache-friendly. It also talks about scalability and security challenges of web applications that rely heavily on web services.

Chapter 8, *Improving Server-Side Performance and Scalability*

An ASP.NET 2.0 web application has many scalability and performance surprises as it grows from a hundred-user to a million-user web site. Learn how to solve performance, reliability, and scalability challenges of a high volume web site.

Chapter 9, *Improving Client-Side Performance*

Ajax web sites provide a lot of functionality on the client-side browser that introduces many browser specific challenges and JavaScript performance problems. This chapter provides many tips and tricks for overcoming speed and memory problems on the browser and making the UI load faster and be more responsive.

Chapter 10, *Solving Common Deployment, Hosting, and Production Challenges*

Last step of a web project development is to successfully deploy the product and run it 24x7. Learn what it takes to deploy and run a high volume production web site solving software, hardware, hosting, and internet infrastructure problems that can bring down your web site and cause great harm to your business.

# What You Need to Use this Book

You need Visual Studio 2008 Professional Edition and SQL Server 2005 Developer Edition. You can download the latest source code of the open source project from *www.codeplex.com/dropthings* and set it up locally.

The open source project running at Dropthings will greatly benefit from your contribution. You are welcome to participate in its development by extending the core framework or building new widgets for the project.

# Conventions Used in This Book

The following typographical conventions are used in this book:

Plain text

Indicates menu titles, menu options, menu buttons, and keyboard accelerators (such as Alt and Ctrl).

*Italic*

Indicates new terms, URLs, email addresses, filenames, file extensions, pathnames, directories, and Unix utilities.

Constant width

Indicates commands, options, switches, variables, attributes, keys, functions, types, classes, namespaces, methods, modules, properties, parameters, values, objects, events, event handlers, XML tags, HTML tags, macros, the contents of files, or the output from commands.

**Constant width bold**

Shows commands or other text that should be typed literally by the user.

*Constant width italic*

Shows text that should be replaced with user-supplied values.

 This icon signifies a tip, suggestion, or general note.

 This icon indicates a warning or caution.

# Using Code Examples

This book is here to help you get your job done. In general, you may use the code in this book in your programs and documentation. You do not need to contact us for permission unless you're reproducing a significant portion of the code. For example, writing a program that uses several chunks of code from this book does not require permission. Selling or distributing a CD-ROM of examples from O'Reilly books *does* require permission. Answering a question by citing this book and quoting example code does not require permission. Incorporating a significant amount of example code from this book into your product's documentation *does* require permission.

We appreciate, but do not require, attribution. An attribution usually includes the title, author, publisher, and ISBN. For example: "*Building a Web 2.0 Portal with ASP. NET 3.5*, by Omar AL Zabir. Copyright 2008 Omar AL Zabir, 978-0-596-51050-3."

If you feel your use of code examples falls outside fair use or the permission given above, feel free to contact us at *permissions@oreilly.com*.

# Safari® Books Online

 When you see a Safari® Books Online icon on the cover of your favorite technology book, that means the book is available online through the O'Reilly Network Safari Bookshelf.

Safari offers a solution that's better than e-books. It's a virtual library that lets you easily search thousands of top tech books, cut and paste code samples, download chapters, and find quick answers when you need the most accurate, current information. Try it for free at *http://safari.oreilly.com*.

# How to Contact Us

Please address comments and questions concerning this book to the publisher:

O'Reilly Media, Inc.
1005 Gravenstein Highway North
Sebastopol, CA 95472
800-998-9938 (in the United States or Canada)
707-829-0515 (international or local)
707-829-0104 (fax)

There is a web page for this book, where we list errata, examples, and any additional information. You can access this page at:

*http://www.oreilly.com/catalog/9780596510503*

To comment or ask technical questions about this book, send email to:

*bookquestions@oreilly.com*

For more information about our books, conferences, Resource Centers, and the O'Reilly Network, see our web site at:

*http://www.oreilly.com*

The author of this book and Dropthings project can be reached at:

*omaralzabir@gmail.com*

The code for this book can be found here:

*www.codeplex.com/dropthings*

# Acknowledgments

My deepest respect and appreciation to my parents for their support in writing this book. Special thanks to Mike Pope at Microsoft and Craig Wills at Infusion for their sincere support, ideas, and thorough reviews.

# CHAPTER 1

# Introducing Web Portals and Dropthings.com

In this book, I will show you how to develop an Ajax-enabled Web 2.0-style portal.

The portal is built using ASP.NET 3.5, ASP.NET AJAX, and .NET 3.5, as well as Language-Integrated Query (LINQ) and SQL Server 2005. While building this application, you'll learn about the:

- Design decisions that must be made for and usability issues involved in a Web 2.0 user interface
- Architectural complexities and development challenges of JavaScript-rich, widget-enabled web sites
- Production and maintenance challenges of running a high-volume web application

Ajax web portals are among the most extreme implementations of client-side technologies you'll find on the Web. They not only use large amounts of JavaScript, CSS, and HTML, but also push the Ajax and server-side technologies to their limits for interactivity, performance, and scalability. By the time you finish reading this book, you will be equipped with enough technical know-how to launch a Web 2.0 Internet startup on your own.

The application example, which I have named Dropthings, for reasons that will become clear shortly, is a reduced feature set prototype of a real web portal, like Google's iGoogle or Pageflakes. You will be able to deploy the Dropthings on a production server and run it as your own personal web site, a group site, or even as a corporate intranet. Including drag-and-drop enabled widgets, complete support for personalization, the ability to place widgets on multiple pages, centralized authentication and authorization, and much more.

As you work through this book, you will see how Dropthings is architected and implemented. It's a real, living, breathing, open source web portal that you'll find at *http://www.dropthings.com*. Although the application does not compare to a real web portal in terms of its code quality, feature set, scalability, performance, and other aspects of the product, it works as a good proof of concept for several nascent technologies.

However, you can use it for your current day-to-day personal use, and you are welcome to support continued development of the project by adding more features to it or by making cool new widgets for it.

 The open source project for Dropthings is hosted at *http://www. codeplex.com/dropthings*. Anyone can contribute.

Figure 1-1 shows the Dropthings site, which you will learn how to build in this book.

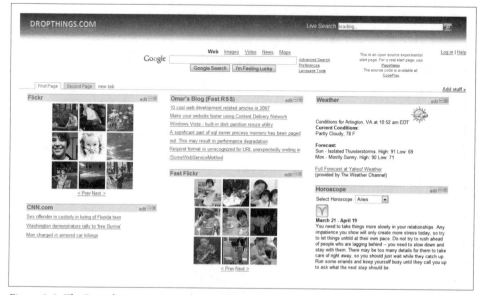

*Figure 1-1. The Dropthings site is a widget-enabled Web 2.0 portal; you'll build one like it using ASP.NET 3.5, ASP.NET AJAX, the .NET Framework 3.5, and SQL Server 2005*

## Defining a Web Portal

A *web portal* is a page that allows a user to customize his homepage by dragging and dropping widgets onto it. This approach gives the user complete control over what content he sees on his home page, where on the page he wants to see it, and how he wants to interact with it.

A *widget* is a discrete piece on a web page that performs a particular function and comes with its own UI and set of features. Examples of widgets include to-do lists, address books, contact lists, RSS feeds, clocks, calendars, playlists, stock tickers, weather reports, traffic reports, dictionaries, games, or almost anything you can imagine that can be packaged up and dropped onto a web page. In a corporate environment, widgets can connect to internal systems; for example, an expense tracker widget can interact directly with the internal accounting system. If you are familiar with the SharePoint Portal, then you already know about widgets, which are called *Web Parts* in SharePoint and ASP.NET 2.0.

Specifically, an Ajax-powered web portal is a web portal that uses Ajax technologies to create richer experiences for its users. It is one step ahead of the previous generation of web portals, including pioneer sites such as MSN or AOL, because it gives you a state-of-the-art UI that behaves more like a Windows client application with widgets, animations, pop ups, client-side data grids, and other effects not usually found on a non-Ajax web portal. Not surprisingly, MSN and AOL have already adopted many of the practices discussed in this book.

Some of the most popular Ajax web portals include iGoogle (*www.google.com/ig*), My Yahoo (*http://my.yahoo.com*), and Pageflakes (*www.pageflakes.com*; see Figure 1-2).

*Figure 1-2. Pageflakes uses widgets to deliver functionality, including local weather, local news, videos, local photos, podcasts, stock portfolio, local events with Google Maps, and more*

A web portal, especially one that is Ajax-powered, gives users a fun way to browse the Internet. Users can add photos, videos, music, podcasts, and video blogs to their Start page. The web portal can also help users become more productive by allowing them to check email, read news, and get weather reports from a single page. They can organize their digital life by putting appointment calendars, to-do-lists, and address books in a central place on the Web. No matter where they happen to be— in the office, home or airport—as long as they can get to the Web, users can access this information directly from their web portal. It's like bringing the whole Internet onto a single page, displayed exactly the way you want it to be. Gone are the days of running after content—now information and entertainment comes to you.

# Defining a Web 2.0 Portal

The term "Web 2.0" defines a set of principles and practices for web applications, which, when followed, entitle a web application to wear the Web 2.0 crown. A web site can claim to be a Web 2.0 site if it:

- Allows users to control data presented on the web site
- Presents a platform that enables the mixing (or *mash-up*) of technologies and data
- Enables services to be consumed that are beyond the boundary of the application
- Harnesses collective intelligence by enabling the following:
  - Aggregation of relevant content from heterogeneous sources
  - User contributed content
  - User moderation of content via tagging and rating
- Uses state-of-the-art technologies that take interactivity on the Web to the next level by use of popular technologies like Ajax, Flash, and Silverlight.

Dropthings, being a web portal, allows a user to control what the user wants to put on the page. The widget architecture allows mashup of technologies in the form of widgets. It exposes web services that external entities can consume. The portal aggregates content from many different sources, such as photos from Flickr, news from CNN, weather reports from Weather.com, and many more. It supports user-submitted content aggregation in the form of RSS feeds. Finally, it pushes inter-activity on the Web to the next level by using Ajax technologies.

# Using a Web Portal

With a web portal, every visitor to your web site will be able to customize and set it up exactly the way they would like to see it the next time they visit. Best of all, the layout is saved per user, so your master layout remains unchanged. Moreover, visitors can add more widgets from a widget catalog and decorate the page as they like.

## How an Ajax-Powered Start Page Is Different

The advantages of Ajax and a rich client-side experience give users a fun and exciting environment to do their regular work. All the functionality is developed as small widgets that perform only a specific job, like showing messages from an Exchange Mail server, assigning tasks from a SharePoint List, or even displaying your expenses from an internal accounting system. Just as with a regular web portal, enterprise users can drag the widgets around and put them anywhere they like. For example, an email inbox can be put on the left, expenses in the middle, and a list of "Phone calls to make" on the right. A key advantage is that these widgets can provide content from different web servers on different platforms, including Linux, Unix, or IBM OS/2 servers. As long as the platform speaks XML and HTTP, any functionality can be provided in the form of a widget. The main framework takes care of authentication, authorization, user profile, communication, and all those cool Ajax effects. As a result, the widgets are a lightweight component with a small amount of code to do exactly what they are supposed to.

An Ajax web portal is also quite useful for group portals or social web sites. For example, say you want to make a .NET developer group portal. You would start with a blank page, add lots of .NET feeds, put a link widget and fill it with useful .NET web site links, add an address book widget and fill in useful contacts, put in a calendar widget to publish events for the group, and so on. With just these basic widgets and some rearranging, you have a dynamic, personalizable developer group portal that is state of the art in both technology and usability.

Enterprise portals especially can benefit from using Ajax web portals. Enterprise portals bring in content from many sources and different platforms. By using an Ajax widget platform, you can make the whole portal in terms of small widgets that connect to different systems and serve content to the page. The benefit of such a platform is that the complexity of the entire portal is dramatically reduced because it's just a generic widget platform.

## Navigating Dropthings

When you first visit Dropthings, which I encourage you to do now, you get a predefined default setup of widgets that you can customize anyway you like. For example, there's a Flickr photo widget, some RSS feeds, and several community contributed widgets for weather, news, and so on (see Figure 1-3).

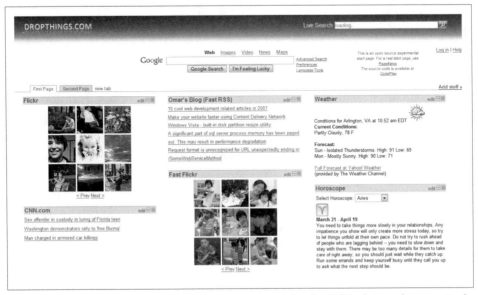

*Figure 1-3. Your initial visit to Dropthings gives you a predefined template that can be customized*

On the Dropthings Start page, you can add widgets, remove widgets that you don't like, and customize individual widgets by clicking on the "edit" link on each title bar. Clicking on the "edit" link brings up the "Settings" area for the widget where you can change its look, feel, and behavior (see Figure 1-4).

Figure 1-4. *The photo widget allows you to change the photo stream by clicking on "edit" link on the title bar of widget*

You can also drag-and-drop widgets from one column to another and reorganize the page as you like. When you come back to the page, your customization is preserved even if you did not sign up. However, when you sign up, your pages are saved permanently and you can access them from anywhere (see Figure 1-5).

It is possible to have more than one tab (page) of widgets. There's already a precreated empty second tab where you can add new widgets. So from there, you can add as many tabs as you like. This helps you keep your tabs clean and light and groups relevant widgets in the same location.

Clicking on the "Add stuff" link on the top right of the web page brings up a pop-up widget gallery that shows the list of available widgets (see Figure 1-6). From the list, you can click anywhere on the widget and have it added to your page. After adding it, you can further customize it by clicking on the "edit" link on the widget's title bar.

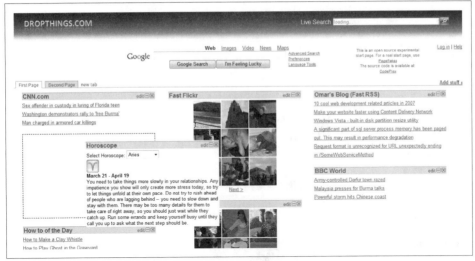

Figure 1-5. You can drag and drop widgets on the page and reorganize the page as you like

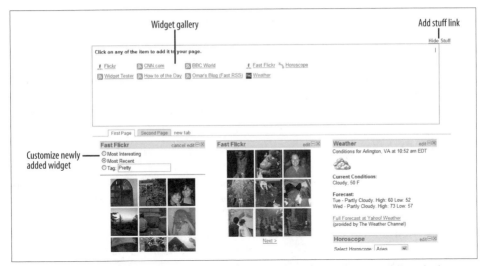

Figure 1-6. Create a "Photo" tab and add a Flickr photo widget to it with Add Stuff; each photo widget shows a specific photo stream from Flickr as defined by the widget's settings

At the top part of the page, there's a bar where you can search the Internet. Search is the most used function on the Web. Therefore, web portals need to have convenient search functionality; otherwise users won't set a web portal as browser homepage. The Live.com search bar on the top provides on-site search functionality where the search results are shown right on the page, which allows the user to perform a search without leaving the web portal (see Figure 1-7).

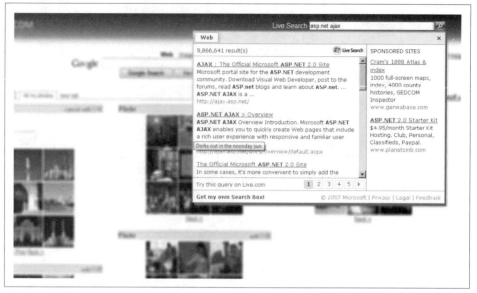

*Figure 1-7. The Live.com search bar provides on-site search functionality*

As you use the site, you will notice there's not a single postback of the page. Operations are performed either via asynchronous postback or via JavaScript calls from the browser. You can add/remove widgets, drag-and-drop widgets, and switch tabs without ever causing a postback or refresh of the page. This is what makes Ajax web portals really convenient and fast to use compared to non-Ajax web portals.

# Using ASP.NET AJAX

The web portal you'll learn how to build is an N-tier application with a user interface (UI) layer, a business layer, and a data access layer. You'll use ASP.NET AJAX to implement the UI layer of the web portal application, which includes the homepage and the widget's UI. ASP.NET AJAX provides the framework (via UpdatePanel) for updating widgets without doing any postbacks, and it changes page layout by dragging and dropping widgets on the page. It also offers a rich collection of Control Extenders that add cool effects like fade in/fade out, smooth transitions, and client-side animations. You can add to the rich client-side experience by providing autocompletion behavior on text boxes, asynchronous data loading via web service calls, client-side paging, sorting, and much more.

The ASP.NET AJAX runtime provides a framework you can use to make XML HTTP calls from within the widgets. It also provides the framework for building client-side effects using Custom Extenders. The drag-and-drop behavior of widgets on the page is built as an Extender. You'll also reuse some extenders from the Ajax Control Toolkit (ACT) to enrich the client user experience within the widgets.

ASP.NET AJAX exposes a handy API that you can use to authenticate against the ASP.NET Membership application service. A good thing about the ASP.NET Membership API is that it's fully compatible with ASP.NET AJAX and providers for Membership, Profile properties, and so on; they all work exactly the same way as a regular ASP.NET web site. This means you can make client-side login and signup forms, and change user preferences without requiring any postback.

# Using C# 3.0 and .NET 3.5

Dropthing's business layer is built with the Windows Workflow Foundation (WF), which was introduced in .NET 3.0. Major operations like a first-time user visit, a subsequent user visit, adding a new widget, and creating a new page are all orchestrated using workflow. The workflows contain all the business rules and activities needed to complete each operation. For example, the *New User Visit* workflow creates the user account, populates the user profile with default values, creates some default pages, populates them with specific widgets, etc. Such compound operations are very easy to build with workflows, which enable you to break the complete operation into smaller chunks called *Activities*. Each Activity does a very small amount of work. It talks to the data access layer and performs the task. The data access layer is built with .NET 3.5, using LINQ to SQL, which vastly simplifies the querying of databases from within your application code.

The web project and the widgets make good use of .NET 3.5 by using new functionality for lambda expressions, LINQ to SQL, and LINQ to XML. You will use LINQ queries to work with collections and database rows. Widgets make good use of LINQ to XML to consume XML from external data sources.

The application is built following a typical N-tier architecture where there's a clear separation between the UI, business logic, and data (see Figure 1-8). For example:

*Web layer*
> Consists of web pages, web services, resources (e.g., graphics, CSS, JavaScript, and *.resx* files), and configuration settings.

*Business layer*
> Provides the entity classes, business rules, and middle-tier caching of data to reduce database roundtrips.

*Data access layer*
> Encapsulates database access and provides an interface that is database and data source independent. It also provides object factories that create Entity classes out of database rows and vice versa.

In Figure 1-8, the technologies are mapped to each layer.

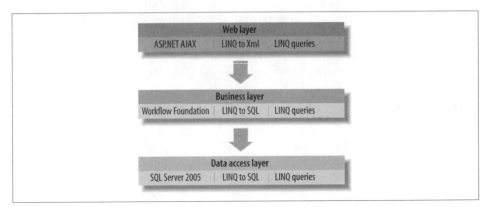

*Figure 1-8. Mapping technologies to the different layers*

The web portal application in this book makes use of some of the newest .NET 3.0 and .NET 3.5 technologies. The web layer uses ASP.NET AJAX for a rich user experience, and the business layer uses the new WF to orchestrate complex operations. All three layers use LINQ to work with data structures.

C# 3.0 language extensions and LINQ queries are used in all layers to work easily with collections, database rows, and XML. WF is used in the business layer to perform complex operations, such as workflows. LINQ to SQL is part of both the data access layer and the business layer. Although the insert, update, and delete operations are mostly encapsulated inside the data access layer, some queries are faster to implement directly from the business layer. That's why LINQ to SQL is also part of the business layer.

## Summary

Ajax web portals push Ajax technologies to their limits. Microsoft's ASP.NET AJAX offers a rich set of Ajax components and a robust cross-browser compatible framework to harness the full power of Ajax in web portals. The new features in .NET 3.0 and 3.5 Frameworks empower architects and developers with features like Workflow Foundation, LINQ to SQL, and LINQ to XML. This chapter, provided a brief overview of what an Ajax web portal can do and what technologies are involved in making such a project. The next chapter will discuss the architectural challenges, performance issues, and security threats that make architecting a web portal more challenging than typical web applications.

## Additional Resources

- "Using LINQ to SQL (Part 1)" from Scott Guthrie's blog (*http://weblogs.asp.net/ scottgu/archive/2007/05/19/using-linq-to-sql-part-1.aspx*)

- LINQ to XML overviews (*http://msdn2.microsoft.com/en-us/library/bb308960.aspx*)

- Workflow Foundation tutorials (*http://wf.netfx3.com*)

- The LINQ Project (*http://msdn2.microsoft.com/en-us/netframework/aa904594.aspx*)

# CHAPTER 2

# Architecting the Web Portal and Widgets

Because it strives to deliver its functionality on a single page, an Ajax web portal that lives up to its promise is invariably a masterpiece of Ajax technology. It is a great architectural challenge to provide so much on one page without compromising the performance of either the server or client. Some of the unique challenges seen only in web portals include incorporating many features into one web application and aggregating content from every kind of web site.

This chapter explains the architecture of the Dropthings portal, which you can also use to design one of your own. We'll examine a number of architectural challenges, including how to run many widgets on one page, load a web portal quickly, and deal with security threats such as denial-of-service (DoS) attacks, attempts to compromise user data, and more.

The heart of any web portal is its support for widgets, which is the mechanism by which users can customize their start pages and the means by which providers can make their services available, whether a department inside a company or a third-party, like Reuters.

In an ASP.NET implementation like the one we use in this book, *Default.aspx* is the homepage that displays the widgets and allows them to be added, removed, moved, customized, and run within the page without ever causing a page refresh or postback.

The application remembers a user's actions and customizations so that on her next visit she sees the exact same widgets she saw when she left, with her customizations preserved. Web portals typically allow anonymous users to use many of their features, including adding widgets, editing, deleting, and creating multiple pages, and changing preferences, without registering.

A *Dropthings widget* is basically an ASP.NET web control. It can be a user control or a server control, but works just like a regular web control participating in the ASP. NET page life cycle. Widgets support postbacks, the ViewState, sessions, and caches. The only difference is that a Dropthings widget must implement IWidget—a custom interface—to integrate with the widget framework and use the services provided by the core framework we use for the application. A custom-built Ajax control extender provides the drag-and-drop feature for the widgets. The widget framework and its core are explained later in this chapter (see the "Using a Widget Framework" section).

A widget is hosted inside a frame or container. The container provides the header bar, which consists of the title, edit link, minimize/maximize buttons, and close button. The widget itself is loaded below the header bar inside the body area. Events, such as changing the title, clicking on the edit link, minimizing/maximizing, and closing are notified via the IWidget interface.

In a web portal, it's important that widgets perform asynchronous postback and fetch data asynchronously so the user experiences as few page refreshes as possible. Widgets are developed as regular ASP.NET controls with support for postback. So, the core widget framework used by Dropthings, which you'll read about shortly, takes care of hosting the widget inside UpdatePanel to ensure all postbacks are asynchronous.

Although you can use a site like Dropthings for quite a while without registering, registration will save the pages permanently so that when you use a different computer, you can log in and get the same pages with the same widget setup. The ASP. NET membership and profile provider allows anonymous users to have a persistent state but convert to a registered user after signup. The page and widget states are stored in their own tables.

## Object Model

The ASP.NET membership provider contributes the user and roles. If the user has one or more pages, each page can contain one or more *widget instances*. The difference between a widget and widget instance is that a widget is like a class, whereas a widget instance is an instance of that class. For example, the Flickr photo widget is a widget that loads photos from Flickr. When a user adds the Flickr photo widget to the page, it becomes an instance of the Flickr widget. Although the term *widget* is used throughout this book, it will actually means an instance of a widget.

Figure 2-1 shows the entire object model.

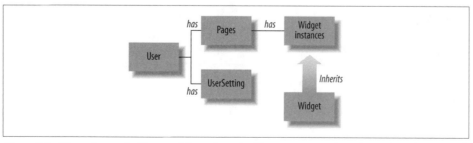

*Figure 2-1. The web portal object model consists of a User, its settings (UserSetting), and associated pages (Pages). A Page can contain Widget instances, each of which is an instance of Widget.*

The object model starts with the user, which can have some settings and one or more pages. Each page contains zero or more widget instances.

## Application Components

Dropthings uses the Facade pattern to provide a single entry point to the business layer. It provides access to internal subsystems, which deal with users, pages, widgets, etc. The façade is named DashboardFacade (see Figure 2-2).

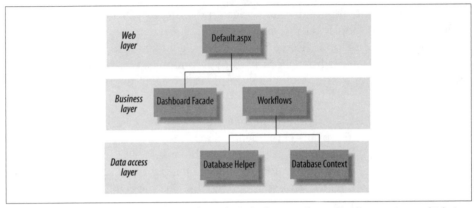

Figure 2-2. Default.aspx calls DashboardFacade in the business layer for all operations, which, in turn, uses workflows that work with databases via DatabaseHelper and DatabaseContext

On the web layer, *Default.aspx* is the entry point. It uses DashboardFacade to perform operations such as adding a new tab or widget, or storing a widget state. DashboardFacade invokes different workflows for different operations. The workflows do the real work and are developed using Windows Workflow Foundation (WF), as explained in Chapter 4. Each workflow consists of one or more activities. Each activity is like a class that performs some unit task. Activities use the DatabaseHelper and DashboardDataContext classes to work with the database. DatabaseHelper is a class used for performing common database operations. DashboardDataContext is generated by LINQ to SQL and maps entities to database tables.

## Data Model

To implement the data model used by the application, we use the ASP.NET membership provider's default database tables—the aspnet_Users table contains all of the user accounts. The schema has been extended with additional tables for other information (see Figure 2-3).

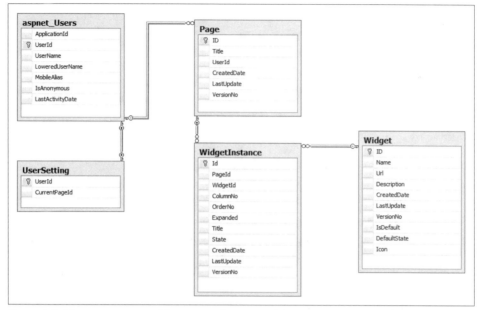

*Figure 2-3. The aspnet_Users table contains the users, while the rest of the tables are for the entities*

Some important details about the tables include:

- aspnet_Users is the default ASP.NET membership table. However, this table contains only the anonymous user accounts. Registered user accounts are in aspnet_membership table. They aren't shown in Figure 2-3 because there's no relationship between aspnet_membership table and the tables.

- The Page table contains foreign key references on the aspnet_users table's UserId column.

- The Widget table contains the widget inventory or master list. It defines each widget's title and the location from where the widget is dynamically loaded. It also defines the widgets created by default during a user's first visit.

- The WidgetInstance table has the foreign key references on the PageId and WidgetId columns, as well as the Page and Widget table's ID columns, respectively.

- The UserSetting table has foreign key references on UserId column with aspnet_users table's UserId column.

Table 2-1 shows the table's index plan and explanations.

*Table 2-1. Index plan*

| Table | Column | Index type | Why |
|-------|--------|------------|-----|
| Page | UserID | Nonclustered | The user pages are loaded by WHERE UserID=<ID>. |
| Page | ID | Clustered | During the page edit, the page is located by its ID, which is also the PK. |

| Table | Column | Index type | Why |
|---|---|---|---|
| Widget | ID | Clustered | ID is the PK and referenced by WidgetInstance. When a widget is added, it is located by its ID. |
| Widget | IsDefault | Nonclustered | On the first visit, default widgets are automatically created on the Start page. IsDefault determines which widgets are defaults. |
| WidgetInstance | PageId | Nonclustered | Widget instances are loaded page by page. |
| WidgetInstance | ID | Clustered | During a single widget instance update or delete, ID is used to identify the instance. |
| UserSetting | UserId | Clustered | User setting is queried by UserId. |

Some common design guidelines for choosing the right index setup:

- A clustered index is used on fields that increase continuously, e.g., auto number integer fields. Because SQL Server physically arranges rows in the database file based on a clustered index field, if I choose some fields that do not continuously increase, it will be rearrange too many pages during the INSERT and DELETE steps.
- Foreign key fields are nonclustered index types because they are not added as increasing values.

## Solution Files

The Dropthings solution consists of an ASP.NET web project and four C# projects, available for download at *www.codeplex.com/dropthings*.

*Default.aspx*
> Controls the widgets on the Start page

*WidgetService.asmx*
> Exposes some web service methods used to access widgets on the Start page

*Proxy.asmx*
> Allows widgets to fetch content from external sources and other web controls that make up different parts of the Start page

*WidgetContainer.ascx*
> The generic widget frame that hosts a widget inside it and works as a bridge between the core framework and the real widget

The widgets are stored inside the *Widgets* folder. Each widget is built as a web control, and all related resources like graphics, CSS, and JavaScript are placed inside subfolders of the *Widgets* folder (see Figure 2-4).

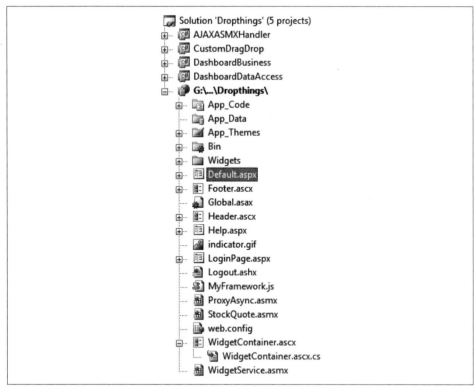

*Figure 2-4. The web project's directory shows the files that make up the site*

## Update Panels

UpdatePanels allow you to update any part of the Start page asynchronously and give any web site an Ajax look-and-feel. However, UpdatePanels are a significant drag on the page. The more UpdatePanels you have, the slower asynchronous postbacks become due to the processing required to locate the page part for postback and re-render. It becomes even more complicated when you put UpdatePanels inside of UpdatePanels. So, it is important to carefully study the layout of the page before making architecture decisions.

On Dropthings, the entire widget area is a good candidate for an UpdatePanel because it needs to reload when a user switches tabs. Also, the page tabs themselves (where new tabs are added and deleted) should also be considered for an UpdatePanel because tab operations can happen without affecting the rest of the page. The Add Stuff widget gallery containing the collection of widgets is also inside an UpdatePanel so that it can asynchronously come and go (see Figure 2-5).

Putting the whole widget area inside one UpdatePanel will result in poor performance when adding and removing widgets because that entire UpdatePanel needs to be refreshed to reflect the current widgets on the page. This would require a large

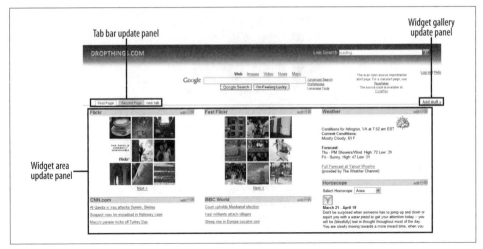

Figure 2-5. The Dropthings home page uses three UpdatePanels

amount of HTML and JavaScript for all the widgets on the page to be delivered during the asynchronous update. So, a better strategy is to put each column inside one UpdatePanel. Any changes made on any column will require an asynchronous update only on the UpdatePanel of that column, not the entire widget area (see Figure 2-6).

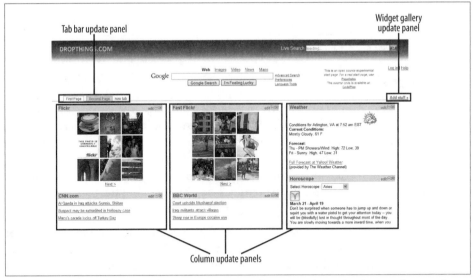

Figure 2-6. Instead of using one UpdatePanel to hold the three widgets, use three UpdatePanels, one for each column. When a widget is added or removed from one column, only the UpdatePanel on that column is refreshed.

When you drag and drop a widget from one column to another, there is no need for an UpdatePanel refresh because the UI is already up-to-date using JavaScript. You just need to inform the server which widget has been moved. The server can also recalculate the new position of all the widgets, just like the client does. So, there's no asynchronous postback on drag and drop; it's only needed when a new widget is added or removed.

## Drag-and-Drop Operations

There are two ways to implement drag-and-drop operations: free form and column-wise. Protopage (*www.protopage.com*) is a site that uses free-form drag-and-drop functionality, where you can drag widgets anywhere on the page. The positions of the widgets are absolute positions. But Live.com, iGoogle, and Pageflakes follow column-wise organization. This allows you to either reorder widgets vertically within a column or drag a widget from one column to another. Column-wise organization maintains a clean setup of the page all the time because the widgets are nicely ordered in columns. This approach is used by most web portals (see Figure 2-7).

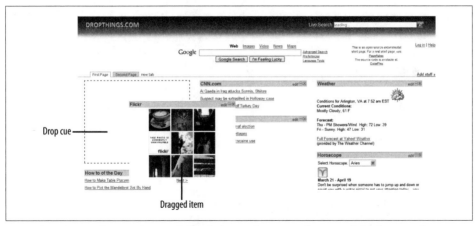

*Figure 2-7. A page showing drag-and-drop behavior between columns and the drop cue that indicates where the widget can be dropped*

To implement drag-and-drop behavior between multiple columns, the page is divided into three columns where each column is an ASP.NET Panel control. Widgets can be added to any of the Panels. The drag-and-drop functionality is provided using a custom-made extender.

There are two types of drag behavior that need to be supported: reordering of widgets on the same column and moving a widget from one column to another. If we make each column a drop zone using the IDropTarget interface in the ASP.NET AJAX framework, then each widget that is an IDragSource can easily be dropped on the columns. The more challenging part is to make widgets switch position within the same column, that is, to reorder them. For example, if you move a widget downward, the widget that was below the dragged widget will jump up to fill the vacant place. Similarly, if you drag one widget over another, the second widget needs to move down and make enough space for the first widget to be dropped. These behaviors are implemented as Extenders, so you can easily attach the Extender to a Panel, and it will act like an IDropTarget and provide the reorder facility.

So, how do you send the position of the widgets asynchronously to the server after a drag-and-drop operation completes? When you complete a drag-and-drop move, it is reflected on the UI, but the server does not know what just happened. Any kind of postback to inform the server of the position of the widget will create a disruptive user experience because the whole page or column will refresh. The server needs to be informed asynchronously behind the scenes so the user doesn't notice the widgets' positions being transmitted to the server and saved after each drag and drop. The second challenge is to provide this entire drag-and-drop functionality in the form of one Extender. The Extender needs to hook onto the Column Panel and make it a drop target, as well as connect to the widget's drag handles, which allows widgets to be moved to any drop target.

In the next section, you'll see how to go about adding widgets and their containers to the Start page.

## Using a Widget Framework

Dropthings makes use of a *widget framework* that allows you to focus on providing features that are relevant to the widget itself without worrying about authentication, authorization, profile, personalization, or storage. Widgets get these functions from the widget framework, or the *core*, shown in Figure 2-8.

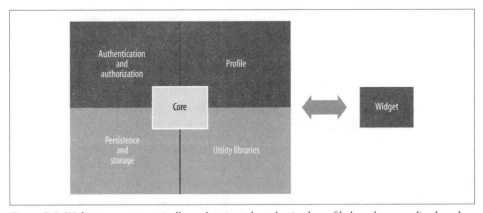

*Figure 2-8. Widgets are automatically authenticated, authorized, profiled, and personalized, and they receive storage and utility libraries from the host, which allows you to easily add more functionality to the web portal in the form of widgets. The core coordinates these services.*

Moreover, you can build widgets independently of the host project. You don't need the whole web portal's web application source code in your local development computer to build widgets. All you have to do is create a regular ASP.NET 2.0 web site, create a user control, make it do what it's supposed to do in a regular postback model (don't worry about JavaScript), implement a little interface, and you are done!

You don't have to worry about Ajax and JavaScript with the widget framework I have created for Dropthings. The architecture allows you to use regular ASP.NET 2.0 controls, *Ajax Control Toolkit* controls (*http://www.asp.net/ajax/ajaxcontroltoolkit/ samples*), and any extender in ASP.NET AJAX. Full server-side programming support is also included, and you can use .NET 2.0, 3.0, or 3.5, as well as regular View-State and store temporary states. ASP.NET Cache can be used to cache widget data. This approach is far better than what you would find in any current web portal where you have to build the whole widget using only JavaScript, abide by specific API guidelines, and follow a strict "no postback" model (see Figure 2-8).

In the Dropthings widget framework, the core does authentication and authorization using the ASP.NET membership provider. This allows the widgets to get the current user's profile when loading. The core also provides widgets with a data storage service to persist their states, as well as the user's actions, such as expanding or collapsing a widget, moving, or deleting. The communication between the widget and the core is done via a *widget container*. The widget container hosts the actual widget and works as a middleman. The widget container knows which widget instance it is hosting and provides it with services like persistence service or event notification. A page hosts one or more widget containers, but each widget container hosts only one widget inside it (see Figure 2-9).

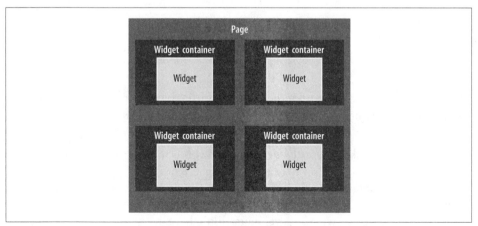

*Figure 2-9. A page contains a collection of widget containers where each widget container contains one widget*

A widget's code is straightforward, and just like a regular web control, you can do stuff inside Page_Load. You can also get events raised from ASP.NET user controls. Widgets are similar to SharePoint Web Parts, but one advantage over Web Parts is that you can use ASP.NET user controls instead of custom controls. User controls give you access to Visual Studio, which you don't have with custom controls. You can also make a widget in one *.ascx* file, which requires no compilation into DLL or deploying that DLL to a server—just copy the *.ascx* file from the web folder and it is ready to use.

For example, say you wanted a widget that shows photos, perhaps from Flickr. You can write the widget as a user control and, in the control code, handle events the usual way for a user control. The following bit of code displays the photos when the control is loaded onto the page:

```
protected void Page_Load(object sender, EventArgs e)
{
    if( !base.IsPostBack )
        this.ShowPictures(0);
    else
        this.ShowPictures(PageIndex);
}
```

To give the widget LinkButton controls to move between photos, write event handlers for the buttons to include navigation code, just as you would for any server-based navigation:

```
protected void LinkButton1_Click(object sender, EventArgs e)
{
    if( this.PageIndex > 0 ) this.PageIndex --;
    this.ShowPictures(this.PageIndex);
}
protected void LinkButton2_Click(object sender, EventArgs e)
{
    this.PageIndex ++;
    this.ShowPictures(this.PageIndex);
}
```

The ASP.NET page cycle works the same as ordinary page processing. Inside the widget, you can use any ASP.NET control and write code for its events.

The Container provides the widget's container and frame, and defines a header and a body area. The actual widget is loaded inside the body area at runtime by the widget container. For each widget on the page, the core creates one widget container, and then the widget container dynamically loads the real widget inside its body area. The widget container is part of the framework and you only have to write it once (see Figure 2-10). However, widget developers don't have to write containers because they write the actual widget.

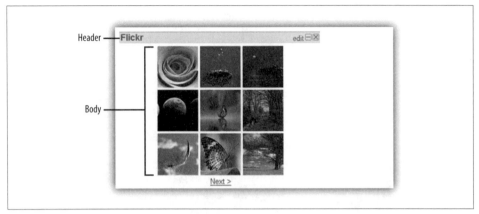

*Figure 2-10. A widget container is an ASP.NET web control that has a header and a body part, which is where the widget is loaded*

The widget container is a user control that is dynamically created on the page for each widget instance while the page loads. The widget itself is also a user control that is loaded dynamically by the widget container via Page.LoadControl("...").

The actual widget hosted inside the container is loaded inside an UpdatePanel control. So, no matter how many times the actual widget performs a postback, the widget container does not perform a postback.

## Designing the Widget Container

Designing a good widget container is a matter of finding the right combination of UpdatePanels. It is a bit difficult to first decide the best distribution of ASP.NET controls inside an UpdatePanel. Putting the whole widget container inside one UpdatePanel works well enough, and there is only one UpdatePanel per widget container, so the overhead is small. But a problem surfaces with the extenders that are attached to the HTML elements inside UpdatePanel. When UpdatePanel refreshes, it removes existing HTML elements rendered by ASP.NET controls and creates new ones. As a result, all the extenders attached to the previous HTML elements are destroyed, unless the extenders are also inside the UpdatePanel. Putting extenders inside the UpdatePanel means that whenever an UpdatePanel control is refreshed, a new instance of the extenders is created and initialized. This slows UI update after a postback, noticeably so when working with widgets on the page.

You could separate the header and body areas into multiple UpdatePanels—one UpdatePanel would host the header area and another would host the actual widget. This would allow you to change something on the widget and refresh the body widget, but not the header, so the extenders that are attached to the header (e.g., an extender for drag and drop) are not lost. But this means that all the extenders attached to the header controls must be inside the header UpdatePanel, which will affect performance. So, although separating header and body areas into multiple extenders does provide some performance improvement, it isn't as much as you need (see Figure 2-11).

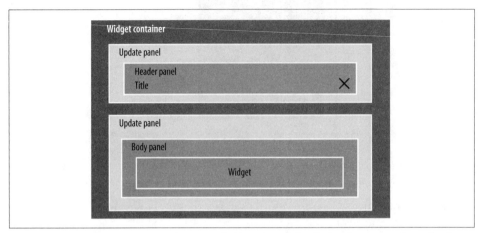

*Figure 2-11. A widget container with two UpdatePanels, one for the header area and one for the body area where the real widget is loaded*

However, for even better performance, what if the header `UpdatePanel` didn't contain the whole header, just the title and header buttons? When the header `UpdatePanel` refreshes (for example, when a user clicks a header button), the whole header is not recreated, only the title and buttons that are inside the `UpdatePanel` control are refreshed. This way, the drag-and-drop extender that attaches to the header panel can be put outside the `UpdatePanel` (see Figure 2-12).

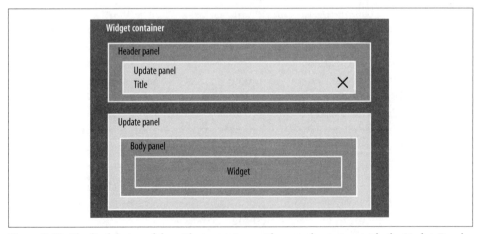

*Figure 2-12. The final design of the widget container with some elements outside the UpdatePanel control to optimize the performance of the widget*

The WidgetContainer implementation is quite simple. There is a header area that contains the title and the expand/collapse/close buttons, and a body area where the actual widget is hosted. In the Dropthings solution folder shown in Figure 2-4, the file *WidgetContainer.ascx* contains the markup for WidgetContainer (see Example 2-1).

*Example 2-1. The .ascx content for the WidgetContainer*

```
<asp:Panel ID="Widget" CssClass="widget" runat="server">
    <asp:Panel id="WidgetHeader" CssClass="widget_header" runat="server">
        <asp:UpdatePanel ID="WidgetHeaderUpdatePanel" runat="server"
                    UpdateMode="Conditional">
        <ContentTemplate>
            <table class="widget_header_table" cellspacing="0"
                    cellpadding="0">

            <tbody>
            <tr>
            <td class="widget_title"><asp:LinkButton ID="WidgetTitle"
                runat="Server" Text="Widget Title" /></td>
            <td class="widget_edit"><asp:LinkButton ID="EditWidget"
                runat="Server" Text="edit" OnClick="EditWidget_Click" /></td>
            <td class="widget_button"><asp:LinkButton ID="CollapseWidget"
                runat="Server" Text="" OnClick="CollapseWidget_Click"
                CssClass="widget_min widget_box" />

                <asp:LinkButton ID="ExpandWidget" runat="Server" Text=""
                CssClass="widget_max widget_box" OnClick="ExpandWidget_Click"/>
            </td>
            <td class="widget_button"><asp:LinkButton ID="CloseWidget"
                runat="Server" Text="" CssClass="widget_close widget_box"
                OnClick="CloseWidget_Click" /></td>
            </tr>
            </tbody>
            </table>
        </ContentTemplate>

        </asp:UpdatePanel>
    </asp:Panel>
    <asp:UpdatePanel ID="WidgetBodyUpdatePanel" runat="server"
        UpdateMode="Conditional" >
        <ContentTemplate><asp:Panel ID="WidgetBodyPanel" runat="Server">
    </asp:Panel>
</ContentTemplate>
    </asp:UpdatePanel>

</asp:Panel>
<cdd:CustomFloatingBehaviorExtender ID="WidgetFloatingBehavior"
DragHandleID="WidgetHeader" TargetControlID="Widget" runat="server" />
```

The whole widget container is inside a panel control named Widget. The first child is the header panel, which includes the WidgetHeaderUpdatePanel and contains the content of the header area. Inside of that is the title of the widget, some buttons to change the edit area, and buttons for expanding and collapsing the widget. The WidgetBodyUpdatePanel, which hosts the real widget at runtime, is also included in the header panel. The real widget is loaded by calling Page.LoadControl(...), and then it's added to the body panel. The CustomFloatingBehavior extender is also included; it attaches to the widget header and makes the whole widget draggable.

## Adding Widgets

A widget is made up of settings and body parts. The body part is always shown as long as the widget is not minimized. The settings part is only shown when user clicks the "edit" link on the widget header. The settings part stores customization options for the widget. For example, with a Flickr photo widget, settings could include allow the user to choose what type of photos to show, to enter tags, or to enter a user ID. The settings area hides customization options from the UI until the user wants them, but there can be as many choices as you like. The settings part can be made using a regular ASP.NET Panel that contains all the elements for the customization area. By default, the Panel is invisible, but the widget makes it visible when it is notified that a user has clicked the "edit" link.

As noted earlier, widgets are created as ordinary web server controls. To integrate widget functionality, implement the IWidget interface, which defines how the widget container communicates with the widget (see Example 2-2).

*Example 2-2. IWidget interface*

```
public interface IWidget
{
    void Init(IWidgetHost host);
    void ShowSettings();
    void HideSettings();
    void Minimized();
    void Maximized();
    void Closed();
}
```

The IWidget interface defines a way to inform the widget when to initialize the widget area and restore its state. When a user clicks the "edit" link, ShowSettings informs the widget to show the settings area. When a user clicks the maximize or minimize links (the plus or minus icons), Maximized and Minimized functions are called. The same happens when a user closes the widget—Closed is called and the widget cleanups any information stored in database. These are all *post-event callback methods*—actions the user has already performed and the widget reacts to.

 Widgets are regular ASP.NET web controls with IWidget—a simple interface implementation.

Widgets get references to an interface implementation named IWidgetHost via the IWidget.Init method. This interface exposes methods to communicate with the container as well as the services provided by the container. IWidgetHost allows the widget to consume services provided by the framework, including authentication, notification, and state persistence. For example:

```
public interface IWidgetHost
{
    void SaveState(string state);
    string GetState();
    void Maximize();
    void Minimize();
    void Close();
    bool IsFirstLoad { get; }
}
```

The various methods IWidgetHost uses are as follows:

SaveState
> Stores arbitrary data as XML (or any other format), but because the data needs to be serialized in a string format, XML is the preferred choice. Whatever is stored as the state can be retrieved using the GetState method on the second-time load.

GetState
> Gets the state that you stored using SaveState.

Maximize
> Maximizes the widget and shows the widget body. It's the same as a user clicking the "+" button, only the widget does it itself from code.

Minimize
> Minimizes the widget and hides the body area. It's the same as a user clicking the "-" button, only the widget does it itself from code.

Close
> Removes the widget from the page permanently.

IsFirstLoad
> Determines whether it's the first-time load on the page or if an asynchronous postback is happening either on the widget or on some other widget.

 The IWidget.Init method executes before the Page_Load method of the web control. By having the reference to IWidgetHost earlier than Page_Load, you can use it to determine whether it's a postback or first-time load.

The IsFirstLoad property is tricky. Think about what happens when a user clicks some button on a widget and the widget goes through a postback. Basically the whole page is instantiated again and all the widgets are loaded on the server side. Because widgets are user controls, ASP.NET fires the Page_Load method of all the widgets on the page. Now, the widgets need to know if it's a postback or a first-time load because the content is loaded from different sources. For example, for a first-time load, the Flickr photo widget loads the photos directly from Flickr, but on post-back it can get the photos from ViewState or some other cache. The IWidgetHost.IsFirstLoad property tells the widget whether it is a first-time or postback load.

You might be wondering, why not use Page.IsPostback, which comes with ASP.NET? It will surely tell whether it's a postback or first visit to the page. The multi-tab nature of the Ajax web portal redefines what a first-time load is because not all tabs are loaded on the first visit; and widgets on a tab are loaded only when the tab is activated. Imagine a user switching tabs and loading a different set of widgets, but all of the tabs are on the same ASP.NET page. So, when you click on a tab, it's a regular ASP.NET asynchronous postback to the ASP.NET page. Now you are loading the widgets on the new tab, not on the old tab. If the widgets on the new tab call Page.IsPostback, they will find it true because clicking on a tab is a regular postback for ASP.NET. But for the widgets that are loading for the first time on the new tab, it's not a postback for them. They will fail when trying to read data from ViewState because no ViewState exists for them yet. This means the user cannot use the regular ASP.NET postback concept for the widgets. This is why the IWidgetHost differentiates regular ASP.NET postback with our own definition of postback for Widgets.

## Maximizing the First-Visit Experience

The most challenging part of a web portal is the first-visit experience. On first visit, a new user gets a page that is set up with predefined widgets that are ready for further customization (see Figure 2-13).

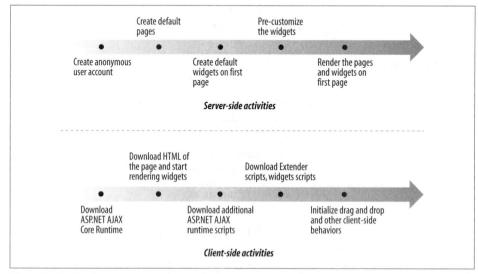

*Figure 2-13. The first visit to a web portal requires setting up the user account, creating pages, and populating with predefined widgets that user can further customize*

During a first-time visit, the page does the following before the user sees it:

- Creates a new user account using a ASP.NET 2.0 membership provider
- Creates a new profile using a ASP.NET 2.0 profile provider
- Creates new pages for the user
- Creates default widgets on the first page
- Sets up widgets with default data, e.g., shows the weather in the user's city by inferring the user's location based on the IP address
- Renders the widgets and any associated client script
- Delivers the entire client framework to support the web portal functionality

The challenge here is to execute server-side tasks instantly so the server does not have a noticeable delay before it starts to deliver the page content to the browser. Once the response is delivered, the browser needs to download the Ajax framework, widget scripts, graphics, CSS, etc., which takes a long time. To give the user perceived fast speed, the server needs to deliver the content almost instantly and progressively download the rest while the user is looking at the content of the page.

Basically, during the first visit, the application needs to deliver almost every aspect of the web portal, because you don't know what user might do once the page becomes functional. With Dropthings, users can use all the features of the application on the first visit. For example, a user can drag widgets, add new pages, and organize the content in pages, and then sign up to continue using the customized page. The user does all of this from a single web page with absolutely zero postback and no navigation to other pages. If postback was allowed on the page or the page was broken into multiple pages, then we could deliver only basic content and client-side features, like drag and drop. The rest of the functionality would be delivered when the user does something that makes a postback to the server or navigates to a different page. Because postback or navigation to other pages is not allowed, if the entire client framework is not ready by the time the user starts interacting with the page, there will be JavaScript errors and actions will fail.

At the same time, you need to ensure that providing all these features on the first visit does not slow down first-time loading of the page. Otherwise, the first visit experience will be slow and the user will lose interest in the site. It's a big challenge to make the first visit as fast as possible for the user so she can use the site immediately without getting bored looking at the browser progress bar.

The following are some ideas on how you can avoid a slow first-visit experience:

- Send HTML of the page and scripts in parallel so that the user sees something is happening on the page while the scripts and pictures download in the background. This increases the site's perceived speed.

- Download the scripts in multiple steps. First, download the core Ajax runtime and then render the UI. This way, the user sees that something is happening and does not become impatient.

- Start downloading the other scripts that add additional features once the widgets are rendered on the UI. For example, extenders can download after the content is rendered.

- Delay downloading scripts that aren't immediately necessarily and download those at a later stage. Generally, users don't use features like drag and drop right away, which allows you to delay scripts for dialog boxes, tool tips, and animations.

- Combine multiple small scripts in one large script file. You could create one JavaScript file for each particular functionality. For example, each ASP.NET extender has one or more JavaScript files. Try to keep JavaScript files small and introduce many small files in the web applications. The browser takes about 200 to 400 ms to reach the server and come back to the browser to download a file. So, each script file can waste 200 to 400 ms, and if there are five scripts, then the application spends one second on each network roundtrip. Now, add the total download time for the files, and it could easily take 10 seconds for 5 large scripts. So, you need to seriously think about (and test) how to optimize script file size and reduce network roundtrips as much as possible. Ideally, you should try to deliver only one large JavaScript file that combines all the smaller JavaScript files that are essential for the web portal to be fully functional on first visit.

## Rendering a Second-Visit Experience

The second visit is piece of cake. The user account is already available from a browser cookie, which you get via the ASP.NET membership provider. All the Ajax scripts are already in the browser's cache. So, you just load existing pages and widgets on the page and render the page to the browser (see Figure 2-14).

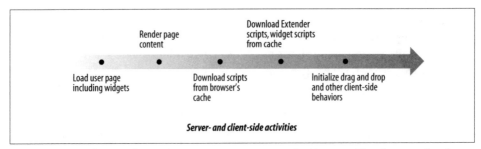

*Figure 2-14. On the second visit, the user account, pages, and widgets are already created so the user page loads very fast*

Here's what the web portal does on the second visit:

- Gets user from encrypted browser cookie via theASP.NET membership provider
- Loads user pages and creates tabs for each page
- Finds the current page
- Loads all widgets on the current page
- Allows widgets to load their previous state
- Renders the widgets and scripts
- Delivers the client-side framework (should be cached on browser already)

Because the client-side framework, widget scripts, and extender scripts are already cached on the browser, the duration of a second-time visit is basically the time spent on the server and the time the browser spends initializing scripts. However, in the meantime, the browser cache might expire and the cached JavaScript can get lost. If this happens, the browser will download the scripts again and the user will notice some delay during the next visit.

# Improving ASP.NET AJAX Performance

There are several ways to improve your ASP.NET AJAX performance.

## Server-Side Rendering Versus Client-Side Rendering

The Ajax web portal can be rendered in two ways: from the server or from the client. Server rendering means that the HTML on a page, along with all the widgets, is created in server code, rendered by the server code, and delivered statically to browser. So, the browser just renders the HTML, loads the JavaScript (or Ajax framework, extenders, widget scripts, etc.), and initializes it. iGoogle is a good example of server-side rendering.

In contrast, client rendering means the content of the widget is not sent along with the page content. Once the scripts download and initialize, the page calls a web service to get the content of the widgets and dynamically creates the widgets on the page, one after another.

The advantages of server rendering include:

- Uses server-side technologies to their full potential. For example, it makes full use of ASP.NET features.
- Renders and delivers entire page to the client in one shot. If the page does not have too many widgets, the perceived speed is better than client-side rendering approach.
- Shows the content and then downloads the Ajax runtime, core scripts, widget scripts, etc., and initializes them later. Because the user sees the widgets before the whole page is downloaded, she feels it is a fast-loading page.

The disadvantages of server-side rendering include:

- The page's cache output is delivered every time the user visits the site because it doesn't know if the user has already changed the page on another computer or if the page's content has changed by other means.
- All widgets need to be developed mostly using server-side technology like ASP. NET. You cannot have JavaScript-only widgets.
- If a widget does not follow the ASP.NET-style postback model, it will need a lot of support from a client-side framework. For example, you will have to provide support for features, such as expanding, collapsing, closing, and resizing, in the client framework and make sure the server is kept in sync with such client-side activities via web service calls.

The advantages of client-side rendering are:

- A server-side framework for widgets is not needed.
- Widgets can provide all functionality from the client side.
- Completely client-side web portals and widgets require zero postback, not even any asynchronous postback, which improves responsiveness.
- The response can be cached via a web service call. Thus, the next time the user comes back, the cached response is loaded from browser cache and rendered very fast. Just as *Default.aspx* is rendered from the server on every visit, you can easily decide whether to load page content from the cache or make a fresh call to get fresh page content if it has changed between the visits.

But the disadvantages of client-side rendering include:

- Widgets are mostly developed with JavaScript so they are a lot more difficult to develop than regular ASP.NET web controls.
- Too much JavaScript on the client side makes the browser slow unless the user has a powerful computer.
- Browsers' debugging support is still very poor compared to server-side debugging support.

## Runtime Size Analysis

ASP.NET AJAX has a pretty big runtime that consists of the core framework, scripts for UpdatePanel, and a preview script that is required for drag-and-drop functionality. Additionally, we need the Ajax Control Toolkit. These requirements total a staggering 564 KB of download for 12 script references on the page. The download size mostly depends on the usage of extenders and Ajax features, so moderately using an extender creates the output in Figure 2-15.

| | | | | | | |
|---|---|---|---|---|---|---|
| 200 | GET | localhost | /Dashboard/Default.aspx | | 5375 ms | 33.93 KB |
| | GET | digg.com | /rss/index.xml | | | 62 bytes |
| 200 | GET | localhost | /Dashboard/App_Themes/Default/StyleSheet.css | | 484 ms | 4.99 KB |
| 200 | GET | localhost | /Dashboard/App_Themes/Default/HeaderBack.png | | 344 ms | 1.73 KB |
| 200 | GET | localhost | /Dashboard/WebResource.axd?d=23LW7YsECi60K6v2dgMDzA2... | | 1172 ms | 21.64 KB |
| 200 | GET | localhost | /Dashboard/ScriptResource.axd?d=KdcUZLR5eO63_3pXb9jDRG... | | 3657 ms | 83.38 KB |
| 200 | GET | localhost | /Dashboard/ScriptResource.axd?d=KdcUZLR5eO63_3pXb9jDRG... | | 1563 ms | 30.16 KB |
| 200 | GET | localhost | /Dashboard/ScriptResource.axd?d=fOZjIoZ-7i0GuWWN54jqOJ3... | | 6500 ms | 136.38 KB |
| 200 | GET | localhost | /Dashboard/ScriptResource.axd?d=fOZjIoZ-7i0GuWWN54jqOFZ... | | 1781 ms | 36.02 KB |
| 200 | GET | localhost | /Dashboard/ScriptResource.axd?d=5spM7i6pb1J9uoE51cNrohQ... | | 2078 ms | 45.25 KB |
| 200 | GET | localhost | /Dashboard/ScriptResource.axd?d=5spM7i6pb1J9uoE51cNrohQ... | | 562 ms | 4.08 KB |
| 200 | GET | localhost | /Dashboard/ScriptResource.axd?d=5spM7i6pb1J9uoE51cNrohQ... | | 5859 ms | 140.86 KB |
| 200 | GET | localhost | /Dashboard/ScriptResource.axd?d=5spM7i6pb1J9uoE51cNrohQ... | | 1156 ms | 18.05 KB |
| 200 | GET | localhost | /Dashboard/ScriptResource.axd?d=5spM7i6pb1J9uoE51cNrohQ... | | 969 ms | 16.48 KB |
| 200 | GET | localhost | /Dashboard/ScriptResource.axd?d=9yoRDWRLh-x24WvIxgMC3... | | 687 ms | 7.32 KB |
| 200 | GET | localhost | /Dashboard/ScriptResource.axd?d=9yoRDWRLh-x24WvIxgMC3... | | 828 ms | 9.73 KB |

*Figure 2-15. A 256 kbps Internet speed simulation shows, which files are downloaded on the first visit to a site*

To capture traffic and simulate slow Internet speed by throttling data transfer speed, I used a tool called Charles (*www.xk72.com/charles*). From the durations, you can see almost 20 seconds is spent on downloading the runtime over a 256 kbps line! Surely this is unacceptable speed.

The following is an explanation of what each script in Figure 2-15 does. Entries starting with */Dashboard/WebResource.axd* or */Dashboard/ScriptResource.axd* are Java-Script and the following list details functions by the size of the file.

*21.64 KB*
> Handy script for postbacks

*83.38 KB*
> Microsoft Ajax core runtime

*30.16 KB*
> UpdatePanel, partial update, asynchronous postback scripts

*136.38 KB*
> Preview version of Ajax that allows drag-and-drop script

*36.02 KB*
> The actual drag-and-drop script in Preview library

*45.25 KB*
> Ajax Control Toolkit

*4.08 KB*
> Timer script

*140.86 KB*
> ACT animation framework

*18.05 KB*

ACT behavior base implementation, which is required for Ajax Control Toolkit behaviors

*16.48 KB*

ACT animation behavior

*7.32 KB*

My custom drag-and-drop behavior

*9.73 KB*

My custom floating behavior

The total payload for the runtime only is too high—you cannot make a user wait 20 seconds just to download Ajax scripts before she can actually start interacting with the page. So, to reduce the size of the download:

- Eliminate the preview version of Ajax completely and use ACT for drag-and-drop functionality
- Use IIS 6 compression to deliver compressed scripts from the client
- Combine multiple script files into one file

ACT comes with its own `DragDropManager`, which is needed for drag-and-drop functionality. You could use `Sys.Preview.UI.DragDropManager`, but the `DragDropManager` alone adds nearly 180 KB of scripts for the entire preview library runtime.

By using ACT's `DrgaDropManager`, you can get rid of the preview runtime and improve response delay by seven seconds.

Without the preview scripts, the scripts downloaded are shown in Figure 2-16.

| | | | | | | |
|---|---|---|---|---|---|---|
| 200 | GET | localhost | /Dashboard/Default.aspx | 4875 ms | 33.98 KB |
| 200 | GET | localhost | /Dashboard/WebResource.axd?d=23LW7YsECi60K6v2dgMDzA2... | 1390 ms | 21.64 KB |
| 200 | GET | localhost | /Dashboard/ScriptResource.axd?d=KdcUZLR5eO63_3pXb9jDRG... | 3281 ms | 83.38 KB |
| 200 | GET | localhost | /Dashboard/ScriptResource.axd?d=KdcUZLR5eO63_3pXb9jDRG... | 1313 ms | 30.16 KB |
| 200 | GET | localhost | /Dashboard/ScriptResource.axd?d=5spM7i6pb1J9uoE51cNrohQ... | 2468 ms | 45.25 KB |
| 200 | GET | localhost | /Dashboard/ScriptResource.axd?d=5spM7i6pb1J9uoE51cNrohQ... | 360 ms | 4.08 KB |
| 200 | GET | localhost | /Dashboard/ScriptResource.axd?d=5spM7i6pb1J9uoE51cNrohQ... | 5328 ms | 140.86 KB |
| 200 | GET | localhost | /Dashboard/ScriptResource.axd?d=5spM7i6pb1J9uoE51cNrohQ... | 875 ms | 18.05 KB |
| 200 | GET | localhost | /Dashboard/ScriptResource.axd?d=5spM7i6pb1J9uoE51cNrohQ... | 828 ms | 16.48 KB |
| 200 | GET | localhost | /Dashboard/ScriptResource.axd?d=5spM7i6pb1J9uoE51cNrohQ... | 328 ms | 3.32 KB |
| 200 | GET | localhost | /Dashboard/ScriptResource.axd?d=5spM7i6pb1J9uoE51cNrohQ... | 1422 ms | 33.13 KB |
| 200 | GET | localhost | /Dashboard/ScriptResource.axd?d=9yoRDWRLh-x24WvixgMC3... | 500 ms | 7.40 KB |
| 200 | GET | localhost | /Dashboard/ScriptResource.axd?d=9yoRDWRLh-x24WvixgMC3... | 562 ms | 9.84 KB |

*Figure 2-16. The scripts loaded without the CTP version of ASP.NET AJAX, which saves about 180 KB*

When IIS 6 compression is enabled, the situation improves dramatically as shown in Figure 2-17.

| | | | | | |
|---|---|---|---|---|---|
| 200 | GET | www.dropthings.com | /ScriptResource.axd?d=GeLuYz0zDZcuWDfnHVHWc-DfmKELuOL... | 4281 ms | 23.90 KB |
| 200 | GET | www.dropthings.com | /ScriptResource.axd?d=GeLuYz0zDZcuWDfnHVHWc-DfmKELuOL... | 1687 ms | 8.35 KB |
| 200 | GET | www.dropthings.com | /ScriptResource.axd?d=lz8Aa0hI23kurdsC5p9mE3bw7rV2WV9G... | 6907 ms | 10.16 KB |
| 200 | GET | www.dropthings.com | /ScriptResource.axd?d=lz8Aa0hI23kurdsC5p9mE3bw7rV2WV9G... | 3000 ms | 1.95 KB |
| 200 | GET | www.dropthings.com | /ScriptResource.axd?d=lz8Aa0hI23kurdsC5p9mE3bw7rV2WV9G... | 4782 ms | 27.30 KB |
| 200 | GET | www.dropthings.com | /ScriptResource.axd?d=lz8Aa0hI23kurdsC5p9mE3bw7rV2WV9G... | 3140 ms | 4.58 KB |
| 200 | GET | www.dropthings.com | /ScriptResource.axd?d=lz8Aa0hI23kurdsC5p9mE3bw7rV2WV9G... | 829 ms | 3.95 KB |
| 200 | GET | www.dropthings.com | /ScriptResource.axd?d=lz8Aa0hI23kurdsC5p9mE3bw7rV2WV9G... | 610 ms | 1.93 KB |
| 200 | GET | www.dropthings.com | /ScriptResource.axd?d=lz8Aa0hI23kurdsC5p9mE3bw7rV2WV9G... | 1109 ms | 7.35 KB |
| 200 | GET | www.dropthings.com | /ScriptResource.axd?d=Az3RulCa6wlfIAm0GTYqIcUCJCayb7mIg... | 656 ms | 2.79 KB |
| 200 | GET | www.dropthings.com | /ScriptResource.axd?d=Az3RulCa6wlfIAm0GTYqIcUCJCayb7mIg... | 656 ms | 3.13 KB |
| 404 | GET | www.dropthings.com | /favicon.ico | 532 ms | 2.24 KB |

*Figure 2-17. IIS compression dramatically decreases the download size of each script*

The total download comes down from 448 KB to 163 KB, which is a 64 percent reduction!

The scripts are downloaded in two steps. First the core runtimes download, and then ACT and other scripts download. The content is displayed after the core runtime is downloaded. So, the time it takes to show content on the browser is reduced significantly because only 50 KB is needed to download before something is visible on the screen, compared to 130 KB in the noncompressed mode.

ScriptManager control has a LoadScriptsBeforeUI property that you can set to false to postpone the download of several scripts after the content is downloaded. This adds the script references to the end of the <body> tag. As a result, you see the content first, and then the additional scripts, extenders, and ACT scripts:

```
<asp:ScriptManager ID="ScriptManager1" runat="server" EnablePartialRendering="true"
LoadScriptsBeforeUI="false" ScriptMode="Release">
```

You can explicitly set ScriptMode=Release to emit highly optimized Ajax runtime scripts during local debugging to gauge their size on a production server.

## Reducing Extenders and UpdatePanels to Improve Browser Response

Because extenders are downloaded and initialized, the fewer you have, and the faster the page will download and initialize. Each extender is initialized using a statement such as the following from the output of *Default.aspx*:

```
Sys.Application.add_init(function() {
    $create(CustomDragDrop.CustomDragDropBehavior, {"DragItemClass":
"widget","DragItemHandleClass":"widget_header","DropCallbackFunction":
"WidgetDropped","DropCueID":"DropCue1","id":"CustomDragDropExtender1"}, null, null,
$get("LeftPanel"));
});
```

Here CustomDragDropBehavior is initialized. If the extender operates a lot during initialization, then browsers will get stuck, especially Internet Explorer 6. Sometimes

IE 6 will freeze while several initializations are happening. To avoid this, you need to avoid putting many extenders on widgets and yet somehow deliver a rich client-side experience. You could load extenders on demand when they are needed, e.g., postpone the drag-and-drop initialization. Generally, a user looks at the page for a while before interacting with it, so you could easily postpone the drag-and-drop initialization using a delay timer. Another idea is to create extenders programmatically instead of putting them on the ASPX or ASCX code, which will group the initialization of extenders for a later time. So, instead of this:

```
<cdd:CustomFloatingBehaviorExtender ID="WidgetFloatingBehavior"
DragHandleID="WidgetHeader" TargetControlID="Widget" runat="server" />
```

You can force it to happen later once the page is fully loaded and the browser is free for some heavy JavaScript operations:

```
var floatingBehavior = $create(CustomDragDrop.CustomFloatingBehavior,
{"DragHandleID":handleId, "id":behaviorId, "name": behaviorId}, {}, {}, child);
```

## Comparing Debug Mode Versus Release Mode

During performance testing, make sure you turn off debug mode. If it is on, Ajax will deliver debugged version of the scripts that are gigantic and full of debug statements. They are so slow that you will hardly be able to drag-and-drop widgets on IE 6, even on a dual-core machine. Once you switch to release mode, an optimized version of the scripts is used, which is quite fast.

# Adding Authentication and Authorization

Because it makes use of web services and asynchronous postbacks, a web portal is faced with four challenges:

- Authenticating the caller and ensuring the caller is a legitimate user on all asynchronous postback and web service calls.
- Authorizing calls to web services and asynchronous postbacks. Making sure the caller has the right to make that call.
- Preventing flooding. Making sure the caller cannot continuously call the service and flood the system.
- Preventing bots from hitting *Default.aspx*.

Web portals treat anonymous users the same way as a registered user. Although you might want to disable some features for anonymous users and make them available only to registered users, the main reason for registering is to save the pages permanently because anonymous cookies can get lost. Almost all web services can be called by any user except a user profile-related service, such as changing a user email address.

Although it sounds like security would be easier with web portal architectures, it is actually more complicated. For security purposes, you need to make sure each and every web service call is made on the caller's pages or widgets. For example, when deleting a widget from a page, you need to verify that the widget belongs to one of the user's pages that just made the call. If it isn't, then it's definitely a hacking attempt. Similarly, when you remove a page, you need to make sure that it belongs to that user and not someone else. This is a big performance concern because such checks always require database calls. If you had a registration-only site or an intranet-only site, you could skip these checks because you trust registered users more than anonymous users. But, since you have to support anonymous users, you cannot leave any web service method call unchecked. For example, when checking for a widget, you need to get the containing page of the widget and make sure it belongs to the user making the call. Once you are satisfied that the call is legitimate, you can update the widget's position. If you don't do this, anyone can run a program and call the service by passing an arbitrary widget ID and change other users' page setups.

Flood attempts are another problem. Anyone can continuously call "create a new widget" to the web service and flood the widget database with garbage widgets and thus make the database large and slow. So, you need to implement a quota on web service calls, e.g., a maximum of 100 calls per minute, 100 widgets per page, or 10 registrations per IP per day, etc.

 Web service calls can be flooded with automated calls. DoS attempts can render the system nonresponsive to valid web requests.

The fourth problem is related to repeated page hits. Imagine hitting a web portal with cookies disabled. Every hit would be a first-time visit, which would force the web portal to generate a new user, create pages, and populate the page with widgets, which would create high database activity and enlarge database tables. So, you need to make sure no one is flooding your system by hitting the *Default.aspx* continuously. Also, you need to:

- Isolate bots and web crawlers
- Deliver different results from *Default.aspx* when a bot visits the site
- Prevent ASP.NET from creating a new anonymous user
- Create a maximum limit of cookieless hits to a page from the same IP

This last point is important, for example, an IP like 192.168.1.1 can only hit *Default.aspx* 50 times an hour. But you can't just set this to a very low value because several users using a proxy server will show the same IP. So, the challenge is to select a threshold value that does not bring down your server but also does not limit users using proxy servers. DoS attacks and prevention are covered in detail in the next section.

# Preventing Denial-of-Service Attacks

Web services are the most attractive target for hackers because even an unsophisticated hacker can bring down a server by repeatedly calling a web service. Ajax web portals are a good target for such DoS attacks because if you just visit the home page repeatedly without preserving a cookie, every hit is producing a new user, a new page setup, and new widgets.

You can try this yourself with a simple code like this:

```
for( int i = 0; i < 100000; i ++ )
{
    WebClient client = new WebClient( );
    client.DownloadString("http://www.dropthings.com/default.aspx");
}
```

To your great surprise, you will notice that after a couple of calls, you will simply get no response. It's not that you brought down the server, but that your requests are being rejected. You no longer get any service, thus you achieve denial of service (for yourself), and the site is happy to deny you of service (DYoS).

A simple trick to remember how many requests are coming from a particular IP is to record a caller's IP in the ASP.NET cache and count the requests per IP. When the count exceeds a predefined limit, reject further requests for a specific duration, say 10 minutes. After 10 minutes, allow requests from that IP again.

The `ActionValidator` class maintains a count of specific actions such as first visit, revisit, asynchronous postbacks, adding a new widget, adding a new page, etc. It checks whether the count for a specific IP exceeds the threshold value or not. The following code shows the enumeration that contains the type of actions to check for and their threshold value for a specific duration, which is 10 minutes:

```
public static class ActionValidator
{
    private const int DURATION = 10; // 10 min period

    public enum ActionTypeEnum
    {
        FirstVisit = 100, // The most expensive one, choose the value wisely
        ReVisit = 1000,  // Welcome to revisit as many times as the user likes
        Postback = 5000,   // Not much of a problem
        AddNewWidget = 100,
        AddNewPage = 100,
    }
```

A static method named `IsValid` does the check. It returns true if the request limit is not passed and false if the request needs to be denied. Once you return false, you can call `Request.End( )` and prevent ASP.NET from proceeding further. You can also switch to a page that shows something like "Congratulations! You have succeeded in a denial-of-service attack (for you)."

```csharp
public static bool IsValid( ActionTypeEnum actionType )
{
    HttpContext context = HttpContext.Current;
    if( context.Request.Browser.Crawler ) return false;

    string key = actionType.ToString( ) + context.Request.UserHostAddress;

    var hit = (HitInfo)(context.Cache[key] ?? new HitInfo( ));

    if( hit.Hits > (int)actionType ) return false;
    else hit.Hits ++;

    if( hit.Hits == 1 )
        context.Cache.Add(key, hit, null, DateTime.Now.AddMinutes(DURATION),
            System.Web.Caching.Cache.NoSlidingExpiration, System.Web.Caching.
            CacheItemPriority.Normal, null);

    return true;
}
```

The cache key is built with a combination of action types and client IP addresses. It first checks if there's any entry in the cache for the action and the client IP. If not, start the count and remember it for the IP cache for the specific duration. The absolute expiration on a cache item ensures that after the duration, the cache item will be cleared and the count will restart. When there's already an entry in the cache, it will get the last hit count and check if the limit has been exceeded. If not, then the counter will be increased. There is no need to store the updated value in the cache again by calling Cache[url]=hit; because the hit object is determined by reference, it is changed in the cache every time as well. In fact, if you put it in the cache again, the cache expiration counter will restart and fail the logic of restarting count after specific duration.

The usage is very simple:

```csharp
protected override void OnInit(EventArgs e)
{
  base.OnInit(e);

  // Check if revisit is valid or not
  if( !base.IsPostBack )
  {
    // Block cookie less visit attempts
    if( Profile.IsFirstVisit )
    {
      if( !ActionValidator.IsValid(ActionValidator.ActionTypeEnum.FirstVisit))
Response.End( );
    }
    else
    {
      if( !ActionValidator.IsValid(ActionValidator.ActionTypeEnum.ReVisit) )
Response.End( );
    }
  }
```

```
    else
    {
      // Limit number of postbacks
      if( !ActionValidator.IsValid(ActionValidator.ActionTypeEnum.Postback) ) Response.
  End();
    }
  }
```

Of course you can put in a Cisco firewall and you get a guarantee from your hosting provider that its entire network is immune to DoS and distributed DoS (DDoS) attacks. But what they guarantee is protection against a network-level attack, such as TCP SYN attacks or malformed packet floods. There is no way your hosting provider can analyze the packet to find out if a particular IP is trying to load the site too many times without supporting cookies or adding too many widgets. These are application-level DoS attacks that cannot be prevented with hardware, operating systems, or firewalls, and must be implemented in your own code.

There are very few web sites that take such precautions against application-level DoS attacks. Therefore, it's quite easy to make servers go mad by writing a simple loop and hitting expensive pages or web services continuously from your home broadband connection.

## Summary

In this chapter you learned the basics of the web portal architecture used to build Dropthings, which encapsulates most of the client functionality that makes it easy for developers to create widgets that plug into a web portal. In particular, you've seen how use of a widget framework greatly facilitates their development and deployment.

It can be quite challenging to provide a rich client-side experience in a web portal; the biggest challenge is the first visit, where huge scripts must be downloaded. A web portal is also vulnerable to certain security risks, so you must implement mitigations that prevent them. Now that you know about the architectural challenges, let's use ASP.NET AJAX to build the web layer in the next chapter.

# CHAPTER 3

# Building the Web Layer Using ASP.NET AJAX

The biggest challenge you'll face developing an Ajax web portal is providing almost all of your web application's functionality on a single page. A web portal is all about aggregating many services in one place. It's a never-ending challenge to have as many features on one page as possible yet keep them small, simple, and fast. So, the *Default.aspx* is the most complicated of all the pages in your application because it does everything from loading Ajax frameworks to serving the widgets on the page. Sometimes it is the only page users will see during their entire stay on the web site.

In this chapter, you will learn to code the Start page *Default.aspx*, the widget container, and the IWidget and IWidgetHost interfaces. Then you will put it all together and build a Flickr photo widget and a RSS widget. Finally, you will use ASP.NET 2.0 Membership and Profile providers to implement authentication, authorization, and profiles.

## Implementing the Start Page of a Web Portal

The *Default.aspx* page in this web project is the Start page of the Ajax web portal. (see Figure 3-1).

It contains the following:

- The header which shows a search box
- The Add Stuff area where users can add more widgets
- The tab bar
- The columns
- The footer

The *Default.aspx* page starts with regular ASP.NET page syntax (see Example 3-1).

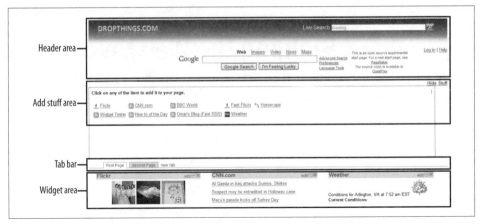

Header area

Add stuff area

Tab bar

Widget area

*Figure 3-1. The Default.aspx page contains almost everything in the Start page*

*Example 3-1. Default.aspx, part 1: Declarations of external components*

```
<%@ Page Language="C#" AutoEventWireup="true" CodeFile="Default.aspx.cs" Inherits="_
Default" Theme="Default" EnableSessionState="False"  %>
<%@ OutputCache Location="None" NoStore="true" %>
<%@ Register Src="Header.ascx" TagName="Header" TagPrefix="uc1" %>
<%@ Register Src="Footer.ascx" TagName="Footer" TagPrefix="uc2" %>
<%@ Register Assembly="AjaxControlToolkit" Namespace="AjaxControlToolkit"
TagPrefix="ajaxToolkit" %>
<%@ Register Assembly="CustomDragDrop" Namespace="CustomDragDrop" TagPrefix="cdd" %>
<%@ Register Src="WidgetContainer.ascx" TagName="WidgetContainer" TagPrefix="widget" %>
<!DOCTYPE html PUBLIC "-//W3C//DTD XHTML 1.0 Transitional//EN" "http://www.w3.org/TR/
xhtml1/DTD/xhtml1-transitional.dtd">
<html xmlns="http://www.w3.org/1999/xhtml">
<head id="Head1" runat="server">
    <title>Ajax Web Portal</title>
```

The code block in Example 3-1 does the following:

- Registers the WidgetContainer control, which is the web control for the widget container.

- Adds a reference to the CustomDragDrop assembly, which contains the CustomDragDropExtender and the CustomFloatingBehavior.

- Turns off all caching because the page must be downloaded from the server every time a user visits. If the page is cached, then users will not see the latest content in widgets after making changes on the page.

- Registers the header and footer web controls.

# Real-Life Example: When Caching Works Against You

Problem: Caching the *Default.aspx* page on the user's browser made site fail to work.

Solution: Turn off caching from *Default.aspx* and serve it directly from the server.

At Pageflakes, we used to cache the *Default.aspx* page on the user's browser. But we began receiving complaints that after the page loaded from the browser's cache, user actions—like clicking a button on a widget or adding a new widget—always failed. We tried our best to locate the problem but could never produce it.

Sometime after this, I was in the U.S. to attend Microsoft's MIX06. While I was at the hotel and using the hotel's Internet connection, I encountered the problem myself. Pageflakes was my browser homepage, and it loaded as soon as I started the browser for the first time. But when I tried to use the site, all XML HTTP calls failed. If I did a hard refresh, everything worked fine. After using the Fiddler Tool for a bit, which shows all HTTP requests and responses, I found that hotel had an intermediate Welcome page that loaded when you accessed the Internet for the first time to make sure the user is legitimate. As the *Default.aspx* page was coming from the cache, there was no request sent to the server and thus the hotel Internet provider could not validate who was using the Internet. So, all XML HTTP calls trying to reach the server were redirected to the Welcome page and failed. The same problem happened when I tried to access Pageflakes from Starbucks or from airport Wi-Fi zones. So, we turned off caching from *Default.aspx* and instead made sure that it was always served from our server and the problem disappeared. We stopped receiving complaints too.

## The Header Area

The header area displays the logo, the search bars for Live.com and Google, and the Login link. After the header area, there's a script block that contains some client-side scripts that I will explain later on. These scripts are used to provide some client-side behaviors like calling a web service when dragging and dropping, showing/hiding elements, and so on.

Example 3-2 shows the start of the <body> tag in *Default.aspx*.

*Example 3-2. Default.aspx, part 2: HTML snippet for the header part*

```
<body>
    <form id="form1" runat="server">

        <!-- Render header first so that user can start typing search criteria while the
        huge runtime and other scripts download -->
        <uc1:Header ID="Header1" runat="server" />
```

*Example 3-2. Default.aspx, part 2: HTML snippet for the header part (continued)*

```
<div id="body">

<asp:ScriptManager ID="ScriptManager1" runat="server"
EnablePartialRendering="true" LoadScriptsBeforeUI="false" ScriptMode="Release">
    <Services>
    <asp:ServiceReference InlineScript="true" Path="WidgetService.asmx" />
    </Services>
</asp:ScriptManager>
```

 Browsers render HTML top to bottom. Put HTML elements before script blocks so that browser can render the HTML block before it starts downloading scripts.

The header control is put before the ScriptManager block. This makes the header emit its HTML right after the body tag. Because browsers render top to bottom, putting the HTML block for the search bar at the top of the page will help the browser render the search bar as soon as the user visits the site. Users typically launch their browsers many times a day for the sole purpose of web searching, so they need to be able to get to the search bar as soon as possible. Otherwise, they will by-pass your page. The HTML block in Example 3-2 gives us the Google and Live.com search bars (see Figure 3-2).

*Figure 3-2. The header needs to be rendered as soon as possible because it contains the search bar, which is usually one of the first tools used*

The Live Search box is pretty cool. It shows the search result in a pop-up right on the page as shown in Figure 3-3.

The HTML snippet shown in Example 3-3 downloads the necessary components for providing the Live.com search functionality right on the page. Just put the snippet anywhere on the page and you have search functionality in that exact spot. Best of all, you don't need to register on the Live.com web site to get code snippets nor do you need to make web service calls to get search result. Both the UI and the functionality is provided inside the snippet.

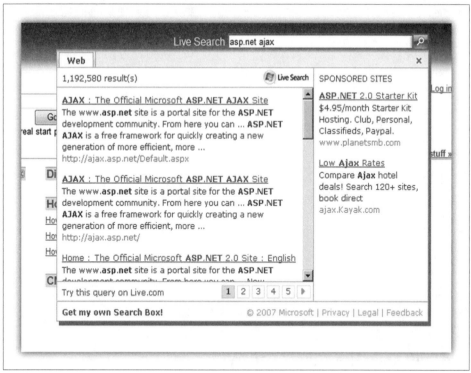

*Figure 3-3. Live.com search shows the results on a popup DIV right on the page, which is very handy for web portals because users can stay on the page and see search results*

*Example 3-3. HTML snippet for adding Live.com search bar on any page*

```
<div id="WLSearchBoxDiv" style="width:325px;">
  <table cellpadding="0px" cellspacing="0px">
    <tr id="WLSearchBoxPlaceholder">
        <td style="white-space:nowrap; color: White; padding-right: 5px; font-size
        12pt">Live Search</td>
        <td style="border-style:solid none solid solid;border-color:#4B7B9F;border
        width:2px;">
        <input id="WLSearchBoxInput" type="text" value="loading..." disabled="disabled"
        style="background-image:url(http://search.live.com/s/siteowner/searchbox_
        background.png);background-position-x:right;background-position-y:50;background-r
        epeat:no-repeat;height:16px;width:293px;border:none 0px #FFFFFF;"/>
        </td>
        <td style="border-style:solid;border-color:#4B7B9F;border-width:2px;">
            <input id="WLSearchBoxButton" type="image" src="http://search.live.com/s/
            siteowner/searchbutton_normal.PNG" align="absBottom" style="border-style:
            none"/>
        </td>
    </tr>
  </table>
</div>
```

*Example 3-3. HTML snippet for adding Live.com search bar on any page (continued)*

```
<script type="text/javascript" charset="utf-8">
  var WLSearchBoxConfiguration=
  {
    "global":{
      "serverDNS":"search.live.com"
    },
    "appearance":{
      "autoHideTopControl":false,
      "width":600,
      "height":400
    },
    "scopes":[
      {
        "type":"web",
        "caption":"Web",
        "searchParam":""
      }
    ]
  }
</script>
<script language="javascript" defer="defer" src="http://search.live.com/bootstrap.
js?ServId=SearchBox&ServId=SearchBoxWeb&Callback=WLSearchBoxScriptReady"></script>
</div>
```

## Add Stuff Area: The Widget Gallery

This pop-up area appears when the user clicks on the Add Stuff link. This widget gallery showcases all the available widgets. Users can choose which widget to add to the page from this area. It renders a five-column view of widgets as shown in Figure 3-4.

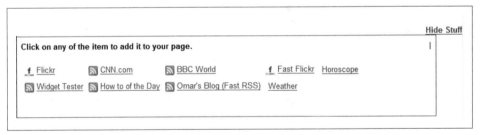

*Figure 3-4. Add Stuff area shows where all the widgets in the database are available*

The Add Stuff area is inside a single `UpdatePanel` control that contains buttons for adding and hiding widgets, plus the collection (list) of available widgets. The `UpdatePanel` control makes sure that user actions, such as adding a widget, happen asynchronously, without any postbacks (see Example 3-4).

*Example 3-4. Default.aspx, part 3(a): HTML snippet for the add stuff area (partial)*

```
<asp:UpdatePanel
        ID="AddContentUpdatePanel"
        runat="server"
        UpdateMode="conditional">

    <ContentTemplate>
        <asp:LinkButton
        ID="ShowAddContentPanel"
        runat="server"
        Text="Add stuff &#187;"
        CssClass="add_stuff_toggle"
        OnClick="ShowAddContentPanel_Click"/>

    <asp:LinkButton
        ID="HideAddContentPanel"
        runat="server"
        Text="Hide Stuff"
        CssClass="add_stuff_toggle"
        Visible="false"
        OnClick="HideAddContentPanel_Click" />
```

The update panel contains the Add Stuff and Hide Stuff link buttons. They toggle on the user's click. When the user clicks the Add Stuff link, the widget collection is loaded and displayed inside a panel named `AddContentPanel`. The HTML markup of `AddContentPanel` is shown in Example 3-5.

*Example 3-5. Default.aspx, part 3(b): AddContentPanel HTML snippet*

```
<asp:Panel ID="AddContentPanel" runat="Server"
    Visible="false"
    CssClass="widget_showcase" >
        <div style="float:left">
            <b>Click on any of the item to add it to your page.</b>
        </div>
    <div style="float:right">
            <asp:LinkButton ID="WidgetListPreviousLinkButton" runat="server"
                Visible="false"
                Text="&lt; Previous"
                OnClick="WidgetListPreviousLinkButton_Click" />
            |
            <asp:LinkButton ID="WidgetListNextButton" runat="server"
                Visible="false"
                Text="Next &gt;"
                OnClick="WidgetListNextButton_Click" />
        </div>
        <br /><br />
        <asp:DataList ID="WidgetDataList" runat="server"
            RepeatDirection="Vertical"
            RepeatColumns="5"
            RepeatLayout="Table"
```

*Example 3-5. Default.aspx, part 3(b): AddContentPanel HTML snippet (continued)*

```
            CellPadding="3"
            CellSpacing="3"
            EnableViewState="False"
            ShowFooter="False"
            ShowHeader="False">
                <ItemTemplate>
                    <asp:Image ID="Icon" runat="server"
                        ImageUrl='<%# Eval("Icon") %>'
                        ImageAlign="AbsMiddle" /> 
                    <asp:LinkButton ID="AddWidget" runat="server"
                        CommandArgument='<%# Eval("ID") %>'
                        CommandName="AddWidget" >
                        <%# Eval("Name") %>
                    </asp:LinkButton>
                </ItemTemplate>
        </asp:DataList>
</asp:Panel>
```

The `AddContentPanel` appears when the user clicks the Add Stuff link. Inside, the `DataList` named `WidgetDataList` is bound to the widget collection in the database at runtime from the code. The Add Stuff area fades in when a user clicks the Add Stuff link. An `AnimationExtender` runs the fade-in and fade-out effect (see Example 3-6).

*Example 3-6. Default.aspx, part 3(c): The AnimationExtender fades in and out in the Add Stuff area*

```
        <ajaxToolkit:AnimationExtender ID="AddContentPanelAnimation" runat="server"
            TargetControlID="AddContentPanel">
            <Animations>
                <OnLoad>
                    <FadeIn minimumOpacity=".2" />
                </OnLoad>
            </Animations>
        </ajaxToolkit:AnimationExtender>
    </ContentTemplate>
</asp:UpdatePanel>
```

The widget list is loaded by the `LoadAddStuff` function in *Default.aspx.cs*. The function just binds a list of widgets to the `DataList` control, and the rendering is done via simple data binding (see Example 3-7).

*Example 3-7. Default.aspx.cs: LoadAddStuff function*

```
private void LoadAddStuff( )
    {
        this.WidgetDataList.ItemCommand += new DataListCommandEventHandler(WidgetDataList_
        ItemCommand);

        var itemsToShow = WidgetList.Skip(AddStuffPageIndex*30).Take(30);
        this.WidgetDataList.DataSource = itemsToShow;
        this.WidgetDataList.DataBind( );

        // Enable/Disable paging buttons based on paging index
```

*Example 3-7. Default.aspx.cs: LoadAddStuff function (continued)*

```
        WidgetListPreviousLinkButton.Visible = AddStuffPageIndex > 0;
        WidgetListNextButton.Visible = AddStuffPageIndex*30+30 < WidgetList.Count;
    }
```

Inside the `LoadAddStuff` function, you will load the widget list from the database.
`List<Widget> WidgetList` is a private variable that loads all the widgets from the database only once and then stores in the cache. Example 3-8 uses the `DashboardFacade` to
load the widget list.

*Example 3-8. Loading WidgetList once and cache it for the lifetime of the application*

```
private List<Widget> WidgetList
{
    get
    {
        List<Widget> widgets = Cache["Widgets"] as List<Widget>;
        if( null == widgets )
        {
            widgets = new DashboardFacade(Profile.UserName).GetWidgetList();
            Cache["Widgets"] = widgets;
        }

        return widgets;
    }
}
```

`WidgetList` returns all the widgets defined in the widget table. You can't show all the
widgets at once on the data list, so you need to do paging on the `WidgetList` collection. Paging can be done by using two new function extensions—`Skip` and `Take`—
that were introduced in LINQ. LINQ adds these two functions on all lists so you can
easily do paging on any `List<>` instance. In the `LoadAddStuff` function, `Skip` skips 30
widgets per page and `Take` takes 30 widgets from the current page. The result after
`Skip` and `Take` is another generic `List<T>` of widgets of type `List<Widget>`, which
always contains 30 or fewer items.

When a user clicks on any of the widget links on the widget list, a new instance of
the widget is added on the first column of the page. This is handled in the
`ItemCommand` event of the `WidgetDataList` as shown in Example 3-9.

*Example 3-9. Creating new widget when user clicks on a widget from the widget list*

```
void WidgetDataList_ItemCommand(object source, DataListCommandEventArgs e)
{
    int widgetId = int.Parse( e.CommandArgument.ToString() );

    DashboardFacade facade = new DashboardFacade(Profile.UserName);
    WidgetInstance newWidget = facade.AddWidget( widgetId );

    ...
    ...
}
```

## The Tab Bar

The tab area shown in Figure 3-5 is inside an UpdatePanel because you want the user to add, edit, and delete tabs without refreshing the page. Actions like adding a new tab or editing a tab title do not require the widget area to be refreshed. However, when the user switches tabs by clicking on another tab, both the tab bar and the widget area refresh to show the new widgets on the new tab.

*Figure 3-5. Each tab represents a virtual page where the user can put more widgets*

The HTML snippet for the tab bar is shown in Example 3-10.

*Example 3-10. Default.aspx, part 4: HTML snippet for the tab bar*

```
<asp:UpdatePanel ID="TabUpdatePanel" runat="server"
    UpdateMode="conditional">
    <ContentTemplate>
        <div id="tabs">
            <ul class="tabs" runat="server" id="tabList">
                <li class="tab inactivetab">
                    <asp:LinkButton id="Page1Tab" runat="server"
                        Text="Page 1">
                    </asp:LinkButton>
                </li>
                <li class="tab activetab">
                    <asp:LinkButton id="Page2Tab" runat="server"
                        Text="Page 2">
                    </asp:LinkButton>
                </li>
            </ul>
        </div>
    </ContentTemplate>
</asp:UpdatePanel>
```

The tabs are generated at runtime inside the <UL> named tabs. Each tab is represented by one <LI> tag containing one LinkButton for the Tab title. Example 3-11 shows how the tab bar is generated from the user's Page collection.

*Example 3-11. Creating tabs dynamically*

```
    private void SetupTabs()
    {
        tabList.Controls.Clear();

        var setup = _Setup;
        var currentPage = setup.CurrentPage;
```

*Example 3-11. Creating tabs dynamically (continued)*

```
foreach( Page page in setup.Pages )
{
    var li = new HtmlGenericControl("li");
    li.ID = "Tab" + page.ID.ToString();
    li.Attributes["class"] = "tab " + (page.ID == currentPage.ID ? "activetab" :
    "inactivetab");

    var linkButton = new LinkButton();
    linkButton.ID = page.ID.ToString();
    linkButton.Text = page.Title;
    linkButton.CommandName = "ChangePage";
    linkButton.CommandArgument = page.ID.ToString();

    if( page.ID == currentPage.ID )
        linkButton.Click += new EventHandler(PageTitleEditMode_Click);
    else
        linkButton.Click += new EventHandler(PageLinkButton_Click);

    li.Controls.Add(linkButton);
    tabList.Controls.Add(li);
}
```

You create one <LI> inside the <UL> for each page. You will notice that I have marked the <UL> tag as runat="server", which means the <UL> tag is now a server control and is available from behind the code. There are two types of <LI> created, one for the active tab (current page) and one for inactive tabs (other pages). Each <LI> contains one LinkButton that acts as a clickable tab title. When you click the title of the active tab, it allows you to change the tab title. But when you click on an inactive tab, it just switches to that tab and loads the widgets on that page.

At the end of the tab bar, there's a "new tab" link that adds one new Page object to the user's Page collection. The new page is represented as a new tab on the tab bar. The "new tab" link is a dynamically created LinkButton, as shown in Example 3-12.

*Example 3-12. Creating a Add New Tab button, which adds a new tab on the tab bar and creates a brand new page for user*

```
var addNewTabLinkButton = new LinkButton();
addNewTabLinkButton.ID = "AddNewPage";
addNewTabLinkButton.Text = "new tab";
addNewTabLinkButton.Click += new EventHandler(addNewTabLinkButton_Click);
var li2 = new HtmlGenericControl("li");
li2.Attributes["class"] = "newtab";
li2.Controls.Add(addNewTabLinkButton);
tabList.Controls.Add(li2);
```

When the user clicks on the Add New Tab link, he creates a new Page object with the default setting, makes the new page a current page, reloads the tab bar, and refreshes columns to show the widgets on the new page. The click handler is defined in Example 3-13.

*Example 3-13. Handling click on "Add New Tab" link and creating new page for user*

*Example 3-13. Handling click on "Add New Tab" link and creating new page for user*

```
void addNewTabLinkButton_Click(object sender, EventArgs e)
{
    new DashboardFacade(Profile.UserName).AddNewPage( );

    this.ReloadPage(wi => true);

    this.RefreshAllColumns( );
}
```

The `ReloadPage` function loads the widgets on the current page. A lambda expression—`wi => true`—is used here. The details of the `ReloadPage` function are explained later in this chapter. But basically, it informs the function that all the widgets on this page will have the `FirstVisit` flag set to `true`. This means the widgets will not see that this is a postback, but instead see it as a first visit. Remember, widgets use `IWidgetHost.IsPostback` to determine whether it's a postback or a first visit. Because tab switching is like a first visit for the widgets on the new tab, you need to tell all widgets that it's a first visit, not a postback. This makes `IWidgetHost.IsPostback` return `false`. Details about how tab switching works and how widgets know whether they should assume that the visit is postback or nonpostback are explained in the upcoming section "Page Switching: Simulating a Nonpostback Experience."

When a user clicks on an inactive tab, it changes to active. The widgets on that page appear on the columns. The new page becomes the user's current page. So, when the user comes back to the site, he is taken to the last active tab, not the first tab. The user's last active tab is stored in a `UserSetting` table. The click handler for inactive tabs is defined in Example 3-14. All inactive tabs call the same event handler.

*Example 3-14. The click handler on the inactive tab makes the tab active when clicked*

```
void PageLinkButton_Click(object sender, EventArgs e)
{
    var linkButton = sender as LinkButton;

    // Get the page ID from the title link button ID
    var pageId = int.Parse(linkButton.ID);

    if( _Setup.UserSetting.CurrentPageId != pageId )
    {
        DatabaseHelper.Update<UserSetting>( _Setup.UserSetting, delegate( UserSetting
        u )
        {
            u.CurrentPageId = pageId;
        });
...


    }
}
```

The user can edit a tab title by clicking on the active tab title. When a user clicks on the title LinkButton, it replaces itself with a text box and a "save" button as shown in Figure 3-6.

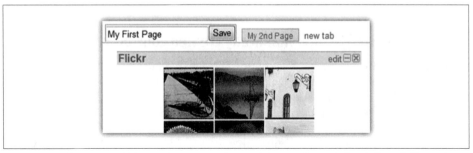

*Figure 3-6. When a user clicks on the My First Page tab, it switches to Edit Mode and allows the user to change the tab title*

The click on the tab is handled by PageTitleEditMode_Click, the server-side event handler, which replaces the title LinkButton with one TextBox and a Button. The event handler is defined in Example 3-15.

*Example 3-15. The event handler when the user switchs to edit mode on a tab*

```
void PageTitleEditMode_Click(object sender, EventArgs e)
{
    var linkButton = sender as LinkButton;

    var editTextBox = new TextBox( );
    editTextBox.ID = "PageNameEditTextBox";
    editTextBox.Text = linkButton.Text;

    var saveButton = new Button( );
    saveButton.Text = "Save";

    linkButton.Parent.Controls.Add(editTextBox);
    linkButton.Parent.Controls.Add(saveButton);
    linkButton.Parent.Controls.Remove(linkButton);
}
```

Because these two controls are created dynamically, they must have a fixed ID. Otherwise they will fail to postback.

Notice that there's no click handler for the saveButton in Example 3-15. So, how does the changed page title get saved? If you use the standard click handler and server-side event approach of ASP.NET, you have to do the following:

- Remember which page is being edited in ViewState
- Render the tabs in SetupTabs function
  - Check to see if the tab is being edited before creating a tab

— Render the LinkButton for the title, instead of rendering a text box and a save button

— Hook the click handler on the button

---

## Why a Fixed ID for Dynamically Created Controls Is Needed

When ASP.NET creates a dynamic control, it assigns a sequential ID to it, e.g., ctrl0. The ID is assigned according to the order it is added in the parent control's Controls collection. This means that if a button is dynamically created on the first visit, it can get an ID like ctrl0. But on a postback, if some other UI elements are created in the same Controls collection before you create the button again, it will get a different ID—say, ctrl1. As a result, when the button tries to restore its state from ViewState, it will look for entries against ID ctrl1, not ctrl0. But on the first visit, the button persisted its state against ctrl0. So, it will fail to restore its state properly. To avoid this, assign a unique ID to each dynamically created control.

---

This was too much effort. So, let's try a quick hack. Whenever there's a postback, you can access the posted controls' values directly from Request object. So, you can easily get the value of the text box when it is posted back (see Example 3-16).

*Example 3-16. Code called during the Page_Load event*

```
if( ScriptManager1.IsInAsyncPostBack )
{
    ...
    ...
    string pageName = Request["PageNameEditTextBox"];
    if( !string.IsNullOrEmpty(pageName) )
    {
        new DashboardFacade(Profile.UserName).ChangePageName(pageName);
        _Setup.CurrentPage.Title = pageName;
        this.SetupTabs();
    }
    ...
}
```

In Example 3-16, the value of the TextBox is read directly from the Request object and the page title in the database is changed accordingly. There's no need to recreate TextBox and Button just to read the page name. Another advantage of this approach is that these functions are never recreated during the postback, so you don't have to remove them and switch back to view mode after the edit. It's a quick way to implement in-place edit modules that pop up and go away. At the click of a button, you can create the controls that will serve the in-place edit area and then read the value of the controls directly from the Request object in the Page_Load handler.

---

However, if you want server-side validation, then you have to go back to complicated approach of always recreating the controls on asynchronous postback because you need to show validation errors, and the controls need to be there to show their invalid content error message. For simplicity, I skipped validation here.

## The Widget Area: The Three-Column Widget View

There are the three columns below the tab bar reserved for widgets, which we will refer to as the widget area. The widget area is a simple three-column HTML table. Each column contains one UpdatePanel and one DropCue, as shown in Example 3-17.

*Example 3-17. Default.aspx, part 7: Defining the three-column view of the widget area*

```
<table width="98%" cellspacing="10" border="0" align="center" class="table_fixed"
height="100%">
<tbody>
    <tr>
        <td class="column">
            <asp:UpdatePanel ID="LeftUpdatePanel" runat="server"
                UpdateMode="Conditional" >
                <ContentTemplate>
                    <asp:Panel ID="LeftPanel" runat="server"
                        class="widget_holder"
                        columnNo="0">
                        <div id="DropCue1" class="widget_dropcue">
                        </div>
                    </asp:Panel>

                    <cdd:CustomDragDropExtender ID="CustomDragDropExtender1"
                    runat="server"
                        TargetControlID="LeftPanel"
                        DragItemClass="widget"
                        DragItemHandleClass="widget_header"
                        DropCueID="DropCue1"
                        OnClientDrop="onDrop" />

                </ContentTemplate>
            </asp:UpdatePanel>
        </td>
```

Widgets are loaded inside Panels named LeftPanel, MiddlePanel, and RightPanel. Each widget is dynamically loaded and added inside these panels. If a widget is on the first column, it is added inside LeftPanel. The CustomDragDropExtender attached to these Panels provides the drag-and-drop support for widgets, as shown in Figure 3-7.

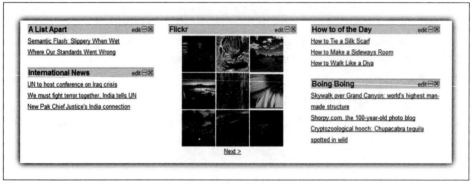

*Figure 3-7. With the three-column view of widgets, each column contains one UpdatePanel where the widgets are loaded*

## Loading the Start Page

Unlike regular ASP.NET pages, there is no code in the Page_Load event; instead, it is in the CreateChildControls function. ASP.NET calls this function when it needs to create server-side controls on the page. During postback processing on a page, unless all the dynamically created controls are already in place by the time the page loads ViewState, the events on those dynamic controls will not get fired properly. The Page_Load event happens too late to do this. In *Default.aspx*, the entire page is constructed dynamically, including the page bar. So, the controls must be created before they load their ViewState and process postback information, as shown in Example 3-18. In the ASP.NET page life cycle, CreateChildControls is the best place to create all dynamic controls that need to load states from ViewState and process postback information.

*Example 3-18. Dynamically create all controls and widgets on the page*

```
protected override void CreateChildControls()
    {
        base.CreateChildControls();

        this.LoadUserPageSetup(false);
        this.SetupTabs();
        this.LoadAddStuff();

        if( ScriptManager1.IsInAsyncPostBack )
        {
...
...
        }
        else
        {
            // First visit, non postback
```

```
            this.SetupWidgets( wi => true );
            this.SetupTabs( );
    }
}
```

There are three steps involved in loading the full page:

1. Load the user page setup and user setting (the `false` passed to the method tells the method not to look for cached information)
2. Render the tabs that shows user's pages
3. Load the widgets on the current page

The first step is to load the user's page setup, which includes the following:

- User's setting, e.g., current page
- User's page collection
- Widgets only on the current page

The `LoadUserPageSetup` method checks whether this is a first-time user visiting the site. On the very first visit, the user's page setup is created. On subsequent visits, the user's existing page setup is loaded, as shown in Example 3-19.

*Example 3-19. For a new user, create the page setup; for an existing user, load the existing page setup*

```
private void LoadUserPageSetup(bool noCache)
    {
        if( Profile.IsAnonymous )
        {
            if( Profile.IsFirstVisit )
            {
                // First visit
                Profile.IsFirstVisit = false;
                Profile.Save( );

                _Setup = new DashboardFacade(Profile.UserName).NewUserVisit( );
            }
            else
            {
                _Setup = Cache[Profile.UserName] as UserPageSetup;
                if( noCache || null == _Setup )
                    _Setup = new DashboardFacade(Profile.UserName).LoadUserSetup( );
            }
        }
        else
        {
            _Setup = Cache[Profile.UserName] as UserPageSetup;
            if( noCache || null == _Setup )
                _Setup = new DashboardFacade(Profile.UserName).LoadUserSetup( );
        }
```

*Example 3-19. For a new user, create the page setup; for an existing user, load the existing page setup (continued)*

```
        // Cache the user setup in order to avoid repeated loading during postback
        Cache[Profile.UserName] = _Setup;
    }
```

In Example 3-19, the user's page setup is stored in an ASP.NET cache so that the whole setup is not repeatedly loaded from the database during asynchronous post-backs from widgets. Because there's no chance of a user's page setup being changed unless the user adds, edits, or deletes widgets or pages, you can safely cache the whole setup. However, the cache works for single-server and single-process hosting. If you have multiple servers in a web farm or if you have just one server, but Application Pool is configured to use multiple processes in web garden mode, then this cache approach will not work. For example, say two servers in your web farm have cached a user's page setup. The user now deletes the current page. Say Server A received the postback. The page is deleted from database and the latest page setup is now cached in Server A. But Server B still has the old page setup cached where the deleted page still exists. If the user adds a new widget and the request goes to Server B, it will try to add the widget on the nonexistent page and fail.

In web garden mode, multiple processes serve the application pool for the web site and suffer from a similar problem as requests from the same user go to different processes. The solution is to use commercial distributed cache solutions, but they are quite expensive. Such solutions give you a cache that is synchronized between all servers. If Server A updates an entry in the cache, it will be synchronized with Servers B, C, and D. When you have a large amount of traffic on the site, you won't be able to repeatedly load the whole page setup because it will put a lot of stress on the database server. In that case, you will have to go for caching the whole setup for as long as possible and use a distributed cache solution.

The next step is to dynamically create the widgets on the three columns. The function SetupWidgets shown in Example 3-20 does this difficult job.

*Example 3-20. Dynamically create widget controls inside column panels*

```
    private void SetupWidgets(Func<WidgetInstance, bool> isWidgetFirstLoad)
    {
        var setup = Context.Items[typeof(UserPageSetup)] as UserPageSetup;

        var columnPanels = new Panel[] {
            this.FindControl("LeftPanel") as Panel,
            this.FindControl("MiddlePanel") as Panel,
            this.FindControl("RightPanel") as Panel };

        // Clear existing widgets if any
        foreach( Panel panel in columnPanels )
```

```
{
    List<WidgetContainer> widgets = panel.Controls.OfType<WidgetContainer>().
    ToList();
    foreach( var widget in widgets ) panel.Controls.Remove( widget );
}

foreach( WidgetInstance instance in setup.WidgetInstances )
{
    var panel = columnPanels[instance.ColumnNo];

    var widget = LoadControl(WIDGET_CONTAINER) as WidgetContainer;
    widget.ID = "WidgetContainer" + instance.Id.ToString();
    widget.IsFirstLoad = isWidgetFirstLoad(instance);
    widget.WidgetInstance = instance;

    widget.Deleted += new Action<WidgetInstance>(widget_Deleted);

    panel.Controls.Add(widget);
}

}
```

The reference to Func<> in the method parameters pertains to new functionality in C#.

This function first clears all the widgets from the three Panels. During asynchronous postback, SetupWidgets is called once to recreate the controls and give ASP.NET the exact same control hierarchy so that it can restore ViewState and fire events properly. After the events are processed, if there's any change on the widget area, such as a widget deleted or added, then SetupWidgets is called again to render the latest widgets. It's like calling a Bind method on a DataGrid or DataList again when something changes on the data source.

When SetupWidgets is called for a second time within the same request, the Panels already have the widgets. Thus, some widgets are created twice unless the Panels are cleared. Example 3-21 uses some C# 3.0 language extensions. We use the OfType<> function to get only the widgets inside the Panels, not any other control. The purpose is to delete only the widgets and preserve everything else, like the extenders and the drop cue.

*Example 3-21. Clearing all WidgetContainers from a panel using the OfType<> extension method in C# 3.0*

```
List<WidgetContainer> widgets = panel.Controls.OfType<WidgetContainer>().
ToList();
foreach( var widget in widgets ) panel.Controls.Remove( widget );
```

After clearing the panels, one widget container is created for each widget instance. Now comes the Func<> part, which is another very useful extension in C# 3.0. It is called *predicate*. You can create lambda expressions and pass them as predicate during a function call. Lambda expressions are shorthand for delegates. Instead of creating a delegate function for simple expressions, you can pass them in a lambda expression form. For example, when a page is loaded for the first time, SetupWidgets is called with a lambda expression, which always returns true for all widget instances.

```
SetupWidgets( wi => true );
```

This means, the following statement is always true for all widget instances:

```
widget.IsFirstLoad = isWidgetFirstLoad(instance);
```

But you can also specify expressions that return true or false based on a specific condition:

```
SetupWidgets( wi => wi.ColumnNo == 1 );
```

This will evaluate as true only for those widget instances that are on the middle column (column 1). By doing this, we are telling the function to load middle column widgets as if they are being loaded for the first time. An equivalent C# 2.0 implementation would be as follows:

```
delegate bool SetupWidgetsDelegate( WidgetInstance wi);

SetupWidgets( new SetupWidgetsDelegate(delegate(WidgetInstance wi)
{
    return wi.ColumnNo == 1;
}));
```

The reason why a lambda expression is used here instead of a simple Boolean true/false is explained in the section "Page Switching: Simulating a Nonpostback Experience" later in this chapter. The idea is to set widget.IsFirstLoad = true for some widget instances and set widget.IsFirstLoad = false for some other widget instances. This decision depends on who is calling the SetupWidgets function. The expression that can take this decision is only known to the function that calls SetupWidgets. Thus, by using predicates, the caller can easily pass the expression to SetupWidgets and simplify the logic inside SetupWidgets.

# Building a Custom Drag-and-Drop Extender for a Multicolumn Drop Zone

I first considered a plain vanilla JavaScript-based solution for my drag-and-drop functionality. It required less code, less architectural complexity, and was faster. Another reason was the high learning curve for properly making extenders in ASP.NET AJAX, given that there's hardly any documentation available on the Web (or at least that was the case when I was writing this book). However, writing a proper extender that pushes ASP.NET AJAX to the limit is a very good way to learn the ASP.NET AJAX framework's under-the-hood secrets. So, the two extenders introduced here will tell you almost everything you need to know about ASP.NET AJAX extenders.

Before I wrote my own implementation of drag and drop, I carefully looked at existing solutions. The Ajax Control Toolkit comes with a DragPanel extender that could be used to provide drag-and-drop support to panels. It also has a ReorderList control, which could reorder the items into a single list. Widgets are basically panels that flow vertically in each column. So, it could be possible to create a reorder list in each column and use the DragPanel to drag the widgets. But ReorderList couldn't be used because:

- It strictly uses the HTML table to render its items in a column. But I have no table inside the columns, only one UpdatePanel per column.

- It takes a drag handle template and creates a drag handle for each item at runtime. But there already is a drag handle created inside a widget, which is the widget header, so ReorderList can't create another drag handle.

- It must have client-side callback to JavaScript functions during drag and drop to make Ajax calls and persist the widget positions. The callback must provide the Panel where the widget is dropped, depending on which widget is dropped, and at what position.

The next challenge is with the DragPanel extender. The default implementation of drag and drop in the Ajax Control Toolkit doesn't work for these reasons:

- When you start dragging, the item becomes absolutely positioned, but when you drop it, it does not become statically positioned. A small hack is needed for restoring the original positioning to static.

- It does not bring the dragging item on top of all the items. As a result, when you start dragging, you see the item being dragged below other items, which makes the drag get stuck, especially when there's an IFrame.

For all these reasons, I made CustomDragDropExtender and CustomFloatingExtender. CustomDragDropExtender is for the column containers where widgets are placed. It provides the reordering support. You can attach this extender to any Panel control.

Example 3-22 shows how you can attach this extender to any Panel and make that Panel support dragging and dropping widgets.

*Example 3-22. How to attach CustomDragDropExtender to a Panel*

```
<asp:Panel ID="LeftPanel" runat="server"  class="widget_holder" columnNo="0">
        <div id="DropCue1" class="widget_dropcue">
        </div>
</asp:Panel>

<cdd:CustomDragDropExtender ID="CustomDragDropExtender1"
    runat="server"
    TargetControlID="LeftPanel"
    DragItemClass="widget"
    DragItemHandleClass="widget_header"
    DropCueID="DropCue1"
    OnClientDrop="onDrop" />
```

`<cdd:CustomDragDropExtender>` offers the following properties:

TargetControlID
> ID of the Panel that becomes the drop zone.

DragItemClass
> All child elements inside the Panel having this class will become draggable, e.g., the widget DIV has this class so that it can become draggable.

DragItemHandleClass
> Any child element having this class inside the draggable elements will become the drag handle for the draggable element, e.g., the widget header area has this class, so it acts as the drag handle for the widget.

DropCueID
> ID of an element inside the Panel, which acts as DropCue.

OnClientDrop
> Name of a JavaScript function that is called when the widget is dropped on the Panel.

LeftPanel becomes a widget container that allows widgets to be dropped on it and reordered. The DragItemClass attribute on the extender defines the items that can be ordered. This prevents nonwidget HTML DIVs from getting ordered. Only the DIVs of the class "widget" are ordered. Say there are five DIVs with the class named widget. It will allow reordering of only the five DIVs, not any other element (see Example 3-23).

*Example 3-23. CustomDragDropExtender allows only drag-and-drop support for elements with a specific class*

```
<div id="LeftPanel" class="widget_holder" >
        <div class="widget"> ... </div>
        <div class="widget"> ... </div>

        <div class="widget"> ... </div>
        <div class="widget"> ... </div>
        <div class="widget"> ... </div>

        <div>This DIV will not move</div>
        <div id="DropCue1" class="widget_dropcue"></div>
</div>
```

When a widget is dropped on the panel, the extender fires the function specified in OnClientDrop. It offers standard Ajax events. But unlike basic Ajax events where you have to programmatically bind to events, you can bind the event handler declaratively. So, instead of doing this:

```
function pageLoad( sender, e ) {

    var extender1 = $get('CustomDragDropExtender1');
```

```
      extender1.add_onDrop( onDrop );

   }
```

you can do this:

```
<cdd:CustomDragDropExtender ID="CustomDragDropExtender1"
    runat="server"
    OnClientDrop="onDrop" />
```

When the event is raised, the function named onDrop gets called. This is done with the help of some library functions available in ACT project. When the event is fired, it passes the container, the widget, and the position of where the widget is dropped as an event argument, as specified by the code in Example 3-24.

*Example 3-24. Client-side JavaScript event handler for receiving drag-and-drop notification*

```
function onDrop( sender, e )
{
    var container = e.get_container( );
    var item = e.get_droppedItem( );
    var position = e.get_position( );


    var instanceId = parseInt(item.getAttribute("InstanceId"));
    var columnNo = parseInt(container.getAttribute("columnNo"));
    var row = position;

    WidgetService.MoveWidgetInstance( instanceId, columnNo, row );
}
```

The widget location is updated on the server by calling the WidgetService.MoveWidgetInstance.

CustomDragDropExtender has three files:

*CustomDragDropExtender.cs*
   The server side extender implementation

*CustomDragDropDesigner.cs*
   Designer class for the extender

*CustomDragDropExtender.js*
   Client-side script for the extender

The code for the server-side class *CustomDragDropExtender.cs* is shown in Example 3-25.

*Example 3-25. Code for CustomDragDropExtender.cs*

```
[assembly: System.Web.UI.WebResource("CustomDragDrop.CustomDragDropBehavior.js", "text/
    javascript")]

namespace CustomDragDrop
```

*Example 3-25. Code for CustomDragDropExtender.cs (continued)*

```csharp
{
    [Designer(typeof(CustomDragDropDesigner))]
    [ClientScriptResource("CustomDragDrop.CustomDragDropBehavior",
    "CustomDragDrop.CustomDragDropBehavior.js")]
    [TargetControlType(typeof(WebControl))]
    [RequiredScript(typeof(CustomFloatingBehaviorScript))]
    [RequiredScript(typeof(DragDropScripts))]
    public class CustomDragDropExtender : ExtenderControlBase
    {
        [ExtenderControlProperty]
        public string DragItemClass
        {
            get
            {
                return GetPropertyValue<String>("DragItemClass", string.Empty);
            }
            set
            {
                SetPropertyValue<String>("DragItemClass", value);
            }
        }

        [ExtenderControlProperty]
        public string DragItemHandleClass
        {
            get
            {
                return GetPropertyValue<String>("DragItemHandleClass", string.Empty);
            }
            set
            {
                SetPropertyValue<String>("DragItemHandleClass", value);
            }
        }

        [ExtenderControlProperty]
        [IDReferenceProperty(typeof(WebControl))]
        public string DropCueID
        {
            get
            {
                return GetPropertyValue<String>("DropCueID", string.Empty);
            }
            set
            {
                SetPropertyValue<String>("DropCueID", value);
            }
        }

        [ExtenderControlProperty()]
        [DefaultValue("")]
        [ClientPropertyName("onDrop")]
```

*Example 3-25. Code for CustomDragDropExtender.cs (continued)*

```
    public string OnClientDrop
    {
        get
        {
            return GetPropertyValue<String>("OnClientDrop", string.Empty);
        }
        set
        {
            SetPropertyValue<String>("OnClientDrop", value);
        }
    }

  }
}
```

Most of the code in the extender defines the properties. The important part is the declaration of the class shown in Example 3-26.

*Example 3-26. Declaration of the class CustomDragDropExtender defines the required scripts for the extender and the type of control it can attach to*

```
[assembly: System.Web.UI.WebResource("CustomDragDrop.CustomDragDropBehavior.js", "text/
    javascript")]

namespace CustomDragDrop
{
    [Designer(typeof(CustomDragDropDesigner))]
    [ClientScriptResource("CustomDragDrop.CustomDragDropBehavior", "CustomDragDrop.
        CustomDragDropBehavior.js")]
    [TargetControlType(typeof(WebControl))]
    [RequiredScript(typeof(CustomFloatingBehaviorScript))]
    [RequiredScript(typeof(DragDropScripts))]
    public class CustomDragDropExtender : ExtenderControlBase
    {
```

The extender class inherits from `ExtenderControlBase` as defined in the Ajax Control Toolkit (ACT) project. This base class has additional features beyond those found with the extender base class that ships with ASP.NET AJAX. The ACT extender allows you to use the `RequiredScript` attribute, which makes sure all the required scripts are downloaded before the extender script is downloaded and initialized. The `CustomDragDrop` extender has a dependency on another extender named `CustomFloatingBehavior`. It also depends on ACT's `DragDropManager`. So, the `RequiredScript` attribute makes sure required scripts are downloaded before the extender script downloads. The `ExtenderControlBase` is a pretty big class and does a lot of work for us. It contains default implementations for discovering all the script files for the extender and then renders them in proper order so that the browser downloads the scripts in correct order.

The [assembly:System.Web.UI.WebResource] attribute defines the script file containing the script for the extender. The script file is an embedded resource file.

The [ClientScriptResource] attribute defines the scripts required for the extender. This class is also defined in ACT. ExtenderControlBase uses this attribute to find out which JavaScript files are working for the extender and renders them properly.

The challenge is in writing the client side JavaScript for the extender. On the *CustomDragDrop.js* file, there's a JavaScript class that is the extender implementation, as shown in Example 3-27.

*Example 3-27. The JavaScript implementation of the extender class's constructor*

```
Type.registerNamespace('CustomDragDrop');

CustomDragDrop.CustomDragDropBehavior = function(element) {

    CustomDragDrop.CustomDragDropBehavior.initializeBase(this, [element]);

    this._DragItemClassValue = null;
    this._DragItemHandleClassValue = null;
    this._DropCueIDValue = null;
    this._dropCue = null;
    this._floatingBehaviors = [];
}
```

During initialization, this extender hooks on the Panel and the DropCue while the widget is being dragged and dropped over the Panel. See Example 3-28.

*Example 3-28. Initialize the CustomDragDrop extender and hook on the items*

```
CustomDragDrop.CustomDragDropBehavior.prototype = {

    initialize : function() {
        // Register ourselves as a drop target.
        AjaxControlToolkit.DragDropManager.registerDropTarget(this);

        // Initialize drag behavior after a while
        window.setTimeout( Function.createDelegate( this, this._initializeDraggableItems
        ), 3000 );

        this._dropCue = $get(this.get_DropCueID( ));
    },
```

After initializing the DragDropManager and marking the Panel as a drop target, a timer is started to discover the draggable items inside the Panel and apply FloatingBehavior to them. FloatingBehavior makes a DIV draggable.

 FloatingBehavior makes one DIV freely draggable on the page. But it does not offer drop functionality. DragDropBehavior offers the drop functionality that allows a freely moving DIV to rest on a fixed position.

Discovering and initializing `FloatingBehavior` for the draggable items is challenging work, as you see in Example 3-29.

*Example 3-29. Discovering draggable items and creating FloatingBehavior for each of item*

```
// Find all items with the drag item class and make each item
// draggable
_initializeDraggableItems : function()
{
    this._clearFloatingBehaviors();

    var el = this.get_element();

    var child = el.firstChild;
    while( child != null )
    {
        if( child.className == this._DragItemClassValue && child != this._dropCue)
        {
            var handle = this._findChildByClass(child, this._
            DragItemHandleClassValue);
            if( handle )
            {
                var handleId = handle.id;
                var behaviorId = child.id + "_WidgetFloatingBehavior";

                // make the item draggable by adding floating behaviour to it
                var floatingBehavior = $create(CustomDragDrop.CustomFloatingBehavior,
                        {"DragHandleID":handleId, "id":behaviorId, "name":
                        behaviorId}, {}, {}, child);

                Array.add( this._floatingBehaviors, floatingBehavior );
            }
        }
        child = child.nextSibling;
    }
},
```

Here's the algorithm:

- Run through all immediate child elements of the control to which the extender is attached.
- If the child item has the class for draggable item, then:
  — Find any element under the child item that has the class for a drag handle; if such an item is found, then attach a `CustomFloatingBehavior` with the child item.

The `_findChildByClass` function recursively iterates through all the child elements and looks for an element that has the defined class. The code is shown in Example 3-30. It's an expensive process. So, it is important that the drag handle is very close to the draggable element. Ideally, the drag handle should be the first child of the draggable element, so the search for a widget header doesn't have to iterate through too many elements.

*Example 3-30. Handy function to find HTML elements by class name*

```
_findChildByClass : function(item, className)
{
    // First check all immediate child items
    var child = item.firstChild;
    while( child != null )
    {
        if( child.className == className ) return child;
        child = child.nextSibling;
    }

    // Not found, recursively check all child items
    child = item.firstChild;
    while( child != null )
    {
        var found = this._findChildByClass( child, className );
        if( found != null ) return found;
        child = child.nextSibling;
    }
},
```

When a user drags an item over the `Panel` to which the extender is attached, `DragDropManager` fires the events shown in Example 3-31.

*Example 3-31. Events raised by DragDropManager*

```
onDragEnterTarget : function(dragMode, type, data) {
    this._showDropCue(data);
},

onDragLeaveTarget : function(dragMode, type, data) {
    this._hideDropCue(data);
},

onDragInTarget : function(dragMode, type, data) {
    this._repositionDropCue(data);
},
```

While drag and drop is going on, you need to deal with the drop cue. The challenge is to find out the right position for the drop cue (see Figure 3-8).

We need to find out where we should show the drop cue based on where the user wants to put the item. The idea is to find the widget that is immediately underneath the dragged item. The item underneath is pushed down by one position and the drop cue takes its place. While dragging, the position of the drag item can be found easily. Based on that, you can locate the widget below the drag item with the `_findItemAt` function shown in Example 3-32.

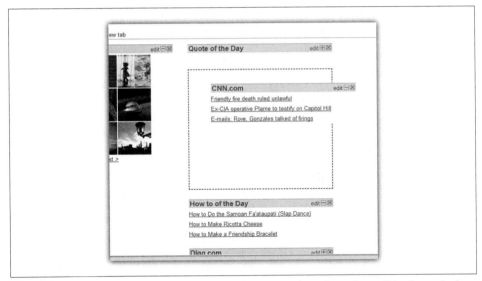

*Figure 3-8. When you drag a widget, a drop cue shows you where the widget will be dropped when mouse is released*

*Example 3-32. Find the widget at the x,y coordinate of the mouse*

```
_findItemAt : function(x, y, item)
    {
        var el = this.get_element();

        var child = el.firstChild;
        while( child != null )
        {
            if( child.className == this._DragItemClassValue && child != this._dropCue &&
            child != item )
            {
                var pos = Sys.UI.DomElement.getLocation(child);

                if( y <= pos.y )
                {
                    return child;
                }
            }
            child = child.nextSibling;
        }

        return null;
    },
```

The _findItemAt function returns the widget that is immediately underneath the dragged item. Now you can add the drop cue immediately above the widget to show the user where the widget being dragged can be dropped. The _repositionDropCue function, whose code is shown in Example 3-33, relocates the drop cue to the position where a widget can be dropped.

*Example 3-33. Move the drop cue to the place where a widget can be dropped*

```
_repositionDropCue : function(data)
    {
        var location = Sys.UI.DomElement.getLocation(data.item);
        var nearestChild = this._findItemAt(location.x, location.y, data.item);

        var el = this.get_element();

        if( null == nearestChild )
        {
            if( el.lastChild != this._dropCue )
            {
                el.removeChild(this._dropCue);
                el.appendChild(this._dropCue);
            }
        }
        else
        {
            if( nearestChild.previousSibling != this._dropCue )
            {
                el.removeChild(this._dropCue);
                el.insertBefore(this._dropCue, nearestChild);
            }
        }
    },
```

One exception to consider here is that there may be no widget immediately below the dragged item. This happens when the user is trying to drop the widget at the bottom of a column. In that case, the drop cue is shown at the bottom of the column.

When the user releases the widget, it drops right on top of the drop cue, and the drop cue disappears. After the drop, the onDrop event is raised to notify where the widget is dropped, as shown in Example 3-34.

*Example 3-34. Place the dropped widget on the right place and raise the onDrop event*

```
_placeItem : function(data)
    {
        var el = this.get_element();

        data.item.parentNode.removeChild( data.item );
        el.insertBefore( data.item, this._dropCue );

        // Find the position of the dropped item
        var position = 0;
        var item = el.firstChild;
        while( item != data.item )
        {
            if( item.className == this._DragItemClassValue ) position++;
            item = item.nextSibling;
        }
        this._raiseDropEvent( /*Container*/ el, /*dropped item*/ data.item, /*position*/
        position );
    }
```

Generally, you can define events in extenders by adding two functions in the extender as shown in Example 3-35.

*Example 3-35. Provide event subscription support in ASP.NET Ajax Extenders*

```
add_onDrop : function(handler) {
    this.get_events().addHandler("onDrop", handler);
},

remove_onDrop : function(handler) {
    this.get_events().removeHandler("onDrop", handler);
},
```

But this does not give you the support for defining the event listener name in the ASP.NET declaration:

```
<cdd:CustomDragDropExtender ID="CustomDragDropExtender1"
    runat="server"
    TargetControlID="LeftPanel"
    DragItemClass="widget"
    DragItemHandleClass="widget_header"
    DropCueID="DropCue1"
    OnClientDrop="onDrop" />
```

Such declarative approaches allows only properties of a control. To support such a declarative assignment of events, you need to first introduce a property named OnClientDrop in the extender. Then, during assignment of the property, you need to find the specified function there and attach an event notification to that function. The discovery of the function from its name is done by CommonToolkitScripts. resolveFunction, which is available in the ACT project and used in Example 3-36.

*Example 3-36. Allow the event name to be specified as a property on the extender*

```
// onDrop property maps to onDrop event
get_onDrop : function() {
    return this.get_events().getHandler("onDrop");
},

set_onDrop : function(value) {
    if (value && (0 < value.length)) {
        var func = CommonToolkitScripts.resolveFunction(value);
        if (func) {
            this.add_onDrop(func);
        } else {
            throw Error.argumentType('value', typeof(value), 'Function', 'resize
            handler not a function, function name, or function text.');
        }
    }
},
```

Raising the event is the same as basic Ajax events:

```
_raiseEvent : function( eventName, eventArgs ) {
        var handler = this.get_events().getHandler(eventName);
```

```
            if( handler ) {
                if( !eventArgs ) eventArgs = Sys.EventArgs.Empty;
                handler(this, eventArgs);
            }
        },
```

The next challenge is to make CustomFloatingBehavior. The server-side class *CustomFloatingBehavior.cs* is declared, as shown in Example 3-37.

*Example 3-37. CustomFloatingBehavior.cs content*

```
[assembly: System.Web.UI.WebResource("CustomDragDrop.CustomFloatingBehavior.js", "text/
javascript")]

namespace CustomDragDrop
{
    [Designer(typeof(CustomFloatingBehaviorDesigner))]
    [ClientScriptResource("CustomDragDrop.CustomFloatingBehavior", "CustomDragDrop.
    CustomFloatingBehavior.js")]
    [TargetControlType(typeof(WebControl))]
    [RequiredScript(typeof(DragDropScripts))]
    public class CustomFloatingBehaviorExtender : ExtenderControlBase
    {
        [ExtenderControlProperty]
        [IDReferenceProperty(typeof(WebControl))]
        public string DragHandleID
        {
            get
            {
                return GetPropertyValue<String>("DragHandleID", string.Empty);
            }
            set
            {
                SetPropertyValue<String>("DragHandleID", value);
            }
        }
    }
}
```

There's only one property—DragHandleID, in which the widget's header works as the drag handle. So, the header ID is specified here. This extender has dependency on DragDropManager, which requires the [RequiredScript(typeof(DragDropScripts))] attribute.

Besides the designer class, there's one more class that CustomDragDropExtender needs to specify its dependency over this FloatingBehavior:

```
[ClientScriptResource(null, "CustomDragDrop.CustomFloatingBehavior.js")]
public static class CustomFloatingBehaviorScript
{
}
```

This class can be used inside the RequiredScript attribute. It defines only which script file contains the client-side code for the extender.

---

The client-side JavaScript is same as FloatingBehavior, which comes with ACT. The only difference is a hack when the drag starts. DragDropManager does not return the item being dragged to the static position once it makes it absolute. It also does not increase the zIndex of the item. If the drag item does not become the top-most item on the page, then it goes below other elements on the page during drag. So, I have made some changes in the mouseDownHandler attribute of the behavior to add these features, shown in Example 3-38.

*Example 3-38. Revised mouseDownhandler in CustomFloatingBehavior.js*

```
function mouseDownHandler(ev) {
    window._event = ev;
    var el = this.get_element();

    if (!this.checkCanDrag(ev.target)) return;

    // Get the location before making the element absolute
    _location = Sys.UI.DomElement.getLocation(el);

    // Make the element absolute
    el.style.width = el.offsetWidth + "px";
    el.style.height = el.offsetHeight + "px";
    Sys.UI.DomElement.setLocation(el, _location.x, _location.y);

    _dragStartLocation = Sys.UI.DomElement.getLocation(el);

    ev.preventDefault();

    this.startDragDrop(el);

    // Hack for restoring position to static
    el.originalPosition = "static";
    el.originalZIndex = el.style.zIndex;
    el.style.zIndex = "60000";
}
```

Setting el.originalPosition = "static" fixes the bug in DragDropManager. It incorrectly stores absolute as the originalPosition when startDragDrop is called. So, after calling this function, reset to the correct originalPosition, which is "static."

When drag starts, zIndex is set to a very high value so that the dragged item remains on top of everything on the page. When drag completes, the original zIndex is restored and the left, top, width, and height attributes are cleared. DragDropManager makes the item position static, but it does not clear the left, top, width, and height attributes. This moves the element away from the place where it is dropped. This bug is fixed in the onDragEnd event, as coded in Example 3-39.

*Example 3-39. onDragEnd event fixes the zIndex related problem*

```
this.onDragEnd = function(canceled) {
    if (!canceled) {
        var handler = this.get_events().getHandler('move');
```

```
        if(handler) {
            var cancelArgs = new Sys.CancelEventArgs();
            handler(this, cancelArgs);
            canceled = cancelArgs.get_cancel();
        }
    }

    var el = this.get_element();
    el.style.width = el.style.height = el.style.left = el.style.top = "";
    el.style.zIndex = el.originalZIndex;
}
```

That's all folks! Now you have two handy extenders that you can attach to HTML elements and provide complete drag-and-drop support.

# Implementing WidgetContainer

WidgetContainer dynamically creates a widget inside its body area. The container consists only of header and body areas. The rest is provided by the actual widget loaded dynamically inside the container's body area. The settings area that you see when you click "edit" on the header also comes from the actual widget. WidgetContainer informs the widget only when to show it. The "Building Widgets" section later in this chapter shows how the widget handles this notification. WidgetContainer acts as a bridge between widgets and the core. The core communicates to the widgets via the container, and the widgets use the core's features via the container.

WidgetContainer's header contains the title text, the expand and collapse button, the "edit" link, and the close button within an UpdatePanel, as shown in Example 3-40.

*Example 3-40. WidgetContainer's header panel*

```
<asp:Panel ID="Widget" CssClass="widget" runat="server">
    <asp:Panel id="WidgetHeader" CssClass="widget_header" runat="server">
        <asp:UpdatePanel ID="WidgetHeaderUpdatePanel" runat="server"
        UpdateMode="Conditional">
        <ContentTemplate>
          ...
          ...
          ...
        </ContentTemplate>
        </asp:UpdatePanel>
    </asp:Panel>
</asp:Panel>
```

By doing this, we are preventing the body area from refreshing when something changes in the header. If the body area refreshes, the widget hosted inside it will unnecessarily refresh. To avoid downloading and refreshing a large amount of data in the whole widget, the header and body contain separate UpdatePanel controls.

There is an UpdateProgress extender attached to the header UpdatePanel, which shows a "Working..." indicator when the header is going through asynchronous postback. This happens when a user clicks on the title to change it or clicks some button on the header area.

```
<asp:UpdateProgress ID="UpdateProgress2" runat="server"
    DisplayAfter="10"
    AssociatedUpdatePanelID="WidgetHeaderUpdatePanel" >
        <ProgressTemplate>
            <center>Working...</center>
        </ProgressTemplate>
</asp:UpdateProgress>
```

After this comes the UpdatePanel body, where the actual widget is loaded.

```
<asp:UpdatePanel ID="WidgetBodyUpdatePanel" runat="server"
 UpdateMode="Conditional" >
    <ContentTemplate>
        <asp:Panel ID="WidgetBodyPanel" runat="Server"></asp:Panel>
    </ContentTemplate>
</asp:UpdatePanel>
```

The widget is not directly added inside the UpdatePanel. Instead it is added inside another regular Panel named WidgetBodyPanel (see Figure 3-9).

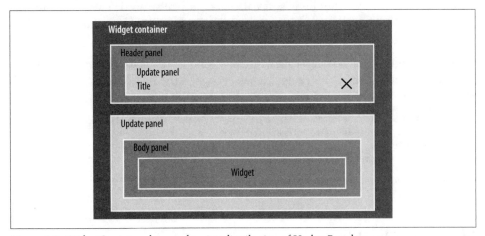

*Figure 3-9. WidgetContainer layout showing distribution of UpdatePanels*

When a widget is collapsed, the body area goes away. This is done by setting Visible=False to the UpdatePanel. But that does not hide the DIV, which is generated for the UpdatePanel, nor does it clear the content of that DIV. But if you put a Panel inside the UpdatePanel and make it invisible, the UpdatePanel will become blank because there's nothing to show anymore. This is exactly what needs to happen when a widget is collapsed. By using an HTTP tracer tool like Fiddler or Charles, you can observe that the following data is transferred by the asynchronous postback when the widget is collapsed and the WidgetBodyPanel is hidden:

```
933|updatePanel|WidgetContainer89605_WidgetHeaderUpdatePanel|
        <table class="widget_header_table" cellspacing="0" cellpadding="0">
        <tbody>
        <tr>
        <td class="widget_title"><a id="WidgetContainer89605_WidgetTitle" ...
         <td class="widget_edit"><a id="WidgetContainer89605_EditWidget" ...
          <td class="widget_button"><a id="WidgetContainer89605_ExpandWidget" ...
          <td class="widget_button"><a id="WidgetContainer89605_CloseWidget" ...
        </tr>
        </tbody>
        </table>
        |20|updatePanel|WidgetContainer89605_WidgetBodyUpdatePanel|

        |0|hiddenField|__EVENTTARGET||0|hiddenField|__EVENTARGUMENT||...
```

The response contains the header UpdatePanel's ID (WidgetContainer89605_
WidgetHeaderUpdatePanel) that was updated, followed by the new HTML snippet
that needs to be placed inside the header update panel. The new HTML contains the
expand button, and the collapse button is no longer present. Once the HTML is set
to the header area, the collapse button disappears and the expand button appears.

After the header's UpdatePanel HTML, the body's UpdatePanel
(WidgetContainer89605_WidgetBodyUpdatePanel) HTML is sent. Because there's no
visible control inside the body's UpdatePanel, there's no HTML sent to the
UpdatePanel. As a result, the representative DIV's innerHTML is set to blank. This
clears the WidgetContainer's body area and the real widget disappears.

After the body area's UpdatePanel, there's only one UpdateProgress extender
attached, which shows a "Working..." message when the body area is going through
any asynchronous postback due to some activity on the widget itself.

```
<asp:UpdateProgress ID="UpdateProgress1" runat="server" DisplayAfter="10"
AssociatedUpdatePanelID="WidgetBodyUpdatePanel" >
    <ProgressTemplate><center>Working...</center></ProgressTemplate>
</asp:UpdateProgress>
```

That's all inside the *WidgetContainer.ascx*. The code behind the file is, however,
quite challenging.

## WidgetContainer.cs

The WidgetContainer class implements the IWidgetHost interface because containers
host widgets.

```
public partial class WidgetContainer : System.Web.UI.UserControl, IWidgetHost
{
```

The container maintains a reference to the hosted widget via the IWidget interface. It
also stores a reference to the WidgetInstance object, which represents the instance of
the widget it contains.

```
private WidgetInstance _WidgetInstance;

public WidgetInstance WidgetInstance
{
    get { return _WidgetInstance; }
    set { _WidgetInstance = value; }
}

private IWidget _WidgetRef;
```

The *Default.aspx* notifies WidgetContainer about a first- or second-time load via a public property called IsFirstLoad.

```
private bool _IsFirstLoad;

public bool IsFirstLoad
{
    get { return _IsFirstLoad; }
    set { _IsFirstLoad = value; }
}
```

WidgetContainer then passes this property's value to the widget via the IWidgetHost.
IsFirstLoad property.

During the OnInit event of WidgetContainer, it loads the widget using LoadControl
and hosts it inside its body area:

```
protected override void OnInit(EventArgs e)
{
    base.OnInit(e);
    var widget = LoadControl(this.WidgetInstance.Widget.Url);

    widget.ID = "Widget" + this.WidgetInstance.Id.ToString();

    WidgetBodyPanel.Controls.Add(widget);
    this._WidgetRef = widget as IWidget;
    this._WidgetRef.Init(this);
}
```

If you do not set the widget.ID to a specific ID that is always the same for the same
widget instance, asynchronous postbacks will fail. You will get a message box saying
an invalid asynchronous postback has been performed. When the asynchronous
postback happens, ASP.NET needs to know which control has produced the postback. To do this, it needs to load the page with all the controls exactly in the same
state as before the postback occurred. Otherwise, it won't be able to find the control
that produced the postback by the ID it received from the Ajax framework.

Also, if the WidgetContainer's ID isn't set to a specific value, ASP.NET will assign
ctrl0 or ctrl1, whatever it finds free. This will vary the ID, and postbacks will map
to nonexistent controls and fail. Setting WidgetContainer's ID to the widget instance
ID ensures the container will always have the same ID for a particular widget
instance.

When the WidgetContainer is expanded or collapsed, the following events get fired:

```
protected void CollapseWidget_Click(object sender, EventArgs e)
{
    (this as IWidgetHost).Minimize();
}

protected void ExpandWidget_Click(object sender, EventArgs e)
{
    (this as IWidgetHost).Maximize();
}
```

Here you call the interface implementations where the actual work is done:

```
void IWidgetHost.Maximize()
{
    DatabaseHelper.Update<WidgetInstance>(this.WidgetInstance,
    delegate(WidgetInstance i)
    {
        i.Expanded = true;
    });

    this.SetExpandCollapseButtons();
    this._WidgetRef.Maximized();

    WidgetBodyUpdatePanel.Update();
    WidgetHeaderUpdatePanel.Update();
}

void IWidgetHost.Minimize()
{
    DatabaseHelper.Update<WidgetInstance>(this.WidgetInstance,
    delegate(WidgetInstance i)
    {
        i.Expanded = false;
    });

    this.SetExpandCollapseButtons();
    this._WidgetRef.Minimized();

    WidgetBodyUpdatePanel.Update();
    WidgetHeaderUpdatePanel.Update();
}
```

## Updating

We now need to update the Expanded property of the WidgetInstance object, as well as the database row to persist the widget's visibility. The details of how the DatabaseHelper works are discussed in Chapter 4. For the time being, let's assume the following code updates one row of WidgetInstance:

```
DatabaseHelper.Update<WidgetInstance>(this.WidgetInstance,
delegate(WidgetInstance i)
```

```
    {
        i.Expanded = false;
    });
```

After updating the database row, update the header area by switching between the expand and collapse buttons, inform the widget about the Minimize or Maximize events, and update both the header and body UpdatePanel. The header update panel is updated to reflect the change in the expand/collapse button. The body update panel is updated to toggle the widget's visibility inside the body area.

### Saving and editing

When a user clicks on the title of the WidgetContainer header, it switches to a text box and a save button. Users can enter a new title and save to set the new title for the widget instance. This is done by switching between LinkButton, TextBox, and Button. When the title LinkButton is clicked, the following event is fired:

```
protected void WidgetTitle_Click(object sender, EventArgs e)
{
    WidgetTitleTextBox.Text = this.WidgetInstance.Title;
    WidgetTitleTextBox.Visible = true;
    SaveWidgetTitle.Visible = true;
    WidgetTitle.Visible = false;
}
```

When the user clicks save, it switches back to the LinkButton showing the new title and hides the text box and save button. After the UI changes, the WidgetInstance object is updated in database with the new title.

```
protected void SaveWidgetTitle_Click(object sender, EventArgs e)
{
    WidgetTitleTextBox.Visible = SaveWidgetTitle.Visible = false;
    WidgetTitle.Visible = true;
    WidgetTitle.Text = WidgetTitleTextBox.Text;

    DatabaseHelper.Update<WidgetInstance>(this.WidgetInstance,
    delegate(WidgetInstance wi)
    {
        wi.Title = WidgetTitleTextBox.Text;
    });
}
```

When a user clicks the edit button, WidgetContainer informs the widget to show its settings area. The edit button then switches itself with "cancel edit" button. Both the edit and cancel edit buttons, when clicked, fire the same event:

```
protected void EditWidget_Click(object sender, EventArgs e)
{
    if( this.SettingsOpen )
    {
        this.SettingsOpen = false;
        this._WidgetRef.HideSettings();
        EditWidget.Visible = true;
```

```
                CancelEditWidget.Visible = false;
            }
            else
            {
                this.SettingsOpen = true;
                this._WidgetRef.ShowSettings( );
                (this as IWidgetHost).Maximize( );
                EditWidget.Visible = false;
                CancelEditWidget.Visible = true;
            }

            WidgetBodyUpdatePanel.Update( );
        }
```

The SettingsOpen property is stored in ViewState to remember whether the settings area is already open or not.

```
    public bool SettingsOpen
        {
            get
            {
                object val = ViewState[this.ClientID + "_SettingsOpen"] ?? false;
                return (bool)val;
            }
            set { ViewState[this.ClientID + "_SettingsOpen"] = value; }
        }
```

Remember, ViewState will always return null until the user clicks the edit button and a true value is set to it. You should always check ViewState entries for null before casting them to a data type. Check whether it's null, and if so, then the default value is false.

### Adding InstanceID

During the rendering of WidgetContainer, one more attribute is added to the DIV: InstanceID. The onDrop event on the client side needs to know the WidgetInstance ID of the widget that is moved so it can call the web service and notify the server about which WidgetInstance was moved. The additional attribute is rendered by overriding the RenderControl function:

```
    public override void RenderControl(HtmlTextWriter writer)
    {
        writer.AddAttribute("InstanceId", this.WidgetInstance.Id.ToString( ));
        base.RenderControl(writer);
    }
```

This results in the following HTML on the client:

```
    <div InstanceId="151" id="WidgetContainer151_Widget" class="widget">
```

The onDrop function on the client side reads this InstanceID and calls the web service:

```
    function onDrop( sender, e )
    {
        var container = e.get_container( );
```

```
                var item = e.get_droppedItem( );
                var position = e.get_position( );

                var instanceId = parseInt(item.getAttribute("InstanceId"));
                var columnNo = parseInt(container.getAttribute("columnNo"));
                var row = position;

                WidgetService.MoveWidgetInstance( instanceId, columnNo, row );
            }
```

### Closing the widget

Closing is more complicated than other behavior because `WidgetContainer` cannot close itself—it needs to be closed from outside and removed from the page's controls collection. The container just raises the `Deleted` event when it is closed, and the *Default.aspx* handles the UI update and database changes. The following is the code when the close button is clicked:

```
        protected void CloseWidget_Click(object sender, EventArgs e)
        {
            this._WidgetRef.Closed( );
            (this as IWidgetHost).Close( );
        }
```

First, the contained widget gets notification and it can then perform cleanup operations, like removing widget-specific information from the database. Then the `Deleted` event is raised:

```
        void IWidgetHost.Close( )
        {
            Deleted(this.WidgetInstance);
        }
```

The *Default.aspx* removes the widget from the database and refreshes the column:

```
      void widget_Deleted(WidgetInstance obj)
      {
          new DashboardFacade(Profile.UserName).DeleteWidgetInstance(obj);

          this.ReloadPage(wi => false);

          this.RefreshColumn(obj.ColumnNo);
      }
```

# Building Widgets

Now that you've seen how to implement `WidgetContainer`, let's look at how you build the widgets it hosts. First, we'll create a simple widget to display Flickr photos, followed by another widget to display RSS and Atom feeds.

## Building a Flickr Photo Widget

Let's look first at a simple Flickr photo widget that downloads photos from Flickr and displays them in a 3×3 grid, as shown in Figure 3-10.

*Figure 3-10. The Flickr widget downloads the Flickr photo stream as XML and parses using LINQ to XML and the photo grid is dynamically rendered*

The widget downloads Flickr photos as an XML feed from the Flickr web site and then renders a 3×3 grid with the pictures. The Flickr photo stream is available as an XML feed (not a RSS feed) at *http://www.flickr.com/services/rest/?method=flickr. photos.getRecent&api_key*.

You need to first obtain an application key from the Flickr developer zone and pass it at the end of the URL. The key I have embedded inside the project may not work if the request quota has already been exceeded.

The URL returns recent Flickr photos uploaded by the user as XML:

```
<?xml version="1.0" encoding="utf-8" ?>
<rsp stat="ok">
<photos page="1" pages="10" perpage="100" total="1000">
  <photo id="431247461" owner="25524911@N00" secret="cb9370fd16" server="162"
  farm="1" title="P1020899" ispublic="1" isfriend="0" isfamily="0" />
  <photo id="431247462" owner="46871506@N00" secret="036edda0e9" server="188"
  farm="1" title="black" ispublic="1" isfriend="0" isfamily="0" />
  <photo id="431247458" owner="91583992@N00" secret="6cd9a27d6d" server="153"
  farm="1" title="DSC00647" ispublic="1" isfriend="0" isfamily="0" />
```

However, the XML does not contain the URL of the photo file. It needs to be built dynamically.

The first step is to download and parse the XML using LINQ to XML, which is available in .NET 3.5. Here's an easy way to prepare a XElement from an URL:

```
var xroot = XElement.Load(url);
```

Next we convert each photo node inside the XML to an object of the PhotoInfo class for convenient processing:

```
var photos = (from photo in xroot.Element("photos").Elements("photo")
select new PhotoInfo
{
        Id = (string)photo.Attribute("id"),
        Owner = (string)photo.Attribute("owner"),
        Title = (string)photo.Attribute("title"),
        Secret = (string)photo.Attribute("secret"),
        Server = (string)photo.Attribute("server"),
        Farm = (string)photo.Attribute("Farm")
})
```

This will produce one PhotoInfo object for each <photo> node in the XML. Paging support has been added to it to select nine photos at a time by using the Skip and Take functions:

```
var photos = (from photo in xroot.Element("photos").Elements("photo")
select new PhotoInfo
{
...
}).Skip(pageIndex*Columns*Rows).Take(Columns*Rows);
```

This takes only nine photos from the current pageIndex. Page index is changed when the user clicks the next or previous links. The Skip method skips the number of items in the XML, and the Take method takes only the specified number of nodes from XML.

A 3×3 HTML table renders the photos from the collection of PhotoInfo objects:

```
foreach( var photo in photos )
{
        if( col == 0 )
                table.Rows.Add( new HtmlTableRow( ) );

        var cell = new HtmlTableCell( );

        var img = new HtmlImage( );
        img.Src = photo.PhotoUrl(true);
        img.Width = img.Height = 75;
        img.Border = 0;

        var link = new HtmlGenericControl("a");
        link.Attributes["href"] = photo.PhotoPageUrl;
        link.Attributes["Target"] = "_blank";
        link.Attributes["Title"] = photo.Title;
        link.Controls.Add(img);

        cell.Controls.Add(link);
        table.Rows[row].Cells.Add(cell);
```

```
        col ++;
        if( col == Columns )
        {
                col = 0; row ++;
        }

        count ++;
    }
```

The reasoning behind using HtmlGenericControl instead of HtmlLink is that HtmlLink does not allow you to add controls inside its Controls collection. This is a limitation of the HtmlLink class in ASP.NET 2.0.

The PhotoPageUrl property of PhotoInfo class gives the URL of the photo. There's no special logic inside the PhotoInfo class besides the public properties:

```
public  class PhotoInfo
{
    private const string FLICKR_SERVER_URL="http://static.flickr.com/";
    private const string FLICKR_PHOTO_URL="http://www.flickr.com/photos/";

    public string Id;
    public string Owner;
    public string Title;
    public string Secret;
    public string Server;
    public string Farm;
    public bool IsPublic;
    public bool IsFriend;
    public bool IsFamily;
    public string PhotoUrl(bool small)
    {
        return FLICKR_SERVER_URL + this.Server + '/' + this.Id + '_' + this.Secret +
    (small ? "_s.jpg" : "_m.jpg");
    }
    public string PhotoPageUrl
    {
        get { return FLICKR_PHOTO_URL + this.Owner + '/' + this.Id; }
    }
}
```

When the widget loads, it checks whether it's a first-time load or a postback. If it's a first-time load, then it fetches the XML photo feed from Flickr and stores it in the cache. When it's a postback, it renders the photos from the cached XML.

```
protected void Page_Load(object sender, EventArgs e)
    {
        if( this._Host.IsFirstLoad )
        {
            this.LoadState();
            this.LoadPictures();
            this.PageIndex = 0;
            this.ShowPictures(0);
```

```
    }
    else
    {
        this.ShowPictures(this.PageIndex);
    }
}
```

First the widget loads its UI state, downloads the Flickr photo XML, and shows the pictures in the grid. But when the page is having a postback, the widget just shows the last pictures. The reason you need to render the pictures again on postback is that the pictures are shown dynamically and are not part of the HTML markups that ASP.NET creates. If they are declaratively specified in the *.ascx* file, then ASP.NET would have created that itself.

The content of the *FlickrWidget.ascx* page is the following:

```
<%@ Control Language="C#" AutoEventWireup="true" CodeFile="FlickrWidget.ascx.cs"
Inherits="FlickrWidget" %>
<asp:Panel ID="settingsPanel" runat="server" Visible="False">
    <asp:RadioButton ID="mostInterestingRadioButton" runat="server"
    AutoPostBack="True"
        Checked="True" GroupName="FlickrPhoto" OnCheckedChanged="photoTypeRadio_
        CheckedChanged"
        Text="Most Interesting" />
        <br />
    <asp:RadioButton ID="mostRecentRadioButton" runat="server" AutoPostBack="True"
    GroupName="FlickrPhoto"
        OnCheckedChanged="photoTypeRadio_CheckedChanged" Text="Most Recent" />
        <br />
    <asp:RadioButton ID="customTagRadioButton" runat="server" AutoPostBack="True"
    GroupName="FlickrPhoto"
        OnCheckedChanged="photoTypeRadio_CheckedChanged" Text="Tag: " />
        <asp:TextBox ID="CustomTagTextBox" runat="server" Text="Pretty" />
        <hr />
</asp:Panel>
<asp:Panel ID="photoPanel" runat="server">

</asp:Panel>
<center>
    <asp:LinkButton ID="ShowPrevious" runat="server" OnClick="ShowPrevious_Click">
    <Prev</asp:LinkButton>
    <asp:LinkButton ID="ShowNext" runat="server" OnClick="ShowNext_Click">Next >
    </asp:LinkButton></center>
```

In the Visual Studio designer, the Flickr widget web control looks pretty simple, as shown in Figure 3-11.

There's a blank panel in the middle of the control that shows the pictures. The Prev and Next LinkButtons do the pagination. The radio buttons are part of the settings area that you see only when you click on the edit link on the widget header area, as shown in Figure 3-12.

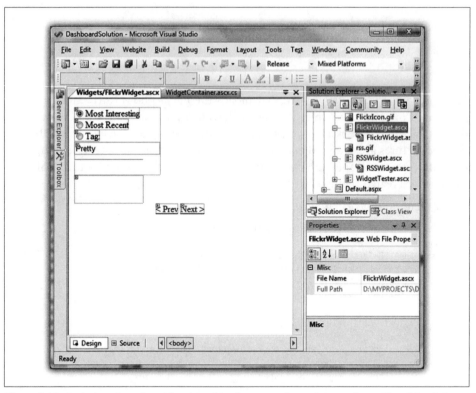

*Figure 3-11. At design view, the widget is nothing but a regular web control; use Visual Studio's Visual Designer to design the UI*

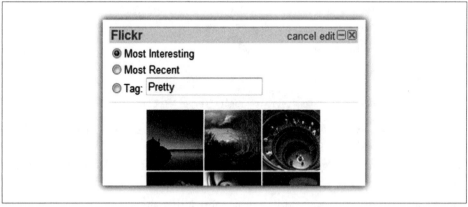

*Figure 3-12. Settings contain options to customize a widget, such as different types of photo streams from Flickr*

## Flickr widget UI controls

Let's explain what the controls do on the Flickr widget UI. The simplest part is the pagination where the click handlers of the Previous and Next LinkButtons do the paging:

```
protected void ShowPrevious_Click(object sender, EventArgs e)
{
    this.PageIndex --;
    this.ShowPictures(this.PageIndex);
}
protected void ShowNext_Click(object sender, EventArgs e)
{
    this.PageIndex ++;
    this.ShowPictures(this.PageIndex);
}
```

When a user changes the type of photo to show, this information is stored in the widget's state. The widget's state is simple XML in this format:

```
<state>
    <type>MostRecent</type>
    <tag>Pretty</tag>
</state>
```

The state is loaded using LINQ to XML's XElement class:

```
private XElement _State;
private XElement State
{
    get
    {
        if( _State == null )
        {
            string stateXml = this._Host.GetState();
            if (string.IsNullOrEmpty(stateXml))
            {
                _State = new XElement("state",
                    new XElement("type", "MostPopular"),
                    new XElement("tag", ""));
            }
            else
            {
                _State = XElement.Parse(stateXml);
            }
        }
        return _State;
    }
}
```

This is a read-only property that loads the widget instance's state XML and returns an XElement reference to it. The host that is the widget container for this widget returns the state content. If no state was stored before, it creates a default state XML with default selections.

Reading and writing to individual properties in the state is very easy when we have a XElement object to work with:

```
public PhotoTypeEnum TypeOfPhoto
{
    get { return (PhotoTypeEnum)Enum.Parse( typeof( PhotoTypeEnum ), State.
        Element("type").Value ); }
    set { State.Element("type").Value = value.ToString( ); }
}
public string PhotoTag
{
    get { return State.Element("tag").Value; }
    set { State.Element("tag").Value = value; }
}
```

After changing the state, it is saved permanently in the database by calling the IWidgetHost.SaveState function. Here's the code that collects current settings from the UI and stores in widget instance's state:

```
private void SaveState( )
{
    if( mostRecentRadioButton.Checked )
        this.TypeOfPhoto = PhotoTypeEnum.MostRecent;
    else if( mostInterestingRadioButton.Checked )
        this.TypeOfPhoto = PhotoTypeEnum.MostPopular;
    else if( customTagRadioButton.Checked )
    {
        this.TypeOfPhoto = PhotoTypeEnum.Tag;
        this.PhotoTag = this.CustomTagTextBox.Text;
    }

    this._Host.SaveState(this.State.Xml);
}
```

Whatever is stored here is stored permanently in the database. If the user closes the browser and visits again, these states will be retrieved from the database. However, temporary state variables, like PageIndex, are not stored as state. They are stored in the ViewState:

```
private int PageIndex
    {
        get
        {
            return (int)(ViewState[this.ClientID + "_PageIndex"] ?? 0);
        }
        set { ViewState[this.ClientID + "_PageIndex"] = value; }
    }
```

So far we made a regular ASP.NET web control. This control becomes a widget when the IWidget interface is implemented on it. The implementation is straightforward:

```
void IWidget.Init(IWidgetHost host)
{
    this._Host = host;
}
```

```
void IWidget.ShowSettings( )
{
    settingsPanel.Visible = true;
}
void IWidget.HideSettings( )
{
    settingsPanel.Visible = false;
}
void IWidget.Minimized( )
{
}
void IWidget.Maximized( )
{
}
void IWidget.Closed( )
{
}
```

Most of implementations are blank because there's nothing special to do here other than show and hide the settings area.

The Flickr photo widget is now ready. Put it in the widgets folder, create a row in widget table in the database, and it's good to go. The user will see the widget listed in the Add Stuff area, as shown in Figure 3-13, and can add it to the page.

| ID | Name | Url | Description | CreatedDate | LastUpdate | VersionNo | IsDefault | DefaultState | Icon |
|----|------|-----|-------------|-------------|------------|-----------|-----------|--------------|------|
| 4 | Flickr | Widgets\FlickrWidget.ascx | Flickr Photo Wi... | 12/7/2006 1... | 12/7/2006 ... | 1 | True | <state> <typ... | Widgets/FlickrIcon.gif |

*Figure 3-13. Widget table entry for the Flickr photo widget*

The widget is marked as IsDefault=True, so it is added automatically to the first page for first-time visitors.

## Building an Atom or RSS Widget

In this section, you will see how to build a simple RSS widget, like the one shown in Figure 3-14.

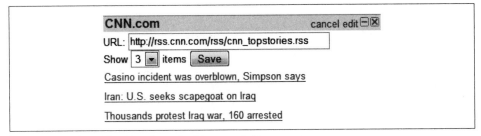

*Figure 3-14. The RSS widget shows feed items as links*

RSS is arguably the most popular widget for a start page because it serves the core functionality of web portals, to aggregate content from different sources. Users use RSS to read news and blogs, and to subscribe to groups, bulletins, notifications, and so on. Nowadays RSS is an almost universal format for content syndication. It is nothing but a fixed and formatted XML feed that is universally agreed upon. Atom, which is another format, is also quite popular. So, the widget you will make will be able to parse both RSS and Atom format feeds.

The RSS widget stores the URL and the number of articles to show on the widget inside its State. Just like a Flickr photo widget, you can customize the number of items you want to see from the settings area. You can also change the feed URL and read a different feed. State handling is handled the same way as a Flickr photo widget, by storing the count and feed URL inside State.

The UI contains the settings panel and a DataList that is bound to a collection of feed items at runtime, as shown in Example 3-41.

*Example 3-41. RSS Widget .ascx content*

```
<%@ Control Language="C#" AutoEventWireup="true" CodeFile="RSSWidget.ascx.cs"
Inherits="Widgets_RSSWidget" EnableViewState="false" %>
<asp:Panel ID="SettingsPanel" runat="Server" Visible="False" >
URL: <asp:TextBox ID="FeedUrl" Text="" runat="server" MaxLength="2000" Columns="40" /><br
/>
Show
<asp:DropDownList ID="FeedCountDropDownList" runat="Server">
<asp:ListItem>1</asp:ListItem>
<asp:ListItem>2</asp:ListItem>
<asp:ListItem>3</asp:ListItem>
<asp:ListItem>4</asp:ListItem>
<asp:ListItem>5</asp:ListItem>
<asp:ListItem>6</asp:ListItem>
<asp:ListItem>7</asp:ListItem>
<asp:ListItem>8</asp:ListItem>
<asp:ListItem>9</asp:ListItem>
</asp:DropDownList>
items
<asp:Button ID="SaveSettings" runat="Server" OnClick="SaveSettings_Click" Text="Save" />
</asp:Panel>


<asp:DataList ID="FeedList" runat="Server" EnableViewState="False">
<ItemTemplate>
<asp:HyperLink ID="FeedLink" runat="server" Target="_blank" CssClass="feed_item_link"
NavigateUrl='<%# Eval("link") %>' ToolTip='<%# Eval("description") %>'>
<%# Eval("title") %>
</asp:HyperLink>
</ItemTemplate>
</asp:DataList>
```

The DataList shows a list of hyperlinks where each hyperlink is bound to a title, description, and a link property at runtime. From the code, a projection with properties named title, description, and link is bound to the DataList. The function ShowFeeds loads the feeds using LINQ to XML and then converts the feed XML to a projection using a LINQ expression, as shown in Example 3-42.

*Example 3-42. Loading feeds and converting to a projection*

```
private void ShowFeeds( )
{
    string url = State.Element("url").Value;
    int count = State.Element("count") == null ? 3 : int.Parse( State.Element("count").
    Value );

    var feed = Cache[url] as XElement;
    if( feed == null )
    {
        if( Cache[url] == string.Empty ) return;
        try
        {
          HttpWebRequest request = WebRequest.Create(url) as HttpWebRequest;
            request.Timeout = 15000;
            using( WebResponse response = request.GetResponse( ) )
            {
                XmlTextReader reader = new XmlTextReader(
                response.GetResponseStream( ) );

                feed = XElement.Load(reader);

                if( feed == null ) return;

                Cache.Insert(url, feed, null, DateTime.MaxValue, TimeSpan.
                FromMinutes(15));
            }
        }
        catch
        {
            Cache[url] = string.Empty;
            return;
        }
    }

    XNamespace ns = "http://www.w3.org/2005/Atom";

    // RSS Format
    if( feed.Element("channel" ) != null )
        FeedList.DataSource = (from item in feed.Element("channel").Elements("item")
                              select new
                              {
                                  title = item.Element("title").Value,
                                  link = item.Element("link").Value,
                                  description = item.Element("description").Value
                              }).Take(this.Count);
```

*Example 3-42. Loading feeds and converting to a projection (continued)*

```
    // Atom format
    else if( feed.Element(ns + "entry") != null )
        FeedList.DataSource = (from item in feed.Elements(ns + "entry")
                               select new
                               {
                                   title = item.Element(ns + "title").Value,
                                   link = item.Element(ns + "link").Attribute("href").
                               Value,
                                   description = item.Element(ns + "content").Value
                               }).Take(this.Count);


    FeedList.DataBind( );
}
```

The `ShowFeeds` function first loads the XML feed from the feed URL using `HttpWebRequest`. Then it passes the response stream to an `XmlReader`, which, in turn, gets passed into a `XElement.Load` function. `XElement.Load` loads the XML, parses it, and builds an `XElement` object model of nodes and attributes. Based on the XML feed format (RSS or Atom), different type of nodes and attributes appear in `XElement`. So, a LINQ expression converts both types of object models to a projection with title, description, and link properties. Once the projection is prepared, it is bound to the `FeedList` `DataList` control. The `DataList` binds one hyperlink for each item in the project and thus shows the feed items.

Now that you have learned how to build widgets, you will learn some framework-level challenges that need to be solved to make widgets work properly on the Start page. Some of these challenges are handling postback in different scenarios, implementing security, and handling `Profile` objects from web services.

# Page Switching: Simulating a Nonpostback Experience

Widgets load on page in three ways:

- The very first time they are created; they have no state at this stage
- When a user revisits the page; they load in nonpostback mode and restore their state from persisted state data
- During asynchronous postback; they load in postback mode and restore their state from both `ViewState` and persisted states

Normally, on a regular visit to the page (i.e., nonpostback, second scenario), widgets load their settings from their persisted state and render the UI for the first time. Upon postback, widgets don't always restore settings from persisted state and instead update the state or reflect small changes on the UI. For example, when you click the Next button on the Flickr photo widget, it's a postback experience for the widget. It does not go and fetch Flickr photos again, it just updates the current page index in its ViewState. So, it's important for widgets to know when they are being rendered for the first time or when it is a postback.

The definition of nonpostback and postback is different when you have multiple tabs on one page. When you click on another tab, it's a regular asynchronous postback for ASP.NET because a LinkButton gets clicked inside an UpdatePanel. This makes the tab's UpdatePanel postback asynchronously, and on the server side you can see which tab is clicked. You can then load the widgets on the newly selected tab. But when widgets load, they call Page.IsPostBack, and they get true. So, widgets assume they are already on the screen and try to do a partial rendering or access their own ViewState. But this is not the case because they are not rendered yet and there's no ViewState. As a result, the widgets behave abnormally and any ViewState access fails.

So, we need to make sure that during the tab switch, even though it's a regular ASP. NET postback, the widgets don't see it as postback. The idea is to inform widgets whether it is a regular visit or a postback via the IWidgetHost interface.

On *Default.aspx*, the SetupWidgets function creates the WidgetContainer and loads the widgets. Here's how it works:

```
private void SetupWidgets(Func<WidgetInstance, bool> isWidgetFirstLoad)
{
...
foreach( WidgetInstance instance in setup.WidgetInstances )
{
var panel = columnPanels[instance.ColumnNo];

var widget = LoadControl(WIDGET_CONTAINER) as WidgetContainer;
widget.ID = "WidgetContainer" + instance.Id.ToString( );
widget.IsFirstLoad = isWidgetFirstLoad(instance);
widget.WidgetInstance = instance;

widget.Deleted += new Action<WidgetInstance>(widget_Deleted);

panel.Controls.Add(widget);
}
```

The public property IsFirstLoad is determined by what calls the SetupWidget and when. SetupWidget's job is to render the widgets on the page. So, it gets called during the first visit and subsequent postbacks. The caller knows whether it's postback or not and can pass a predicate, which decides the value of the IsFirstLoad property. WidgetContainer just passes the value of the property to its contained widget via the IWidgetHost interface.

So, why not just send true when it's postback and false when it's not and declare the function as SetupWidgets(bool)?

When a new widget is added on the page, it is a first-time loading experience for the newly added widget, but it's a regular postback for existing widgets already on the page. If true or false is passed for all widgets, then the newly added widget will see it as a postback just like all other existing widgets on the page and thus fail to load properly. To make sure it's a nonpostback experience for *only* the newly added widget, and a postback experience for existing widgets already on the page, use this predicate feature:

```
DashboardFacade facade = new DashboardFacade(Profile.UserName);
WidgetInstance newWidget = facade.AddWidget( widgetId );

this.ReloadPage(wi => wi.Id == newWidget.Id);
```

Here the predicate will return true for the newly added widget, but false for any other widget. As a result, the newly added widget get IsFirstLoad = true, where existing widgets get IsFirstLoad = false.

# Using the Profile Object Inside a Web Service

The web project uses a Profile object like IsFirstVisit to store a user's state. Profile object is also used to get the currently visiting user's name from the Profile. UserName property. The *Default.aspx* is already full of Profile.Something, and so are the widget container and the widgets. The next step is to add a new web service and access the Profile object, but when you type context.Profile from the web service code, IntelliSense doesn't show any of your custom properties.

At runtime, ASP.NET generates a class looking at the specification provided in *web. config*, which becomes the Profile object in *.aspx* pages and *.ascx* controls. But this object is not available in the web service (*.asmx.cs*) and you cannot see the custom properties you have added in the Profile object. Although HttpContext.Current. Profile will reference the Profile object, its type is ProfileBase, which does not show your custom properties because the class is generated at runtime.

To overcome this problem, you have to handcode the profile class in your *App_Code* folder and then configure *web.config* so it doesn't autogenerate a class but instead uses yours. Here's what you do in *web.config*:

```
<profile enabled="true" inherits="UserProfile">
```

Now go to *App_Code* and make a UserProfile class like this:

```
public class UserProfile : System.Web.Profile.ProfileBase
{
[SettingsAllowAnonymousAttribute(true)]
public virtual int Timezone
{
get
{
return ((int)(this.GetPropertyValue("Timezone")));
}
set
```

```
    {
    this.SetPropertyValue("Timezone", value);
    }
  }
```

This is an example property implementation. Don't forget to add the [SettingsAllowAnonymousAttribute(true)] to the properties that you want to make available to anonymous users. At the end of the class, add this method:

```
public virtual ProfileCommon GetProfile(string username)
{
return ((ProfileCommon)(ProfileBase.Create(username)));
}
```

Here's an easy way to avoid handcoding this class and generate it automatically instead. Before you make the changes in *web.config* and create the UserProfile class, run your web project as it was before. But before running it, turn off SQL Server. This will make the ASP.NET execution break on the first call to a Profile object's property. For example, if you have defined a custom property TimeZone in the Profile object in *web.config*, execution will break on this line:

```
public virtual int Timezone
{
get
{
return ((int)(this.GetPropertyValue("Timezone")));
```

It will fail to load the Profile object values from the database because the database is down. If you scroll up, you will see that this is the class that ASP.NET generates at runtime. All the properties are already declared on this class. So, you can just copy and paste it in your own class easily! However, after copying, you will realize there's no [SettingsAllowAnonymousAttribute(true)] attribute in the generated class. So, you will have to add it manually. Once you have made the class, you will have to remove all the custom properties declared inside <properties> node in the *web.config*.

Now that you have your own Profile class, you can cast (HttpContext.Current. Profile as UserProfile) and use all the custom properties inside the web service.

If you don't want to have strict coding on the web service, then you can use the old way of accessing the Profile properties via Profile.GetPropertyValue("TimeZone"). This will work for both web pages and web services. You don't need to handcode a Profile class if you go for this approach, then again you don't get the strong typing and the IntelliSense feature.

# Implementing Authentication and Authorization

The ASP.NET membership provider and profile provider take care of the authentication and authorization for the application. In addition to this, an anonymous identification provider is used, which is not common among web applications because, unlike web portals, other web apps don't require anonymous user creation on the first visit. The anonymous identification provider creates anonymous users whenever there is a cookieless visit, and takes care of creating entries in the aspnet_users table for the new anonymous user.

The *web.config* defines the providers in Example 3-43.

*Example 3-43. Defining the providers with web.config*

```
<authentication mode="Forms">
    <forms
        name=".DBAUTH" loginUrl="Login.aspx"
        protection="All" timeout="20160"
        path="/" requireSSL="false"
        slidingExpiration="true" defaultUrl="Default.aspx"
        cookieless="UseDeviceProfile" enableCrossAppRedirects="false"/>
    </authentication>
    <membership defaultProvider="DashboardMembershipSqlProvider"
    userIsOnlineTimeWindow="15">
      <providers>
        <add name="DashboardMembershipSqlProvider"
            type="System.Web.Security.SqlMembershipProvider,
                System.Web, Version=2.0.0.0,
                Culture=neutral, PublicKeyToken=b03f5f7f11d50a3a"
            connectionStringName="DashboardConnectionString"
            enablePasswordRetrieval="true"
            enablePasswordReset="true"
            requiresQuestionAndAnswer="false"
            applicationName="Dashboard"
            requiresUniqueEmail="false"
            passwordFormat="Clear"
            minRequiredPasswordLength="1"
            passwordStrengthRegularExpression=""
            minRequiredNonalphanumericCharacters="0"/>
      </providers>
    </membership>
    <roleManager enabled="true" cacheRolesInCookie="true"
        defaultProvider="DashboardRoleManagerSqlProvider"
        cookieName=".ASPXROLES" cookiePath="/"
        cookieTimeout="30" cookieRequireSSL="false"
        cookieSlidingExpiration="true" createPersistentCookie="false"
        cookieProtection="All">
      <providers>
        <add name="DashboardRoleManagerSqlProvider"
            type="System.Web.Security.SqlRoleProvider, System.Web,
                Version=2.0.0.0, Culture=neutral,
                PublicKeyToken=b03f5f7f11d50a3a"
            connectionStringName="DashboardConnectionString"
            applicationName="Dashboard"/>
      </providers>
    </roleManager>
    <profile enabled="true" automaticSaveEnabled="false"
        defaultProvider="DashboardProfileSqlProvider"
        inherits="UserProfile">
```

*Example 3-43. Defining the providers with web.config (continued)*

```
<providers>
  <clear/>
  <add name="DashboardProfileSqlProvider"
       type="System.Web.Profile.SqlProfileProvider"
       connectionStringName="DashboardConnectionString"
       applicationName="Dashboard"
       description="SqlProfileProvider for Dashboard"/>
</providers>
</profile>
```

However, there are several performance issues involved with anonymous identification providers, which are addressed later.

The anonymous identification provider is defined as:

```
<anonymousIdentification
       enabled="true"
       cookieName=".DBANON"
       cookieTimeout="43200"
       cookiePath="/"
       cookieRequireSSL="false"
       cookieSlidingExpiration="true"
       cookieProtection="All"
       cookieless="UseCookies"/>
```

An anonymous identification provider generates a cookie in the browser that identifies the anonymous user for 43,200 minutes (a little over 29 days) after the last hit. (The timeout is on a sliding scale, so each visit restarts the 29-day clock.) This means if a user closes the browser and comes back within a month, the user will be identified and will get the same page setup as it before. As a result, users can keep using the web portal without actually ever signing up. But if the browser cookie is cleared, the page setup will be lost forever. The only solution is to register using a login name and password, so even if the cookie is lost, the user can log in to see his pages.

Web services, which let you modify data, are vulnerable to malicious attacks. For example, there is a web service method that moves a widget from one position to another. Imagine someone trying to call this web service with an arbitrary widget instance ID. The attacker will be able to mess up page setups by trying instance IDs from 1 to 1,000. To prevent such attempts, each web service operation needs to ensure operations are performed only on the objects that the caller owns. Remember from the previous example that you cannot the move position of a widget unless you are the owner. Such security checks are implemented in the business layer because if they were implemented in web layer, the logic for checking ownership, which is a business rule, would get into the web layer. Some might argue that such checks can easily be put on the web layer to kick out malicious calls before they reach the business layer. But this pollutes the web layer with business rules. Besides maintaining such architectural purity, business layer methods are called from many sources, such as a Windows service or a different web frontend. So, it becomes a maintenance issue to preserve conformance to such validations in all places. This topic is covered in more detail in Chapter 7.

# Implementing Logout

Wait, wait! Don't skip this section. A simple logout can be very cool.

First question: why do people implement a logout page as an *.aspx* file when it just calls FormsAuthentication.Signout and redirects to a homepage? You really don't need to make ASP.NET load an *.aspx* page, produce HTML, and process through the page life cycle only to do a cookie cleanup and redirect. A simple HTTP 302 can tell the browser to go back to the homepage. So, the logout page is a great candidate for HTTP handlers without any UI.

Example 3-44 shows how to implement a logout handler inside a file named *Logout.ashx*:

*Example 3-44. Implementing a logout handler in the web application*

```
<%@ WebHandler Language="C#" Class="Logout" %>

using System;
using System.Web;
using System.Web.Security;
using System.Collections.Generic;

public class Logout : IHttpHandler {

    public void ProcessRequest (HttpContext context) {

        /// Expire all the cookies so browser visits us as a brand new user
        List<string> cookiesToClear = new List<string>();
        foreach (string cookieName in context.Request.Cookies)
        {
            HttpCookie cookie = context.Request.Cookies[cookieName];
            cookiesToClear.Add(cookie.Name);
        }

        foreach (string name in cookiesToClear)
        {
            HttpCookie cookie = new HttpCookie(name, string.Empty);
            cookie.Expires = DateTime.Today.AddYears(-1);

            context.Response.Cookies.Set(cookie);
        }

        context.Response.Redirect("~/Default.aspx");
    }
```

*Example 3-44. Implementing a logout handler in the web application (continued)*

```
    public bool IsReusable {
        get {
            return true;
        }
    }

}
```

# Handlers

Handlers are a lot lighter than the *.aspx* page because they have a very simple life cycle, are instance reusable, and generate a small amount of code when compiled at runtime.

The idea here is to remove all cookies related to the site instead of just removing the forms authentication cookie. When you use an anonymous identification provider, you will find two cookies: .DBAUTH and .DBANON. The form's authentication provider generates the first one and the other one is from the anonymous identification provider. These cookies are because an anonymous user is different than the user that is logged in. If you call FormAuthentication.Signout( ), it will just clear the .DBAUTH cookie, but the other one will remain as is. So, after logout, instead of getting a brand new setup, you will get the old setup that you saw when you were an anonymous user during your first visit. The anonymous user is converted to a registered user by directly modifying the aspnet_users table. So, the anonymous user no longer exists in the database. This means the cookie for the anonymous user points to something that no longer exists. So, when the ASP.NET membership provider tries to find the user from the anonymous cookie, it fails.

In a web portal, we want the user to start over with a fresh setup. So, we need to clear both cookies and any other cookie that the widget scripts have used for storing temporary states. You never know what widgets will do with the cookie. Some widgets can secretly keep track of your logged-in session by storing info in a different cookie. When you log out and become an anonymous user, the widget can still access that secret cookie and find out about you. For example, it can easily store your email address when it is loaded in a logged-in session, and after you log out, it can still read that email address from the cookie. It's a security risk to have any cookie left from your logged-in session after logging out.

# Summary

The web layer is the most difficult part of a web portal application because it is so UI intensive. Although ASP.NET AJAX offers a lot of off-the-shelf features, there are some tweaks that need to be made when using it in a real application. The business and the data access layers that I explain in next chapter are quite simple compared to the web layer. However, they use two hot technologies—Workflow Foundation and LINQ to SQL. Brace yourself for some really cool implementation of these cutting-edge technologies.

## Additional Resources

- ASP.NET AJAX Control Toolkit Project (*http://www.asp.net/ajax/ajaxcontroltoolkit*)
- AJAX Application Architecture, Part 1 on MSDN (*http://msdn.microsoft.com/ msdnmag/issues/07/09/cuttingedge/default.aspx*)
- AJAX Application Architecture, Part 2 on MSDN (*http://msdn.microsoft.com/ msdnmag/issues/07/10/cuttingedge/default.aspx*)
- Scott Guthrie's blog post, "ASP.NET AJAX in .NET 3.5 and VS 2008" (*http:// weblogs.asp.net/scottgu/archive/2007/07/30/asp-net-ajax-in-net-3-5-and-vs-2008.aspx*)
- My article on CodeProject, "ASP.NET AJAX Under the Hood Secrets" (*www. codeproject.com/Ajax/aspnetajaxtips.asp*)

# CHAPTER 4

# Building the Data and Business Layers Using .NET 3.5

The data and business layers of the Dropthings portal use two of the hottest features of the .NET 3.0 and 3.5 frameworks: Windows Workflow Foundation (WF) and LINQ. The data layer makes good use of LINQ to SQL, a feature of .NET 3.5. The business layer is built largely with the WF released with .NET 3.0, using new language extensions in C# 3.0.

## Introducing LINQ to SQL

LINQ, or Language integrated query, is a set of C# 3.0 language and .NET 3.5 framework features for writing structured queries over local object collections and remote data sources. With LINQ, you can query any collection that implements IEnumerable<>, including tables in a database.

LINQ to SQL is a lot of fun to work with and makes the task of writing a data access layer that generates highly optimized SQL amazingly simple. If you haven't used LINQ to SQL before, brace yourself.

With LINQ to SQL, you design the database that the application will use and then use the Visual Studio 2008 Object/Relational Designer (*sqlmetal.exe* in LINQ Preview) to generate a class that represents the database with an appropriate object model. This is a giant step beyond having to handcode the entity and data access classes. Formerly, whenever the database design changed, you had to modify the entity classes and modify the insert, update, delete, and get methods in the data access layer. Of course, you could use third-party object-relational mapping (ORM) tools or some kind of code generator that generates entity classes from database schema and data access layer code. But now, LINQ to SQL does it all for you!

A great thing about LINQ to SQL is that it can generate objects known as *projections* that contain only the fields you want to receive from a specific query, not the entire row. There's no ORM tool or object-oriented database library that can do this today because the operation requires a custom compiler to support it. The benefit of projection is pure performance. You select only fields that you need, and you don't have to build a jumbo-sized object with every field from the tables you query. LINQ to SQL selects only the required fields and creates objects that contain only the selected fields. Let's take a look at some example queries used in the business layer. Example 4-1 shows how easy it is to create a new Page object in a database.

*Example 4-1. Inserting a new Page object in a database using LINQ to SQL*

```
var db = new DashboardData(ConnectionString);

var newPage = new Page();
newPage.UserId = UserId;
newPage.Title = Title;
newPage.CreatedDate = DateTime.Now;
newPage.LastUpdate = DateTime.Now;

db.Pages.Add(newPage);
db.SubmitChanges();
NewPageId = newPage.ID;
```

Here DashboardData is the DataContext generated by the Visual Studio 2008 Object Relational Designer. It contains all the database access methods and entities for tables in the database. DataContext takes care of generating queries for objects that are requested from the database, executing the queries, and populating objects from the database. It also keeps track of changes made to the objects and when they are updated, and knows exactly which fields to update in the tables. DataContext completely encapsulates database access and provides a nice, clean, object-oriented way of working with data that is persisted in a database. Moreover, DataContext allows you to run arbitrary queries as well; you can use regular stored procedures to read and write rows in database tables.

Example 4-2 shows how to get a Page and change its name. You can use lambda expressions similar to those you have seen in Chapter 3 to define the condition for the where clause.

*Example 4-2. Get an object by primary key and updating*

```
var page = db.Pages.Single( p => p.ID == PageId );
page.Title = PageName;
db.SubmitChanges();
```

Another option is to select only a scalar value from the database. Reading scalar values directly from a database is faster than reading a row and then converting it to an object repeatedly. Example 4-3 shows how to do it.

*Example 4-3. Read scalar values*

```
var UserGuid = (from u in db.AspnetUsers
where u.LoweredUserName == UserName
select u.UserId).Single();
```

You can also read specific fields and create an object on the fly that contains only the specific fields. This is called *projection* and is shown in Example 4-4.

*Example 4-4. Create projection*

```
var users = from u in db.AspnetUsers
select { UserId = u.UserId, UserName = u.LoweredUserName };

foreach( var user in users )
{
Debug.WriteLine( user.UserName );
}
```

In Example 4-4, only two fields from the Aspnet_Users table are selected. LINQ to SQL returns an object that has only these two fields, and not all the fields in the table.

Database paging is very easy in LINQ to SQL. For example, if you want to select 20 rows starting at the 100th row, just use the Skip and Take functions as shown in Example 4-5.

*Example 4-5. Paging using Skip and Take*

```
var users = (from u in db.AspnetUsers
select { UserId = u.UserId, UserName = u.LoweredUserName }).Skip(100).Take(20);

foreach( var user in users )
{
Debug.WriteLine( user.UserName );
}
```

It's easy to provide transaction support in LINQ to SQL. You just write code inside a using block, and the code inside it falls into a transaction scope (see Example 4-6).

*Example 4-6. Using transaction*

```
using( var ts = new TransactionScope( ) )
{
List<Page> pages = db.Pages.Where( p => p.UserId == oldGuid ).ToList( );
foreach( Page page in pages )
page.UserId = newGuid;

// Change setting ownership
UserSetting setting = db.UserSettings.Single( u => u.UserId == oldGuid );
db.UserSettings.Remove(setting);

setting.UserId = newGuid;
db.UserSettings.Add(setting);
db.SubmitChanges( );

ts.Complete( );
}
```

When there's any exception, the using block will call the `Dispose` function on `ts`, and the transaction will abort unless it is already completed. But if the code reaches the end of the block, it calls `ts.complete( )` and the transaction commits.

# Building the Data Access Layer Using LINQ to SQL

The first step to using LINQ to SQL is to build a `DataContext`, which contains all entity classes and their data access methods. You will generate one `Entity` class per table, e.g., the `Page` Entity class for the `Page` table in the database. Visual Studio 2008's ORM designer allows you to easily drag and drop tables onto a designer surface and generate entity classes. The next step will be to create a simple helper class that makes working with LINQ to SQL even easier. Let's start with designing the ORM in Visual Studio 2008.

## Generating a Data Model Using the Visual Studio 2008 Designer

Visual Studio 2008 comes with an object relational mapping designer, which allows you to create a LINQ to SQL classes file and then drag and drop tables from the server explorer to the designer surface. Visual Studio will then automatically generate classes from those tables. You can further modify the associations, turn on or off lazy loading of properties, add validation, and much more. Nothing special was done to generate Figure 4-1 in the data model, besides putting all the tables from the database onto the designer surface.

After you create the designer and build the project, the data access and entity classes will be ready for use. `DashboardData` is the data context class that's included in the project.

## Manipulating Data with a Database Helper

Example 4-7 shows the code for a `DatabaseHelper` that makes working with LINQ to SQL a lot easier.

*Example 4-7. DatabaseHelper, part 1*

```
public static class DatabaseHelper
{
  public const string ConnectionStringName = "DashboardConnectionString";
  public const string ApplicationID = "fd639154-299a-4a9d-b273-69dc28eb6388";
  public readonly static Guid ApplicationGuid = new Guid(ApplicationID);

  public static DashboardData GetDashboardData( )
  {
    var db = new DashboardData(ConfigurationManager.
  ConnectionStrings[ConnectionStringName].ConnectionString);
    return db;
  }
```

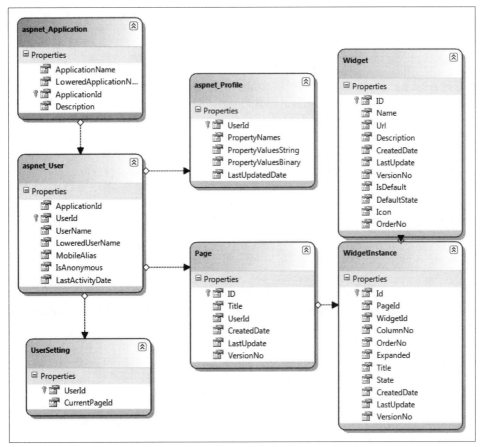

*Figure 4-1. Database model that shows LINQ to SQL classes*

DatabaseHelper also takes care of configuration management and initialization of the DataContent class. It has a GetDashboardData function that returns a reference to the DashboardData instance already configured with the connection string. Insert, Update, and Delete methods offer shortcuts for performing common database operations.

DatabaseHelper reads the connection string from the <connectionString> block in the *web.config* or *app.config* file. It also stores the ApplicationId for the ASP.NET membership provider.

> Although it would be sensible to place the ApplicationID in *web.config*, I've placed it in DatabaseHelper just to simplify this discussion.

Whenever you create a new application using an ASP.NET membership, ASP.NET creates an entry in the Aspnet_Applications table. This ApplicationID is also used in the aspnet_users table to identify which application a user belongs to.

The membership provider is built for hosting multiple applications in the same database. So, all the root objects such as user, personalization, etc. belong to an application.

Here's a problem with LINQ to SQL. If an entity travels through multiple tiers, then it gets detached from the DataContext that created it. This means that as soon as an entity is out of the data access layer and into the business or web layer, it is detached from the DataContext because the DataContext is only available within the data access layer. So, when you try to update entities again using a different DataContext, you first need to attach the entity instance to the new data context, then make the changes and call SubmitChanges. Now the problem is that from the business layer you do not have access to the DataContext, which is created by the data access layer when the entity object is being updated. The business layer will just send the entity object to the data access component, and then the component will update by creating a new DataContext.

LINQ to SQL requires that you attach the entity object *before* making changes to it so that it can track which properties are being changed and determine what kind of UPDATE or INSERT statement to generate. However, a typical business layer will make the object modifications first and then send them to the data access component. So, a traditional attempt like Example 4-8 will fail.

*Example 4-8. Common way of updating objects in the database*

```
Page p = DashboardData.GetSomePage( );
...
...

// Long time later may be after a page postback
p.Title = "New Title";
DashboardData.UpdatePage( p );
```

Somehow you need to do what is shown in Example 4-9.

*Example 4-9. Proper way of updating objects in the database using LINQ to SQL*

```
Page p = DashboardData.GetSomePage( );
...
...
// Long time later may be after a page postback
DashboardData.AttachPage( p );
p.Title = "New Title";
DashboardData.UpdatePage( p );
```

However, Example 4-9 is not possible because you can't make DashboardData stateless. You need to create DataContext inside methods and then store the reference to DataContext between function calls. This will be fine for a single-user scenario, but not an acceptable solution for multiuser web sites. So, I made a workaround (see Example 4-10).

*Example 4-10. Workaround for stateless data persistence*

```
// Load the object from database
Page p = DashboardData.GetSomePage( );
...
...
// Long time later may be after a page postback
DashboardData.Update<Page>( p, delegate( Page p1 )
{
  p1.Title = "New Title";
});
```

Here, the Update<> method first attaches the page object to DataContext and then calls the delegate passing the reference to the attached object. You can now modify the passed object as if you were modifying the original object inside the delegate. Once the delegate completes, the object will be updated using DataContext.SubmitChanges( );.

The implementation of the Update<> method is shown in Example 4-11.

*Example 4-11. The DashboardData.Update<T> updates an object in the database*

```
public static void Update<T>(T obj, Action<T> update)
{
  var db = GetDashboardData( );
  db.GetTable<T>( ).Attach(obj);
  update(obj);
  db.SubmitChanges( );
}
```

The widget container uses DatabaseHelper to update objects in the database as shown in Example 4-12.

*Example 4-12. The widget container uses DatabaseHelper to update objects*

```
WidgetInstance widgetInstance = DatabaseHelper.GetDashboardData( ).
             WidgetInstances.Single( wi => wi.Id == WidgetInstanceId );

DatabaseHelper.Update<WidgetInstance>( widgetInstance,
                               delegate( WidgetInstance wi )
{
      wi.ColumnNo = ColumnNo;
      wi.OrderNo = RowNo;
});
```

The delegate in Update<T> allows you to be in the context of the business layer or the caller. So, you can access the UI elements or other functions/properties that you need to update the entity's properties.

Similarly, there's an UpdateAll<> function that updates a list of objects in the database (see Example 4-13).

*Example 4-13. DashboardData.UpdateAll<T> updates multiple objects*

```
public static void UpdateAll<T>(List<T> items, Action<T> update)
{
  var db = GetDashboardData();

  foreach( T item in items )
  {
    db.GetTable<T>().Attach(item);
    update(item);
  }

  db.SubmitChanges();
}
```

For convenience, I have made Insert<> an Delete<> also. But they are not required because they do not have an "Attach first, modify later" requirement (see Example 4-14).

*Example 4-14. Insert<> and Delete<> functions in DashboardData*

```
public static void Delete<T>(Action<T> makeTemplate) where T:new()
{
  var db = GetDashboardData();
  T template = new T();
  makeTemplate(template);
  db.GetTable<T>().Remove(template);
  db.SubmitChanges();
}
public static void Insert<T>(T obj)
{
  var db = GetDashboardData();
  db.GetTable<T>().Add(obj);
  db.SubmitChanges();
}
```

The Delete<> method is a tricky one. First you need to attach the object to the Table and then call the table's Remove function. This means you need to first get the object before you can call Delete, which adds a read overhead while deleting an object (see Example 4-15).

*Example 4-15. Delete<T> takes the object to delete and then removes it from the database*

```
public static void Delete<T>(T entity) where T : class,new()
{
    using (var db = GetDashboardData())
    {
        db.GetTable<T>().Attach(entity);
        db.GetTable<T>().Remove(entity);
        db.SubmitChanges();
    }
}
```

Now that you have learned how to build the data access layer, let's address some of the challenges you'll face while running the portal project in a production environment.

## Cleaning Up Inactive User and Related Data

An Ajax web portal has a unique challenge when it comes to cleaning up unused data that is generated by anonymous users who never return. Every first visit creates one anonymous user, a page setup, widgets, etc. If the user doesn't come back, that information remains in the database permanently. It is possible that the user might come back within a day, or a week or a month, but there's no guarantee. Generally, *sticky users*—users who return to your site frequently—make up 30 to 50 percent of the total users who come to an Ajax web portal. So, you end up with 50 to 70 percent unused data. Dropthings requires daily data cleanup to keep the database size down—user accounts expire, RSS feeds get old, anonymous sessions expire, and users never come back.

This is a huge cleanup operation once a web portal becomes popular and starts receiving thousands of users every day. Think about deleting millions of rows from 20 or 30 tables, one after another, while maintaining foreign key constraints. Also, the cleanup operation needs to run while the site is running, without hampering its overall performance. The whole operation results in heavily fragmented index and space in the MDF file. The log file also becomes enormous to keep track of the large transactions. Hard drives get really hot and sweat furiously. Although the CPU keeps going, it's really painful to watch SQL Server go through this every day. But there is no alternative to keep up with SQL Server's RAM and disk I/O requirements. Most importantly, this avoids counting users in monthly reports that are not valid users.

When a user visits the site, the ASP.NET membership provider updates the LastActivityDate of the aspnet_users table. From this field, you can find out how long the user has been idle. The IsAnonymous bit field shows whether the user account is anonymous or registered. If it is registered, then there is no need to worry. But if it is anonymous and more than 30 days old, you can be sure that the user will never come back because the cookie has already expired. However, we can't avoid creating an anonymous user because the user might want a fresh start (see the "Implementing Authentication and Authorization" section in Chapter 3). Another scenario is a user logging out on a shared computer (e.g., a cyber café) and the next person using it as an anonymous user.

Here's how the whole cleanup process works:

1. Find out the users that are old enough to be discarded and are anonymous
2. Find out the pages the user has
3. Delete all of the widget instances on those pages
4. Delete those pages

5. Remove rows from child tables related to aspnet_users like aspnet_profile, aspnet_UsersInRoles, and aspnet_PersonalizationPerUser

6. Remove rows for users to be deleted

7. Remove the users from aspnet_users

Example 4-16 is the giant DB script that does it all. I have added inline comments to explain what the script is doing.

*Example 4-16. Cleaning up old anonymous users and their related data*

```
-- Number of days after which we give users the 'bye bye'
DECLARE @Days int
SET @Days = 29

-- Number of users to delete per run. If it's too high, the database will get stuck
-- for a long time. If it's too low, you will end up having more trash than
-- you can clean up. Decide this number based on how many anonymous users are
-- created per day and how frequently you run this query. The correct formula
-- for this number is: @NoOfUsersToDelete > AnonUsersPerDay / FrequencyOfRun
DECLARE @NoOfUsersToDelete int
SET @NoOfUsersToDelete = 1000

-- To find other tables, create temporary tables that hold users and pages to delete
-- as the user and page are used.
-- Having them in a temp table is better than repeatedly running SELECT ID FORM ...
IF  EXISTS (SELECT * FROM sys.objects WHERE object_id = OBJECT_ID(N'[dbo].
[PagesToDelete]') AND type in (N'U'))
DROP TABLE [dbo].[PagesToDelete]
IF  EXISTS (SELECT * FROM sys.objects WHERE object_id = OBJECT_ID(N'[dbo].
[aspnetUsersToDelete]') AND type in (N'U'))
DROP TABLE [dbo].[AspnetUsersToDelete]

create table PagesToDelete (PageID int NOT NULL PRIMARY KEY)
create table AspnetUsersToDelete (UserID uniqueidentifier NOT NULL PRIMARY KEY)

-- Find inactive anonymous users and store the UserID in the temporary
-- table
insert into AspnetUsersToDelete
select top(@NoOfUsersToDelete) UserID from aspnet_Users where
(isAnonymous = 1) and (LastActivityDate < (getDate( )-@Days))
order by UserID -- Saves SQL Server from sorting in clustered index again

print 'Users to delete: ' + convert(varchar(255),@@ROWCOUNT)
GO

-- Get the user pages that will be deleted
insert into PagesToDelete
select ID from Page where UserID in
(
select UserID from AspnetUsersToDelete
)
```

*Example 4-16. Cleaning up old anonymous users and their related data (continued)*

```
print 'Pages to delete: ' + convert(varchar(255),@@ROWCOUNT)
GO

-- Delete all widget instances on the pages to be deleted
delete from WidgetInstance where PageID IN
( SELECT PageID FROM PagesToDelete )

print 'Widget Instances deleted: ' + convert(varchar(255), @@ROWCOUNT)
GO

-- Delete the pages
delete from Page where ID IN
( SELECT PageID FROM PagesToDelete )
GO

-- Delete UserSetting
delete from UserSetting WHERE UserID IN
( SELECT UserID FROm AspnetUsersToDelete )
GO

-- Delete profile of users
delete from aspnet_Profile WHERE UserID IN
( SELECT UserID FROm AspnetUsersToDelete )
GO

-- Delete from aspnet_UsersInRoles
delete from aspnet_UsersInRoles WHERE UserID IN
( SELECT UserID FROm AspnetUsersToDelete )
GO

-- Delete from aspnet_PersonalizationPerUser
delete from aspnet_PersonalizationPerUser WHERE UserID IN
( SELECT UserID FROm AspnetUsersToDelete )
GO

-- Delete the users
delete from aspnet_users where userID IN
( SELECT UserID FROm AspnetUsersToDelete )

PRINT 'Users deleted: ' + convert(varchar(255), @@ROWCOUNT)
GO


drop table PagesToDelete
drop table AspnetUsersToDelete
GO
```

Now the question is, when can I run this script? The answer depends on several factors:

- The period of lowest traffic on your site. For example, in the U.S., most users are asleep at midnight. Of course, that works only if the majority of your users are from the U.S.

- Other maintenance tasks, such as index defrag or database backup, are the least likely to be running. If by any chance any other maintenance task conflicts with this enormous delete operation, SQL Server is dead.

- The time it takes to run the script. The operation will take anywhere from 10 minutes to a number of hours depending on the volume of trash to clean up. So, consider the amount of time it will take to run this script and plan other maintenance jobs accordingly.

- When you typically run index defrag. It's best to run the script 30 minutes before the index defrag jobs run, because after the script completes, the tables will be heavily fragmented. So, you need to defrag the indexes.

Before running this script, first:

- Turn off auto shrink from database property. Database size will automatically reduce after the cleanup. Shrinking a database requires a lot of disk I/O activity and it slows the database down. Turn off auto shrink because the database will eventually grow again.

- Ensure that the log file's initial size is big enough to hold such enormous transactions. You can specify one-third of the MDF size as LDF's initial size. Also make sure the log file did not shrink—let it occupy HD space. It saves SQL Server from expanding and shrinking the file. Both of these require high disk I/O.

Once the cleanup job is done and the index defrag runs, the performance of your database will improve significantly. Because the tables are now smaller, the indexes are smaller, and SQL Server doesn't have to run through large indexes anymore. Future index defrags take less time because there's not much data left to optimize. SQL Server also takes less RAM because it has to work with much less amount of data. Database backup size is also reduced because the MDF size does not keep increasing indefinitely. As a result, the significant overhead of this cleanup operation is quite acceptable when compared to all the benefits.

# Introducing Windows Workflow Foundation

Windows Workflow Foundation (WF), included in .NET 3.0, provides the programming model, engine, and tools for quickly building workflow-enabled applications. It gives developers the ability to model business processes in a visual designer by drawing flow chart diagrams. Complex business operations can be modeled as a workflow in the visual workflow designer included in Visual Studio 2008, and coded using any .NET programming language. WF consists of the following parts:

*Activity model*

Activities are the building blocks of workflow—think of them as a unit of work that needs to be executed. Activities are easy to create, either from writing code or by composing them from other activities. Out of the box, there are a set of activities that mostly provide structure, such as parallel execution, if/else, and calling a web service.

*Workflow designer*

This is the design surface in Visual Studio, which allows for the graphical composition of workflow, by placing activities within the workflow model.

*Workflow runtime*

Workflow runtime is a lightweight and extensible engine that executes the activities that make up a workflow. The runtime is hosted within any .NET process, enabling developers to bring workflow to anything, from a Windows forms application to an ASP.NET web site or a Windows service.

*Rules engine*

WF has a rules engine that enables declarative, rule-based development for workflows and any .NET application to use. Using the rule engine, you can eliminate hardcoded rules in your code and move them from the code to a more maintainable declarative format on the workflow diagram.

Although a workflow is mostly used in applications that have workflow-type business processes, you can use a workflow in almost any application as long as the application does complex operations. In this Start page application, some operations, like first visit, are complex and require multistep activities and decisions. So, such applications can benefit from workflow implementation.

# Building the Business Layer Using WF

The entire business layer is developed using WF. Each of the methods in the DashboardFacade do nothing but call individual workflows. There's absolutely no business code that is not part of any workflow.

"This is insane!" you are thinking. I know. Please listen to why I went for this approach. Architects can "design" business layer operations in terms of activities, and developers can just fill in a small amount of unit code to implement each activity.

This is actually a really good reason because architects can save time by not having to produce Word documents on how things should work. They can directly go into Workflow designer, design the activities, connect them, design the data flow, and verify whether all input and output are properly mapped or not. This is lot better than drawing flow charts, writing pseudocode, and explaining in stylish text how an operation should work. It's also helpful for developers because they can see the workflow and easily understand how to craft the whole operation. They just open up each activity and write a small amount of very specific reusable code inside each one. They know what the activity's input (like function parameters) will be and they know what to produce (return value of function). This makes the activities reusable, and architects can reuse an activity in many workflows.

Workflows can be debugged right in Visual Studio Designer for WF. So, developers can easily find defects in their implementation by debugging the workflow. Architects can enforce many standards like validations, input output check, and fault handling on the workflow. Developers cannot but comply and, therefore, produce really good code. Another great benefit for both architect and developer is that there's no need to keep a separate technical specification document up to date because the workflow is always up to date and it speaks for itself. If someone wanted to study how a particular operation works, they could just print out the workflow and read it through.

---

### Performance Concerns with WF

But what about performance? You will read from some blog posts that WF is a pretty big library and can be a memory hog. Also, the workflow runtime is quite big and takes time to start up. So, I did some profiling on the overhead of workflow execution, and it is actually very fast for synchronous execution. Here's proof from Visual Studio's output window log:

```
334ec662-0e45-4f1c-bf2c-cd3a27014691 Activity: Get User Guid       0.078125
b030692b-5181-41f9-a0c3-69ce309d9806 Activity: Get User Pages       0.0625
b030692b-5181-41f9-a0c3-69ce309d9806 Activity: Get User Setting     0.046875
b030692b-5181-41f9-a0c3-69ce309d9806 Activity: Get Widgets in page: 189 0.0625
334ec662-0e45-4f1c-bf2c-cd3a27014691 Total: Existing user visit     0.265625
```

The first four entries are the time taken by individual activities during data access only, not the total time it takes to execute the whole activity. The time entries here are in seconds, and the first four entries represent the duration of database operations inside the activities. The last one is the total time for running a workflow with the four activities shown and some extra code. If you sum up all of the individual activity execution time for only database operations, it is 0.2500, which is just 0.015625 seconds less than the total execution time. This means that executing the workflow itself along with the overhead of running activities takes about 0.015 seconds, which is almost nothing (around 6 percent) compared to the total effort of doing the complete operation.

---

## Mapping User Actions to a Workflow

Each user action can be mapped to a workflow that responds to that action. For example, when a user wants to add a new widget, a workflow can take care of creating the widget, positioning it properly on the page, and configuring the widget with the default value. The first visit of a brand new user to the site is a complex operation, so it is a good candidate to become a workflow. This makes the architecture quite simple on the web layer—just call a workflow on various scenarios and render the UI accordingly, as illustrated in Figure 4-2.

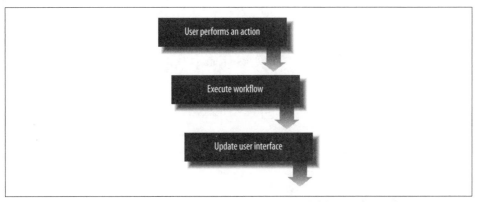

*Figure 4-2. User actions are mapped to a workflow. For example, when a user adds a new tab, the request goes to a workflow. The workflow creates a new tab, makes it current, configures tab default settings, adds default widgets, etc. Once done, the workflow returns success and the page shows the new tab.*

Instead of using complex diagrams and lines of documentation to explain how to handle a particular user or system action, you can draw a workflow and write code inside it. This serves both as a document and a functional component that does the job. The next sections show scenarios that can easily be done in a workflow.

## Dealing with First Visit by a New User (NewUserSetupWorkflow)

Handling the first visit of a brand new user is the most complex operation your web site will handle. It's a good candidate for becoming a workflow. Figure 4-3 shows a workflow that does all the business layer work for the first-time visit and returns a complete page setup. The *Default.aspx* just creates the widgets as it receives them from the workflow and is not required to perform any other logic.

The operations involved in creating the first-visit experience for a new user are as follows:

1. Create a new anonymous user
2. Create two default pages
3. Put some default widgets on the first page
4. Construct a object model that contains user data, the user's page collection, and the widgets for the first page

If you put these operations in a workflow, you get the workflow shown in Figure 4-3.

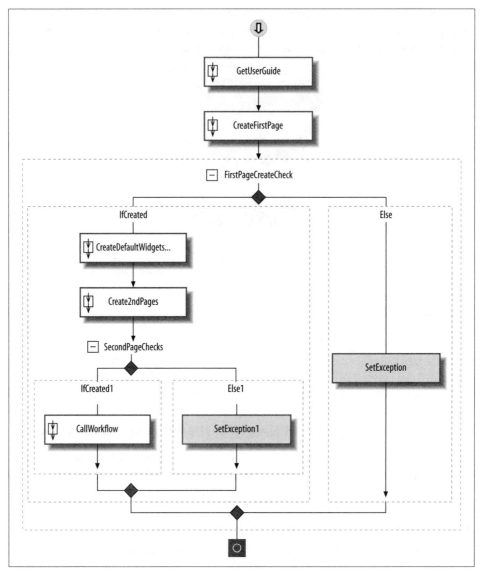

*Figure 4-3. New user visit workflow creates a new user account and configures the account with the default setup*

The workflow takes the ASP.NET anonymous identification provider generated by UserName as an input to the workflow from the *Default.aspx* page.

The first step in passing this input parameter to the workflow while running the workflow is to call the GetUserGuidActivity to get the UserId from the aspnet_users table for that user (see Example 4-17).

*Example 4-17. GetUserGuidActivity Execute function*

```
protected override ActivityExecutionStatus Execute(ActivityExecutionContext
executionContext)
{
  using( new TimedLog(UserName, "Activity: Get User Guid") )
  {
    var db = DatabaseHelper.GetDashboardData();

    this.UserGuid = (from u in db.AspnetUsers
      where u.LoweredUserName == UserName && u.ApplicationId == DatabaseHelper.
    ApplicationGuid
      select u.UserId).Single();

    return ActivityExecutionStatus.Closed;
  }
}
```

This activity is used in many places because it is a common requirement to get the UserId from the username found from the ASP.NET Context object. All the tables have a foreign key in the UserId column but ASP.NET gives only the UserName. So, in almost all the operations, UserName is passed from the web layer and the business layer converts it to UserId and does its work.

 The using(TimedLog) block records the execution time of the code inside the using block. It prints the execution time in the debug window as you read earlier in the "Performance Concerns with WF" section.

The next step is to create the first page for the user using CreateNewPageActivity shown in Example 4-18.

*Example 4-18. CreateNewPageActivity Execute function*

```
protected override ActivityExecutionStatus Execute(ActivityExecutionContext
executionContext)
{
  DashboardData db = DatabaseHelper.GetDashboardData();

  var newPage = new Page();
  newPage.UserId = UserId;
  newPage.Title = Title;
  newPage.CreatedDate = DateTime.Now;
  newPage.LastUpdate = DateTime.Now;

  db.Pages.Add(newPage);
  db.SubmitChanges(ConflictMode.FailOnFirstConflict);
  NewPageId = newPage.ID;

  return ActivityExecutionStatus.Closed;
}
```

This activity takes the UserID as input and produces the NewPageId property as output. It creates a new page, and default widgets are added on that page. CreateDefaultWidgetActivity creates the default widgets on this page as shown in Example 4-19.

*Example 4-19. CreateDefaultWidgetActivity Execute function*

```
protected override ActivityExecutionStatus Execute(ActivityExecutionContext
executionContext)
{
  var db = DatabaseHelper.GetDashboardData( );

  var defaultWidgets = db.Widgets.Where( w => w.IsDefault == true ).ToList( );
  var widgetsPerColumn = (int)Math.Ceiling((float)defaultWidgets.Count/3.0);

  var row = 0;
  var col = 0;

  foreach( Widget w in defaultWidgets )
  {
    var newWidget = new WidgetInstance( );
    newWidget.PageId= this.PageId;
    newWidget.ColumnNo = col;
    newWidget.OrderNo = row;
    newWidget.CreatedDate = newWidget.LastUpdate = DateTime.Now;
    newWidget.Expanded = true;
    newWidget.Title = w.Name;
    newWidget.VersionNo = 1;
    newWidget.WidgetId = w.ID;
    newWidget.State = w.DefaultState;

    db.WidgetInstances.Add(newWidget);

    row ++;
    if( row >= widgetsPerColumn )
    {
      row = 0;
      col ++;
    }
  }

  db.SubmitChanges( );

  return ActivityExecutionStatus.Closed;
}
```

This is what needs to happen next:

1. Decide how many widgets to add per column.

2. Compute the number of widgets to put in each column so they have an even distribution of widgets based on the number of default widgets in the database.

3. Run the foreach loop through each default widget and created widget instances.

4. Create the second empty page.

5. Call another workflow named `UserVisitWorkflow` to load the page setup for the user. This workflow was used on both the first visit and subsequent visits because loading a user's page setup is same for both cases.

The `InvokeWorkflow` activity that comes with WF executes a workflow asynchronously. So, if you are calling a workflow from ASP.NET that in turn calls another workflow, the second workflow is going to be terminated prematurely instead of executing completely. This is because the workflow runtime will execute the first workflow synchronously and then finish the workflow execution and return. If you use `InvokeWorkflow` activity to run another workflow from the first workflow, it will start on another thread, and it will not get enough time to execute completely before the parent workflow ends, as shown in Figure 4-4.

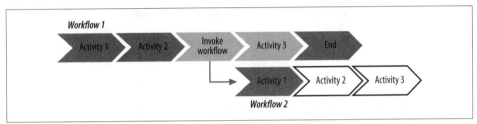

*Figure 4-4. InvokeWorkflow executes a workflow asynchronously, so if the calling workflow completes before the called workflow, it will terminate prematurely*

So, `InvokeWorkflow` could not be used to execute the `UserVisitWorkflow` from `NewUserSetupWorkflow`. Instead it is executed using the `CallWorkflow` activity, which takes a workflow and executes it synchronously. It's a handy activity I found on Jon Flanders' blog (*http://www.masteringbiztalk.com/blogs/jon/PermaLink,guid,7be9fb53-0ddf-4633-b358-01c3e9999088.aspx*).

The beauty of this activity is that it properly maps both inbound and outbound properties of the workflow that it calls, as shown in Figure 4-5.

The `UserName` property is passed from the `NewUserVisitWorkflow`, and it is returning the `UserPageSetup`, which contains everything needed to render the page for the user.

## Dealing with the Return Visit of an Existing User (UserVisitWorkflow)

`UserVisitWorkflow` creates a composite object named `UserPageSetup` that holds the user's settings, pages, and widgets on the current page. The *Default.aspx* gets everything it needs to render the whole page from `UserPageSetup`, as shown in Figure 4-6.

*Figure 4-5. You can map CallWorkflow to a workflow and it will call that workflow synchronously. You can also see the parameters of the workflow and map them with properties in the current workflow.*

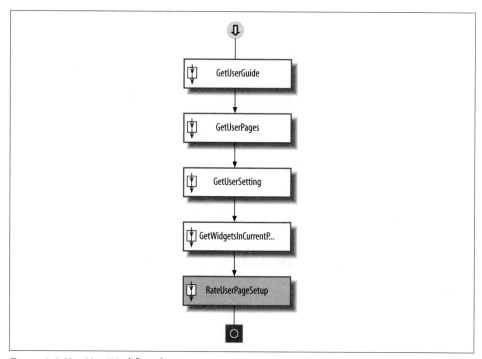

*Figure 4-6. UserVisitWorkflow design view*

Just like the previous workflow, UserVisitWorkflow takes UserName and converts it to UserGuid. It then calls the GetUserPagesActivity, which loads the pages of the user (see Example 4-20).

*Example 4-20. GetUserPagesActivity's Execute function*

```
protected override ActivityExecutionStatus Execute(ActivityExecutionContext
executionContext)
{
  using( new TimedLog(UserGuid.ToString( ), "Activity: Get User Pages") )
  {
    var db = DatabaseHelper.GetDashboardData( );

    this.Pages = (from page in db.Pages
           where page.UserId == UserGuid
           select page).ToList( );

    return ActivityExecutionStatus.Closed;
  }
}
```

After that, it calls the GetUserSettingActivity, which gets or creates the user's setting. The UserSetting object contains the user's current page, which is used by GetUserSettingActivity to load the widgets of the current page.

The code in GetUserSettingActivity is not straightforward (see Example 4-21). It first checks if UserSetting has been created for the user and, if not, GetUserSettingActivity creates it.

*Example 4-21. GetUserSettingActivity Execute function*

```
protected override ActivityExecutionStatus Execute(ActivityExecutionContext
executionContext)
{
  using( new TimedLog(UserGuid.ToString( ), "Activity: Get User Setting") )
  {
    DashboardData db = DatabaseHelper.GetDashboardData( );

    var query = from u in db.UserSettings
           where u.UserId == UserGuid
           select u;

    IEnumerator<UserSetting> e = query.GetEnumerator( );

    if( e.MoveNext( ) )
    {
      this.UserSetting = e.Current;
    }
    else
    {
      // No setting saved before. Create default setting
```

*Example 4-21. GetUserSettingActivity Execute function (continued)*

```
    UserSetting newSetting = new UserSetting( );
    newSetting.UserId = UserGuid;
    newSetting.CurrentPageId = (from page in db.Pages
                  where page.UserId == UserGuid
                  select page.ID).First( );

    db.UserSettings.Add(newSetting);
    db.SubmitChanges( );

    this.UserSetting = newSetting;
  }

  this.CurrentPage = db.Pages.Single(page => page.ID == this.UserSetting.CurrentPageId);

  return ActivityExecutionStatus.Closed;
 }
}
```

Loading the existing user's settings is optimized by getting only the CurrentPageId instead of the whole UserSetting object. This results in a very small query that does a scalar selection, which is a bit faster than a row selection because it doesn't involve constructing a row object or sending unnecessary fields to a row.

The final activity loads the widgets on the current page (see Example 4-22). It takes the PageId and loads widget instances on the page, including the widget definition for each instance.

*Example 4-22. GetWidgetsInPageActivity Execute function*

```
protected override ActivityExecutionStatus Execute(ActivityExecutionContext
executionContext)
{
  using( new TimedLog(UserGuid.ToString( ), "Activity: Get Widgets in page: " + PageId) )
  {
    var db = DatabaseHelper.GetDashboardData( );

    // Load widget instances along with the Widget definition
    // for the specified page
    this.WidgetInstances = (from widgetInstance in db.WidgetInstances
            where widgetInstance.PageId == this.PageId
            orderby widgetInstance.ColumnNo, widgetInstance.OrderNo
            select widgetInstance)
            .Including(widgetInstance => widgetInstance.Widget)
            .ToList( );

    return ActivityExecutionStatus.Closed;
  }
}
```

The LINQ query that loads the widget instances has two important actions:

- Loads widget instances on the page and orders them by column, and then row. As a result, you get widget instances from left to right and in proper order within each column.
- Fetches the widget object by producing an INNER JOIN between Widget and the WidgetInstance table.

The collection of the widget instance is mapped to the WidgetInstance property of the activity. The final code block—ReturnUserPageSetup—populates the UserPageSetup property of the workflow with loaded data (see Example 4-23).

*Example 4-23. PopulateUserPageSetup property with widgets, pages, and user settings needed to render the page*

```
private void ReturnUserPageSetup_ExecuteCode(object sender, EventArgs e)
{
  this.UserPageSetup.Pages = this.GetUserPages.Pages;
  this.UserPageSetup.UserSetting = this.GetUserSetting.UserSetting;
  this.UserPageSetup.WidgetInstances = this.GetWidgetsInCurrentPage.WidgetInstances;
}
```

The workflow takes an empty UserPageSetup object; when it completes, it populates the empty object with the loaded data. So, from ASP.NET, the UserPageSetup object is passed and emptied. Once the workflow completes, the instance is fully populated.

## Adding a New Tab (AddNewTabWorkflow)

Adding a new tab is quite simple, requiring only two steps, after the GUID is assigned (see Figure 4-7):

1. Create a new blank page.
2. Update the user settings and set the new page as the current page.

## Moving Widgets (MoveWidgetInstanceWorkflow)

To move a widget, you must do the following (see Figure 4-8):

1. Ensure the current user who is calling the workflow owns the widget instance.
2. Fetch the widget instance and put in workflow context so that other activities can use it.
3. Pull the widget up from its previous position, which means all the widgets below are shifted up.
4. Push the widget onto its new position so that all widgets on the new column move down.
5. Update the widget's position.

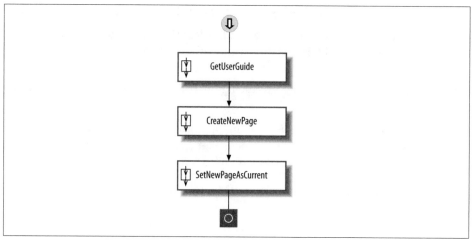

*Figure 4-7. AddNewTabWorkflow design view*

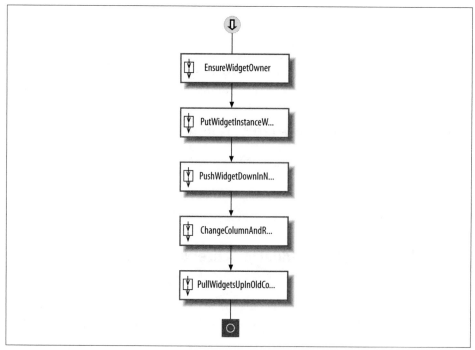

*Figure 4-8. MoveWidgetInstanceWorkflow design view*

MoveWidgetInstanceWorkflow verifies whether the widget being moved is really the current user's widget. This is necessary to prevent malicious web service hacking (see the "Implementing Authentication and Authorization" section in Chapter 3). The EnsureOwnerActivity can check both the page and the widget's ownership (see Example 4-24).

*Example 4-24. EnsureOwnerActivity Execute function*

```
protected override ActivityExecutionStatus Execute(ActivityExecutionContext
executionContext)
{
  var db = DatabaseHelper.GetDashboardData( );

  if( this.PageId == 0 && this.WidgetInstanceId == 0 )
  {
    throw new ApplicationException("No valid object specified to check");
  }

  if( this.WidgetInstanceId > 0 )
  {
    // Gets the user who is the owner of the widget. Then sees if the current user is the
    same.
    var ownerName = (from wi in db.WidgetInstances
        where wi.Id == this.WidgetInstanceId
        select wi.Page.AspnetUser.LoweredUserName).First( );

    if( !this.UserName.ToLower( ).Equals( ownerName ) )
      throw new ApplicationException(string.Format("User {0} is not the owner of the
      widget instance {1}", this.UserName, this.WidgetInstanceId));
  }


  if( this.PageId > 0 )
  {
    // Gets the user who is the owner of the page. Then sees if the current user is the
    same.
    var ownerName = (from p in db.Pages
        where p.ID == this.PageId
        select p.AspnetUser.LoweredUserName).First( );

    if( !this.UserName.ToLower( ).Equals( ownerName ) )
      throw new ApplicationException(string.Format("User {0} is not the owner of the page
      {1}", this.UserName, this.PageId));
  }

  return ActivityExecutionStatus.Closed;
}
```

EnsureOwnerActivity takes UserName and either WidgetInstanceId or PageId and verifies the user's ownership. It should climb through the hierarchy from WidgetInstance to the Page and then to AspnetUser to check whether the username matches or not. If the username is different than the one specified, then the owner is different and it's a malicious attempt.

Checking Page ownership requires just going one level up to AspnetUser. But checking WidgetInstance ownership requires going up to the container page and then checking ownership of the page. This needs to happen very fast because it is called on almost every operation performed on Page or WidgetInstance. This is why you want to make sure it does a scalar select only, which is faster than selecting a full row.

Once the owner has been verified, the widget can be placed on the right column. The next activity, `PutWidgetInstanceInWorkflow`, does nothing but put the `WidgetInstance` object into a public property according to its ID so the object can be manipulated directly. The other activities in the workflow work with the object's `ColumnNo` and `OrderNo` properties. The next step, `PushWidgetsDownInNewColumn`, calls the `PushDownWidgetsOnColumnActivity`, which pushes widgets down one row so there's a room for a new widget to be dropped (see Example 4-25).

*Example 4-25. PushDownWidgetsOnColumnActivity Execute function*

```
protected override ActivityExecutionStatus Execute(ActivityExecutionContext
executionContext)
{
  var db = DatabaseHelper.GetDashboardData( );
  var query = from wi in db.WidgetInstances
        where wi.PageId == PageId && wi.ColumnNo == ColumnNo && wi.OrderNo >= Position
        orderby wi.OrderNo
        select wi;
  List<WidgetInstance> list = query.ToList( );

  int orderNo = Position+1;
  foreach( WidgetInstance wi in list )
  {
    wi.OrderNo = orderNo ++;
  }

  db.SubmitChanges( );

  return ActivityExecutionStatus.Closed;
}
```

The idea is to move all the widgets right below the position of the widget being dropped and push them down one position. Now we have to update the position of the dropped widget using the activity `ChangeWidgetInstancePositionActivity` (see Example 4-26).

*Example 4-26. ChangeWidgetInstancePositionActivity Execute function*

```
protected override ActivityExecutionStatus Execute(ActivityExecutionContext
executionContext)
{
  WidgetInstance widgetInstance = DatabaseHelper.GetDashboardData( ).WidgetInstances.
  Single( wi => wi.Id == WidgetInstanceId );

  DatabaseHelper.Update<WidgetInstance>( widgetInstance, delegate( WidgetInstance wi )
  {
    wi.ColumnNo = ColumnNo;
    wi.OrderNo = RowNo;
  });

  return ActivityExecutionStatus.Closed;
}
```

The widget is placed on a new column, and the old column has a vacant place. But now we need to pull the widgets one row upward on the old column. `ReorderWidgetInstanceOnColumnActivity` fixes row orders on a column, eliminating the gaps between them (see Example 4-27). The gap in the column will be fixed by recalculating the row number for each widget on that column, starting from zero.

*Example 4-27. ReorderWidgetInstanceOnColumnActivity Execute function*

```
protected override ActivityExecutionStatus Execute(ActivityExecutionContext
executionContext)
{
  var db = DatabaseHelper.GetDashboardData( );
  var query = from wi in db.WidgetInstances
        where wi.PageId == PageId && wi.ColumnNo == ColumnNo
        orderby wi.OrderNo
        select wi;
  List<WidgetInstance> list = query.ToList( );

  int orderNo = 0;
  foreach( WidgetInstance wi in list )
  {
    wi.OrderNo = orderNo ++;
  }

  db.SubmitChanges( );

  return ActivityExecutionStatus.Closed;
}
```

That's all that is required for a simple drag-and-drop operation.

# Implementing the DashboardFacade

`DashboardFacade` provides a single entry point to the entire business layer. It provides easy-to-call methods that run workflows. For example, the `NewUserVisit` function executes the `NewUserSetupWorkflow` (see Example 4-28).

*Example 4-28. DashboardFacade.NewUserVisit calls NewUserSetupWorkflow and creates a complete setup for a new user on the first visit*

```
public UserPageSetup NewUserVisit( )
{
  using( new TimedLog(this._UserName, "New user visit") )
  {
    var properties = new Dictionary<string,object>( );
    properties.Add("UserName", this._UserName);
    var userSetup = new UserPageSetup( );
    properties.Add("UserPageSetup", userSetup);

    WorkflowHelper.ExecuteWorkflow( typeof( NewUserSetupWorkflow ), properties );
```

*Example 4-28. DashboardFacade.NewUserVisit calls NewUserSetupWorkflow and creates a complete setup for a new user on the first visit (continued)*

```
    return userSetup;
  }
}
```

Here the input parameter to the workflow is UserName. Although the UserPageSetup object is passed as if it was an input parameter, it's not an input. You are passing a null object, which the workflow will populate with loaded data. It's like an out parameter in function calls. The workflow will populate this parameter's value once it completes the execution.

Other methods, like LoadUserSetup, DeleteWidgetInstance, and MoveWidgetInstance, behave the same way. They take necessary parameters as input and pass them to their own workflows, e.g., the MoveWidgetInstance function (see Example 4-29).

*Example 4-29. DashboardFacade.MoveWidgetInstance calls MoveWidgetInstanceWorkflow to move a widget from one position to another*

```
public void MoveWidgetInstance( int widgetInstanceId, int toColumn, int toRow )
{
  using( new TimedLog(this._UserName, "Move Widget:" + widgetInstanceId) )
  {
    var properties = new Dictionary<string,object>( );
    properties.Add("UserName", this._UserName);
    properties.Add("WidgetInstanceId", widgetInstanceId);
    properties.Add("ColumnNo", toColumn);
    properties.Add("RowNo", toRow);

    WorkflowHelper.ExecuteWorkflow( typeof( MoveWidgetInstanceWorkflow ), properties );
  }
}
```

However, getting a return object from a workflow is quite complicated. The AddWidget function in the façade needs to get the newly added widget instance out of the workflow (see Example 4-30).

*Example 4-30. DashboardFacade.AddWidget function calls AddWidgetWorkflow to add a new widget for the user's current page*

```
public WidgetInstance AddWidget(int widgetId)
{
  using( new TimedLog(this._UserName, "Add Widget" + widgetId) )
  {
    var properties = new Dictionary<string,object>( );
    properties.Add("UserName", this._UserName);
    properties.Add("WidgetId", widgetId);

    // New Widget instance will be returned after the workflow completes
    properties.Add("NewWidget", null);
```

```
    WorkflowHelper.ExecuteWorkflow( typeof( AddWidgetWorkflow ), properties );

    return properties["NewWidget"] as WidgetInstance;
  }
}
```

A null object is being passed here to the `NewWidget` property of the workflow: `AddWidgetWorkflow`, which will populate this property with a new instance of `Widget` when it completes. Once the workflow completes, the object can be taken from the dictionary.

## Implementing the WorkflowHelper Class

`WorkflowHelper` is a handy class that makes implementing a workflow a breeze, especially when used with ASP.NET. In the business layer, the workflow needs to be synchronously executed, but the default implementation of WF is to work asynchronously. Also, you need return values from workflows after their execution is complete, which is not so easily supported due to the asynchronous nature of the workflow. Both of these tasks require some tweaking with the workflow runtime to successfully run in the ASP.NET environment.

The `WorkflowHelper.Init` function initializes workflow runtime for the ASP.NET environment. It makes sure there's only one workflow runtime per application domain. Workflow runtime cannot be created twice in the same application domain, so it stores the reference of the workflow runtime in the application context. Example 4-31 shows its partial code.

*Example 4-31. WorkflowHelper.Init, part 1*

```
public static WorkflowRuntime Init()
{
  WorkflowRuntime workflowRuntime;

  // Running in console/winforms mode, create an return new runtime and return
  if( HttpContext.Current == null )
    workflowRuntime = new WorkflowRuntime();
  else
  {
    // running in web mode, runtime is initialized only once per
    // application
    if( HttpContext.Current.Application["WorkflowRuntime"] == null )
      workflowRuntime = new WorkflowRuntime();
    else
      return HttpContext.Current.Application["WorkflowRuntime"] as WorkflowRuntime;
  }
```

The initialization takes care of both ASP.NET and the Console/Winforms mode. You will need the Console/Winforms mode when you test the workflows from a console application or from unit tests. After the initialization, it registers ManualWorkflowSchedulerService, which takes care of synchronous execution of the workflow. CallWorkflow activity, which is explained in NewUserSetupWorkflow, uses the Activities.CallWorkflowService to run another workflow synchronously within a workflow. These two services make WF usable from the ASP.NET environment (see Example 4-32).

*Example 4-32. WorkflowHelper.Init, part 2*

```
var manualService = new ManualWorkflowSchedulerService( );
workflowRuntime.AddService(manualService);

var syncCallService = new Activities.CallWorkflowService( );
workflowRuntime.AddService(syncCallService);

workflowRuntime.StartRuntime( );

// on web mode, store the runtime in application context so that
// it is initialized only once. On console/winforms mode, e.g., from unit tests, ignore
if( null != HttpContext.Current )
  HttpContext.Current.Application["WorkflowRuntime"] = workflowRuntime;

return workflowRuntime;
}
```

Workflow runtime is initialized from the Application_Start event in Global.asax. This ensures the initialization happens only once per application domain (see Example 4-33).

*Example 4-33. Initializing WorkflowHelper from Global.asax*

```
void Application_Start(object sender, EventArgs e)
{
  // Code that runs on application startup

  DashboardBusiness.WorkflowHelper.Init( );
}
```

The runtime is disposed from the Application_End event in *Global.asax* (see Example 4-34).

*Example 4-34. Disposing the workflow runtime from Global.asax*

```
    void Application_End(object sender, EventArgs e)
    {
        // Code that runs on application shutdown
        DashboardBusiness.WorkflowHelper.Terminate( );
    }
```

Inside the WorkflowHelper, most of the work is done in the ExecuteWorkflow function. DashboardFacade calls this function to run a workflow, which:

1. Executes the workflow synchronously

2. Passes parameters to the workflow

3. Gets output parameters from the workflow and returns them

4. Handles exceptions raised in the workflow and passes to the ASP.NET exception handler

In the first step, ExecuteWorkflow creates an instance of workflow and passes input parameters to it as shown in Example 4-35.

*Example 4-35. ExecuteWorkflow function takes care of initializing workflow runtime and preparing a workflow for execution*

```
public static void ExecuteWorkflow( Type workflowType, Dictionary<string,object>
properties)
{
  WorkflowRuntime workflowRuntime = Init();

  ManualWorkflowSchedulerService manualScheduler = workflowRuntime.
GetService<ManualWorkflowSchedulerService>();

  WorkflowInstance instance = workflowRuntime.CreateWorkflow(workflowType, properties);
  instance.Start();
```

Then ManualWorkflowSchedulerService service executes the workflow synchronously. Next, hook the workflow runtime's WorkflowCompleted and WorkflowTerminated events to capture output parameters and exceptions and handle them properly, as shown in Example 4-36.

*Example 4-36. Handle the workflow completion event to capture the output parameters from the workflow instance*

```
EventHandler<WorkflowCompletedEventArgs> completedHandler = null;
completedHandler = delegate(object o, WorkflowCompletedEventArgs e)
{
  if (e.WorkflowInstance.InstanceId ==instance.InstanceId)
  {
    workflowRuntime.WorkflowCompleted -= completedHandler;

    // copy the output parameters in the specified properties dictionary
    Dictionary<string,object>.Enumerator enumerator = e.OutputParameters.GetEnumerator();
    while( enumerator.MoveNext() )
    {
      KeyValuePair<string,object> pair = enumerator.Current;
      if( properties.ContainsKey(pair.Key) )
      {
        properties[pair.Key] = pair.Value;
      }
    }
  }
};
```

When the workflow completes, WorkflowCompletedEventArgs produces the OutputParameters dictionary, which contains all of the workflow's public properties. Next, read all of the entries in OutputParameters and update the InputParameters dictionary with the new values. This is required in the AddWidget function of DashboardFacade, where you need to know the widget instance created by the workflow.

WorkflowTerminated fires when there's an exception. When any activity inside the workflow raises an exception, this event fires and the workflow execution aborts. This exception is captured and thrown again so ASP.NET can trap it using its default exception handler, as shown in Example 4-37.

*Example 4-37. Handle exceptions raised by the workflow runtime to find out whether there are any exceptions in a particular execution of a workflow instance*

```
Exception x  = null;
EventHandler<WorkflowTerminatedEventArgs> terminatedHandler = null;
terminatedHandler = delegate(object o, WorkflowTerminatedEventArgs e)
{
  if (e.WorkflowInstance.InstanceId == instance.InstanceId)
  {
    workflowRuntime.WorkflowTerminated -= terminatedHandler;
    Debug.WriteLine( e.Exception );

    x = e.Exception;
  }
};
workflowRuntime.WorkflowCompleted += completedHandler;
workflowRuntime.WorkflowTerminated += terminatedHandler;

manualScheduler.RunWorkflow(instance.InstanceId);

if (null != x)
  throw new WorkflowException(x);
```

This helps show exceptions in the ASP.NET exception handler. Exceptions thrown from workflow instances are captured and rethrown. As a result, they jump up to the ASP.NET exception handler, and you see the "yellow page of death" on your local computer (see Figure 4-9).

```
Test Exception

Description: An unhandled exception occurred during the execution of the current web request. Please review the stack trace for more information about the error and where it originated in the code.

Exception Details: System.ApplicationException: Test Exception

Source Error:


  Line 64:            NewPageId = newPage.ID;
  Line 65:
  Line 66:            throw new ApplicationException("Test Exception");
  Line 67:
  Line 68:            return ActivityExecutionStatus.Closed;


Source File: d:\MYPROJECTS\Dashboard\src\DashboardBusiness\Activities\CreateNewPageActivity.cs    Line: 66

Stack Trace:


[ApplicationException: Test Exception]
   DashboardBusiness.Activities.CreateNewPageActivity.Execute(ActivityExecutionContext executionContext) in d:\MYPROJECTS\Dashboard\src\Dashbo
   System.Workflow.ComponentModel.ActivityExecutor`1.Execute(T activity, ActivityExecutionContext executionContext) +40
   System.Workflow.ComponentModel.ActivityExecutor`1.Execute(Activity activity, ActivityExecutionContext executionContext) +31
   System.Workflow.ComponentModel.ActivityExecutorOperation.Run(IWorkflowCoreRuntime workflowCoreRuntime) +488
   System.Workflow.Runtime.Scheduler.Run() +611

[WorkflowException: Test Exception]
   DashboardBusiness.WorkflowHelper.ExecuteWorkflow(Type workflowType, Dictionary`2 properties) in d:\MYPROJECTS\Dashboard\src\DashboardBusine
   DashboardBusiness.DashboardFacade.NewUserVisit() in d:\MYPROJECTS\Dashboard\src\DashboardBusiness\DashboardFacade.cs:31
   _Default.LoadUserPageSetup(Boolean noCache) in d:\MYPROJECTS\Dashboard\src\Dashboard\Default.aspx.cs:121
   _Default.CreateChildControls() in d:\MYPROJECTS\Dashboard\src\Dashboard\Default.aspx.cs:82
   System.Web.UI.Control.EnsureChildControls() +87
   System.Web.UI.Control.PreRenderRecursiveInternal() +41
   System.Web.UI.Page.ProcessRequestMain(Boolean includeStagesBeforeAsyncPoint, Boolean includeStagesAfterAsyncPoint) +1360
```

*Figure 4-9. Handling exceptions in the workflow and escalating them so that they propagate to ASP.NET's exception handler*

# Summary

In this chapter, you learned how to harness the power of LINQ to SQL to build a data access layer. You used Workflow Foundation to create a well-designed and well-implemented business layer. WF makes it easy for both architects and developers to be in sync during the design and implementation of an application, which leaves little room for developers to do anything outside the scope and functional requirements of the project. This saves time for architects, developers, and unit testers. In the next chapter, we will make some cool widgets that put the core to its practical use and delivers rich features to the users.

# CHAPTER 5

# Building Client-Side Widgets

In Chapter 3, you learned how to build two server-side widgets: one for RSS/Atom feeds and one to display Flickr photos. The benefit of a server-side widget is that you can use Visual Studio's comfortable development environment to write and debug code, but also use your favorite programming language, like C# or VB.NET. However, server-side widgets slow down page loading and require too many postbacks. All the widgets on the page are loaded on the server side during page load and asynchronous postback. So, if the widgets load data from an external source, the page load time becomes the cumulative loading time of all widgets. Moreover, server-side widgets require too many postbacks on simple actions like paging or editing items on a grid. There's no way to avoid the postback because you are storing the object model on the server side and you fetch data from server side. Nothing is stored on the client that can help facilitate client-side operations. Although server-side widgets are easier to develop and maintain, they actually offer poor performance compared to client-side widgets.

On the other hand, client-side widgets use mostly JavaScript, so they can offer a lot more interactivity and functionality on the browser without requiring any postback. Because client-side widgets fetch data from external sources right from the JavaScript and maintain object model and state on the client, they offer functionality like paging, editing, and sorting right on the client without making any postback. Moreover, client-side widgets can cache external data on the browser, so subsequent visits for client-side widgets become a lot faster than for server-side widgets because the data needed for the widget is cached on the browser. In this chapter, you will see how you can improve page load time by delaying server-side widget loading. You will also learn how to make page loading much faster by making client-side RSS and Flickr photo widgets, you will develop a proxy web service for client-side widgets that can be used to fetch content from external sources and cache on the browser.

# Delaying Server-Side Widget Loading

When a page executes on the server side, it executes all the widgets on the page. This makes the first-time visit, future visits, and tab switching slower because the server-side execution takes quite some time. Because widgets fetch data from the database or external sources right on Page_Load event, it takes quite some time to fire Page_Load for all the widget web controls on the page. To improve the perceived speed of page load, first you need to deliver the page on the browser with a widget skeleton and some loading progress messages and then incrementally populate the widgets with their content.

Sites like Pageflakes exhibit this behavior; the widget skeletons download first, and each widget shows a loading progress message. Then each widget makes a web service call to fetch its data and show its content. Although the page's total load time is quite high with this approach (there is at least one web service call per widget), the perceived speed is lot better because the user sees the page downloading. As previously mentioned, loading widgets from top to bottom will also give the page a fast-loading feel.

Delayed loading means widgets will not load their content at the Page_Load event, but will instead load after receiving an asynchronous postback from a timer. The widget will first deliver a loading progress message and then use the Timer object to fire an asynchronous postback. During that asynchronous postback, the widget will fetch external data and render the output. This ensures Page_Load is not stuck waiting for external data and the page's load time is not affected by the delay in fetching external content. One easy way to do this is to use a MultiView control where one view contains a progress message and the next view contains the main UI. A Timer control could fire a postback after, say, 100 ms, which will then change the view to the main UI and disable itself.

## Delaying RSS/Atom Widget Loading

First, we will convert the RSS widget to delay loading and make a page full of RSS widgets load in two phases. The page will load instantly and show a "Loading..." script in the RSS widgets. Then each widget will load one after another in a progressive manner.

The UI of the RSS widget is split into two views using a MultiView control: a progress message and the FeedList DataList control, as shown in Example 5-1.

*Example 5-1. RSS widget in two views for delay loading*

```
<%@ Control Language="C#" AutoEventWireup="true" CodeFile="RSSWidget.ascx.cs"
Inherits="Widgets_RSSWidget" EnableViewState="false" %>
<asp:Panel ID="SettingsPanel" runat="Server" Visible="False" >
...
</asp:Panel>

<asp:MultiView ID="RSSMultiview" runat="server" ActiveViewIndex="0">

<asp:View runat="server" ID="RSSProgressView">
```

*Example 5-1. RSS widget in two views for delay loading (continued)*

```
<asp:image runat="server" ID="image1" ImageAlign="middle"
    ImageUrl="~/indicator.gif" />
<asp:Label runat="Server" ID="label1" Text="Loading..." Font-Size="smaller"
    ForeColor="DimGray" />
</asp:View>

<asp:View runat="server" ID="RSSFeedView">

    <asp:DataList ID="FeedList" runat="Server" EnableViewState="False">
    <ItemTemplate>
    <asp:HyperLink ID="FeedLink" runat="server" Target="_blank" CssClass="feed_item_link"
        NavigateUrl='<%# Eval("link") %>' ToolTip='<%# Eval("description") %>'>
    <%# Eval("title") %>
    </asp:HyperLink>
    </ItemTemplate>
    </asp:DataList>

</asp:View>

</asp:MultiView>

<asp:Timer ID="RSSWidgetTimer" Interval="1" OnTick="LoadRSSView" runat="server" />
```

The timer calls the LoadRSSView function on the server by doing an asynchronous postback. This function changes the current view to RSSFeedView and shows the feed, as seen in Example 5-2. This function is defined in the code behind the RSS web control's file.

*Example 5-2. TheLoadRSSView function in the RSS widget code is fired by the timer*

```
protected void LoadRSSView(object sender, EventArgs e)
{
    this.ShowFeeds();
    this.RSSMultiview.ActiveViewIndex = 1;
    this.RSSWidgetTimer.Enabled = false;
}
```

So now Page_Load does nothing on first load. It loads only the feed during the asynchronous postback. As the Page_Load event completes instantly, the load time of the widget no longer depends on fetching external content, as shown in Example 5-3.

*Example 5-3. The widget's Page_Load event does nothing on first load*

```
protected void Page_Load(object sender, EventArgs e)
{
    if (!this._Host.IsFirstLoad) this.LoadRSSView(sender, e);
}
```

Page_Load fires only the LoadRSSView function during postback. On subsequent postback, LoadRSSView will execute instantly because the content will be already cached in the ASP.NET cache.

---

## Delay Flickr Photo Widget Loading

It is exactly the same process to delay loading the Flickr photo widget. `MultiView` is used to show a progress message, and then on the second view, the page loads the photos. During `Page_Load`, the widget does absolutely nothing on first load so there isn't any delay on first-time page load. Once the progress message is delivered on the UI, a timer fires an asynchronous postback and only then is the photo stream loaded from Flickr and the UI rendered.

## Problems with Delaying Widget Loading

Although the page-loading speed seems faster, the total load time is significantly higher because it requires one asynchronous postback per widget. Moreover, it's a significant load on *Default.aspx* because each widget makes an asynchronous postback during the first load. So, instead of *Default.aspx* being hit once, it is actually hit *n* times with *n* widgets delaying the loading feature. Asynchronous postbacks are HTTP POST, so there's no way to cache the content on the browser that widgets fetch from external sources. So, if one RSS feed doesn't change for a week, the asynchronous postback for the RSS widget returns the same output for seven days. The output does not get cached on the browser so it doesn't improve the widget's second-time loading.

Figure 5-1 shows four asynchronous postbacks to *Default.aspx* because there are four RSS widgets on the page delaying loading, which are all HTTP POST.

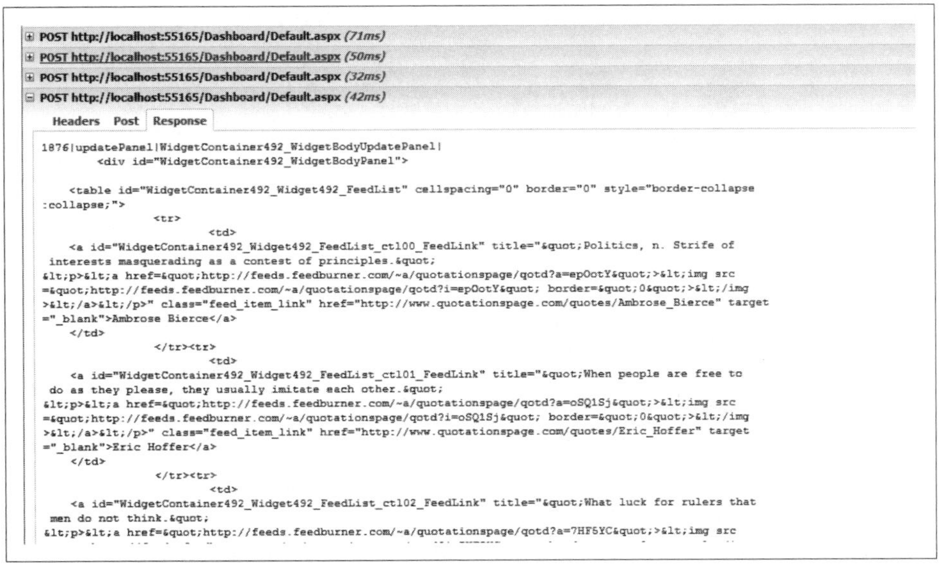

*Figure 5-1. Asynchronous postback's response content while delaying a widget's loading*

On subsequent visits, these four asynchronous postbacks repeatedly return the exact same data from the server because the feed source isn't changing as frequently.

However, there's no way to cache the response and avoid repeated postbacks because asynchronous postback, being HTTP POST, is not cacheable, as we noted previously.

To improve widget load time on subsequent visits, you need to fetch data from the browser via a HTTP GET call and produce response headers that indicate the response to the browser's cache. You need to use JavaScript to fetch data from the original source, parse it, and render the HTML. And because you cannot use server-side rendering logic, you need to make client-side widgets to benefit from fast subsequent visits.

However, the browser does not allow cross-domain calls. So, you cannot use XML HTTP to get data from external domains directly. For example, you cannot fetch an XML feed from *http://msdn.microsoft.com/rss.xml*. You need to make a call to one of your own web services, which will act as a proxy (bridge) to fetch data from original source. In the next section, we will build such a proxy that can serve data from external URLs and perform intelligent caching.

# Content Proxy

Content proxy is a web service on your server that can fetch data from external URLs and return it to the browser (see Figure 5-2).

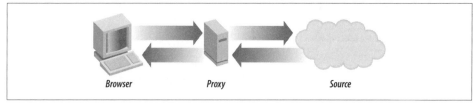

Browser            Proxy                     Source

*Figure 5-2. The browser makes a call to the proxy to fetch data from an external URL*

The proxy can cache the response on the server for some period and thus save repeated calls to same external URL. For example, if a hundred users subscribe to the same RSS feed and the feed does not change for days, the proxy can cache the response from the feed source for one day and serve hundreds and thousands of users directly from its server-side cache (see Figure 5-3).

Server-side caching greatly improves load time for users because there's only one network roundtrip. The server doesn't have to go to the external source. The proxy can also produce response headers that will tell the browser to cache the response on the browser for a period of time. During this time, the same call to the proxy will be served from the browser cache and complete blazingly fast. There'll be no network roundtrip at all on subsequent calls to same data from the proxy (see Figure 5-4).

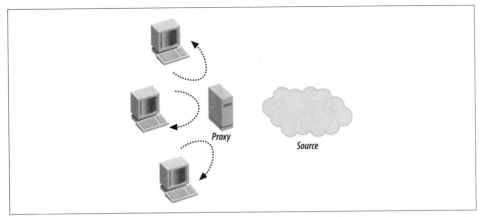

Figure 5-3. *The proxy caches data on the server and prevents repeatedly calling the same external source for multiple users*

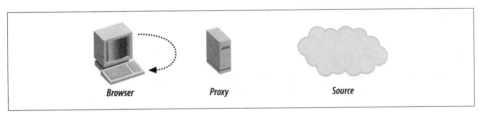

Figure 5-4. *When a response is cached on the browser, it does not make call to the proxy and thus there's no network roundtrip at all*

This means if we use a proxy to fetch RSS feeds and cache the response in the browser for an hour, and the user goes to another web site and comes back, the RSS widgets will load instantly without making a call to the server. So, if you have only RSS widgets on your page, the whole page will load in just one call to *Default.aspx*. Everything else is already cached on the browser. Chapter 9 explains how client-side caching can be used to speed up RSS loading.

## Content Proxy Web Service

*Proxy.asmx* is the content proxy web service. It has three methods:

GetString( url, cacheDuration )
> Returns data from the URL in string format and caches on the browser for a specified duration

GetXml( url, cacheDuration )
> Returns XML from a specified URL and caches the response on the browser for a specified duration

```
GetRss( url, count, cacheDuration)
```
Returns the RSS feed converted to a LINQ projection (discussed in Chapter 3) from a specified URL and caches the feed on the server for 15 minutes and on the client for a specified cache duration

GetString and GetXml are simple; they just use WebClient to get data from the original URL and cache the response (see Example 5-4).

*Example 5-4. GetString and GetXml methods of the proxy web service*

```
[WebMethod]
[ScriptMethod(UseHttpGet=true)]
public string GetString(string url, int cacheDuration)
{
    using( WebClient client = new WebClient() )
    {
        string response = client.DownloadString(url);
        this.CacheResponse(cacheDuration);
        return response;
    }
}

[WebMethod]
[ScriptMethod(UseHttpGet = true, ResponseFormat=ResponseFormat.Xml)]
public string GetXml(string url, int cacheDuration)
{
    return GetString(url, cacheDuration);
}
```

The only difference between GetString and GetXml is that GetString returns a JSON representation of string content, whereas GetXml returns XML content as a string. The ResponseFormat attribute on the GetXml method tells ASP.NET AJAX to emit XML in plain-text format instead of delivering JSON.

However, GetRss is a bit more complicated. It downloads the feed and caches it using ASP.NET cache for 15 minutes. So, subsequent calls to the same feed are returned from the ASP.NET cache. GetRss also generates a proper response cache header to cache the response on the browser for a specified duration. So, the widget consuming RSS via proxy can control how long to cache the response on the browser.

Example 5-5 shows the same RSS loading and parsing code that was in the RSS widget in Chapter 3.

*Example 5-5. GetRss on a proxy web service*

```
[WebMethod]
[ScriptMethod(UseHttpGet = true)]
public object GetRss(string url, int count, int cacheDuration)
{
    var feed = Context.Cache[url] as XElement;
    if( feed == null )
```

*Example 5-5. GetRss on a proxy web service (continued)*

```
{
    if( Context.Cache[url] == string.Empty ) return null;
    try
    {
        HttpWebRequest request = WebRequest.Create(url) as HttpWebRequest;

        request.Timeout = 15000;
        using( WebResponse response = request.GetResponse( ) )
        {
            using( XmlTextReader reader = new XmlTextReader( response.
            GetResponseStream( ) ) )
            {
                feed = XElement.Load(reader);
            }
        }

        if( feed == null ) return null;
        Context.Cache.Insert(url, feed, null, DateTime.MaxValue, TimeSpan.
            FromMinutes(15));

    }
    catch
    {
        Context.Cache[url] = string.Empty;
        return null;
    }
}

XNamespace ns = "http://www.w3.org/2005/Atom";

// see if RSS or Atom

try
{
    // RSS
    if( feed.Element("channel" ) != null )
        return (from item in feed.Element("channel").Elements("item")
                        select new
                        {
                            title = item.Element("title").Value,
                            link = item.Element("link").Value,
                            description = item.Element("description").Value
                        }).Take(count);

    // Atom
    else if( feed.Element(ns + "entry") != null )
        return (from item in feed.Elements(ns + "entry")
                        select new
                        {
                            title = item.Element(ns + "title").Value,
                            link = item.Element(ns + "link").
                            Attribute("href").Value,
```

*Example 5-5. GetRss on a proxy web service (continued)*

```
                                        description = item.Element(ns + "content").Value
                                    }).Take(count);

            // Invalid
            else
                return null;
        }
        finally
        {
            this.CacheResponse(cacheDuration);
        }
    }
}
```

## Challenges with the Proxy Web Service

The proxy web service will become your most frequently used web service once you start making client-side widgets. Anytime the browser's JavaScript needs to fetch content from an external domain, it will have to call the proxy service. As a result, you will hit scalability challenges with the proxy web service. Thousands of widgets making calls to this service, which, in turn, results in external web service calls, will create a significant load on the ASP.NET process. The external services' response time is unpredictable and unreliable. Sometimes a heavily loaded external service might take 20 to 30 seconds to complete, which means the call to the proxy will get stuck for 20 to 30 seconds. If that happens to 100 incoming requests within a 20-second period, all of the available ASP.NET worker thread will be used. Your web application will no longer serve any requests until the proxy requests either complete or timeout and release the ASP.NET worker thread. This will create a slow-loading web site or a completely nonresponsive web site. Chapter 6 discusses the scalability challenges web applications have that heavily depend on web services and fetch a majority of the content from external services.

Now we have the necessary methods to download data from external domains directly from the browser using the proxy. The next step is to make a JavaScript client-side widget that uses the proxy to download and cache data on the browser.

# Building a Client-Side RSS Widget

First, let's make a client-side RSS widget. RSS will benefit from client-side caching because not all RSS feeds change frequently, e.g., you can safely cache a feed for an hour. Also, popular RSS feeds are subscribed by many users, so caching a popular feed on the server and serving it to hundreds of thousands users will save the server from fetching the same feed again and again from the source.

Some fundamental differences in a client-side RSS widget include:

- It does not load the RSS feed from the server-side code. So, there's no LINQ to XML code in the widget's code that downloads the RSS XML. The LINQ to XML code is now inside the proxy service.
- It does not have MultiView. Instead, client-side JavaScript shows the progress message.
- It has no DataList on the widget web control because JavaScript generates the HTML for the feeds.
- A JavaScript class named FastRssWidget in *FastRssWidget.js* takes care of loading the feed on the browser by calling a proxy web service and rendering the feed.
- The server-side control creates an instance of the FastRssWidget JavaScript class and injects the necessary startup script to pass the feed's URL and load it on the client.

In Example 5-6, you will see that there's no UI except a blank Panel, other than the settings area. This Panel acts as a container for the rendering.

*Example 5-6. FastRssWidget.ascx now contains almost no UI elements*

```
<%@ Control Language="C#" AutoEventWireup="true" CodeFile="FastRssWidget.ascx.cs"
Inherits="Widgets_FastRssWidget" EnableViewState="false" %>
<asp:Panel ID="SettingsPanel" runat="Server" Visible="False" >
...
</asp:Panel>

<asp:Panel ID="RssContainer" runat="server"></asp:Panel>
```

On the widget server-side code, the Page_Load event registers a script include tag for the *FastRssWidget.js* (see Example 5-7).

*Example 5-7. The Page_Load event of FastRssWidget control adds a script tag to download FastRssWidget.js and then initializes the class to show the feeds on the client*

```
protected void Page_Load(object sender, EventArgs e)
{
    if (this._Host.IsFirstLoad)
    {
        ScriptManager.RegisterClientScriptInclude(this,
            typeof(Widgets_FastRssWidget),
            "FastRssWidget",
            this.ResolveClientUrl(
                this.AppRelativeTemplateSourceDirectory
                + "FastRssWidget.js"));

        ScriptManager.RegisterStartupScript(this,
            typeof(Widgets_FastRssWidget),
            "LoadRSS",
            string.Format("
                var rssLoader{0} =
                    new FastRssWidget( '{1}', '{2}', {3} );
```

*Example 5-7. The Page_Load event of FastRssWidget control adds a script tag to download FastRssWidget.js and then initializes the class to show the feeds on the client (continued)*

```
                rssLoader{0}.load( );",
                this.UniqueID,
                this.Url,
                this.RssContainer.ClientID,
                this.Count),
            true);
    }
}
```

It then injects a JavaScript statement that constructs an instance of the class and passes the URL, the container panel's client ID, and the number of feed items to show. This only happens once on the first load of the widget. The client-side class uses these parameters to make a call to the proxy, downloads the RSS, and renders the feed item links inside the container panel. The ID of the panel is passed down to the client-side JavaScript class. From this ID, the class knows which div to use to render the feed links.

However, during postback we need to render the content again on the client-side because an asynchronous postback will send a blank container panel to the browser and remove the links that were created by the JavaScript. In fact, any work that the client-side JavaScript does on the UI is undone whenever an asynchronous postback happens. So, we need to inform the JavaScript to restore the UI after every asynchronous postback. This is done in the OnPreRender event. A script block is sent to the client to reset the URL and count parameter and then fire the load function on the previously created class instance. It is the same as first load where the class is constructed with parameters and the load function is called. The only difference is that this time no new instance of the class is created, and instead an existing instance is assumed to be there already (see Example 5-8).

*Example 5-8. During OnPreRender a script block is sent to refresh UI on the client*

```
protected override void OnPreRender(EventArgs e)
{
    base.OnPreRender(e);

    if (!this._Host.IsFirstLoad)
        ScriptManager.RegisterStartupScript(this,
            typeof(Widgets_FastRssWidget),
            "LoadRSS",
            string.Format("
                rssLoader{0}.url = '{1}';
                rssLoader{0}.count = {2};
                rssLoader{0}.load( );",
                this.UniqueID,
                this.Url,
                this.Count),
            true);
}
```

That's all on the server. However, the client-side class is a bit more complicated as we move most of the code to the client from the server. The class is available in the *FeedRssWidget.js* file.

Example 5-9 shows the constructor and load function.

*Example 5-9. The client-side FeedRssWidget class*

```
var FastRssWidget = function(url, container, count)
{
    this.url = url;
    this.container = container;
    this.count = count;
}

FastRssWidget.prototype = {

    load : function( )
    {
        var div = $get( this.container );
        div.innerHTML = "Loading...";

        Proxy.GetRss ( this.url, this.count, 10, Function.createDelegate( this, this.
        onContentLoad ) );
    },
```

The constructor takes the parameters like the URL, container ID, and number of feed links to show. Then the load function calls the Proxy.GetRss function to get the feed. It passes the URL, the number of feed items to return, and the cache duration in minutes. The response is cached for 10 minutes, so loading the page again or returning to the page from another web site within 10 minutes will deliver the response directly from the browser cache without making any call to the proxy web service (see Example 5-10).

*Example 5-10. Proxy.GetRss fires the onContentLoad function as callback and it renders the feed links*

```
onContentLoad : function( rss )
{
    var div = $get( this.container );
    div.innerHTML = "";

    for( var i = 0; i < rss.length; i ++ )
    {
        var item = rss[i];

        var a = document.createElement("A");
        a.href = item.link;
        a.innerHTML = item.title;
        a.title = item.description;
        a.className = "feed_item_link";
        a.target = "_blank";
```

*Example 5-10. Proxy.GetRss fires the onContentLoad function as callback and it renders the feed links (continued)*

```
            div.appendChild(a);
        }
}
```

On the `onContentLoad` function, it creates the hyperlinks for the feed items on the client side. There are some benefits to this client-side widget over the server-side widget:

- No ViewState is delivered because there's minimal UI on the web control, so first load and asynchronous postback have very little payload

- Content is cached on the browser and saves roundtrips to the network

- Content is fetched via the proxy instead of asynchronous postback, so it benefits from server-side caching

## Building a Client-Side Flickr Widget

The client-side Flickr widget is developed following the same principles as the client-side RSS widget. The server-side code does not fetch the Flickr HTML; instead, the client-side class does this via the `Proxy.GetXml` method. It downloads the entire Flickr feed's XML to the client, which allows the client-side class to offer paging functionality through all the photos it received right on the browser without making any asynchronous postbacks or proxy calls. The user can look through the photos very quickly, and the returned XML is cached on the browser for 10 minutes. Subsequent visits within 10 minutes delivers the photo's XML from browser cache, and the widget loads instantly on the client without requiring any asynchronous postback or proxy calls.

The client-side class `FastFlickrWidget` is in the same format as the `FastRssWidget` class. It's available in *Widgets\FastFlickrWidget.js* (see Example 5-11).

*Example 5-11. Constructor of load function of FastFlickrWidget*

```
var FastFlickrWidget = function(url, container, previousId, nextId)
{
    this.url = url;
    this.container = container;
    this.pageIndex = 0;
    this.previousId = previousId;
    this.nextId = nextId;
    this.xml = null;
}

FastFlickrWidget.FLICKR_SERVER_URL="http://static.flickr.com/";
FastFlickrWidget.FLICKR_PHOTO_URL="http://www.flickr.com/photos/";

FastFlickrWidget.prototype = {
```

*Example 5-11. Constructor of load function of FastFlickrWidget (continued)*

```
load : function( )
{
    this.pageIndex = 0;

    var div = $get( this.container );
    div.innerHTML = "Loading...";

    Proxy.GetXml( this.url, 10, Function.createDelegate( this, this.onContentLoad ) );
},
onContentLoad : function( xml )
{
    this.xml = xml;
    this.showPhotos();
},
```

It takes the Flickr feed URL, a container div ID, and the next and previous link ID. These links are needed because the class toggles previous/next links based on page index during paging.

The showPhotos function (shown in Example 5-12) does all the work for creating a 3 × 3 table, images, and hyperlinks for the photo items.

*Example 5-12. The showPhotos function inFastFlickrWidget.js*

```
showPhotos : function( )
{
    var div = $get( this.container );
    div.innerHTML = "";

    if( null == this.xml )
        return (div.innerHTML = "Error occured while loading Flickr feed");

    var photos = this.xml.documentElement.getElementsByTagName("photo");

    var row = 0, col = 0, count = 0;

    var table = document.createElement("table");
    table.align = "center";
    var tableBody = document.createElement("TBODY");
    table.appendChild( tableBody );
    var tr;

    for( var i = 0; i < 9; i ++ )
    {
        var photo = photos[i + (this.pageIndex * 9)];

        if( photo == null )
        {
            Utility.nodisplay( this.nextId );
            break;
        }
```

*Example 5-12. The showPhotos function inFastFlickrWidget.js (continued)*

```
            if( col == 0 )
            {
                tr = document.createElement("TR");
                tableBody.appendChild(tr);
            }

            var td = document.createElement("TD");

            var img = document.createElement("IMG");
            img.src = this.getPhotoUrl(photo, true);
            img.style.width = img.style.height = "75px";
            img.style.border = "none";

            var a = document.createElement("A");
            a.href = this.getPhotoPageUrl(photo);
            a.target = "_blank";
            a.title = this.getPhotoTitle(photo);

            a.appendChild(img);
            td.appendChild(a);
            tr.appendChild(td);

            if( ++ col == 3 ) { col = 0; row ++ }

        }

        div.appendChild(table);

        if( this.pageIndex == 0 ) Utility.nodisplay(this.previousId);
},
previous : function( )
{
        this.pageIndex --;
        this.showPhotos( );

        Utility.display( this.nextId, true );
        if( this.pageIndex == 0 )
            Utility.nodisplay( this.previousId );

},

next : function( )
{
        this.pageIndex ++;
        this.showPhotos( );
        Utility.display( this.previousId, true );
}
```

This is basically a direct convert of the server-side Flickr photo widget's C# code to equivalent JavaScript code. You will see some reference to the Utility class in JavaScript. It's a custom-made class that has some handy JavaScript functions like displaying/hiding UI elements, dealing with DOM elements in a cross-browser fashion, and more. The Utility class is defined in the *MyFramework.js* file, which is available at the web root of the project.

The server-side web control contains minimal UI besides the settings panel. It contains an empty container and the previous/next links (see Example 5-13).

*Example 5-13. FastFlickrWidget.ascx*

```
<%@ Control Language="C#" AutoEventWireup="true" CodeFile="FastFlickrWidget.ascx.cs"
Inherits="Widgets_FastFlickrWidget" EnableViewState="false" %>
<asp:Panel ID="settingsPanel" runat="server" Visible="False">
...
</asp:Panel>

<asp:Panel ID="FlickrPhotoPanel" runat="server">

</asp:Panel>

<div style="text-align: center; width:100%; white-space:nowrap">
<asp:LinkButton ID="ShowPrevious" runat="server" >< Prev</asp:LinkButton>
 
<asp:LinkButton ID="ShowNext" runat="server" >Next ></asp:LinkButton></center>
</div>
```

In Page_Load event's code behind class the FastFlickrWidget JavaScript class is constructed with parameters from State (shown in Example 5-14). It also injects some script on the previous/next link's click event so that it fires the client-side class's previous and next function.

*Example 5-14. FastFlickrWidget web control's Page_Load event*

```
protected void Page_Load(object sender, EventArgs e)
{
    if (this._Host.IsFirstLoad)
    {
        ScriptManager.RegisterClientScriptInclude(this,
        typeof(Widgets_FastFlickrWidget),
        "FastFlickrWidget",
        this.ResolveClientUrl(
            this.AppRelativeTemplateSourceDirectory + "FastFlickrWidget.js"));

        ScriptManager.RegisterStartupScript(this,
            typeof(Widgets_FastFlickrWidget),
            "LoadFlickr",
            string.Format("
                var flickrLoader{0} =
                    new FastFlickrWidget( '{1}', '{2}', '{3}', '{4}' );
                flickrLoader{0}.load( );",
            this.UniqueID,
            this.GetPhotoUrl( ),
            this.FlickrPhotoPanel.ClientID,
```

*Example 5-14. FastFlickrWidget web control's Page_Load event (continued)*

```
                this.ShowPrevious.ClientID,
                this.ShowNext.ClientID),
            true);

        this.ShowPrevious.OnClientClick =
            string.Format("flickrLoader{0}.previous( ); return false;", this.UniqueID);
        this.ShowNext.OnClientClick =
            string.Format("flickrLoader{0}.next( ); return false;", this.UniqueID);
    }
}
```

Page_Load event produces the necessary script block to instantiate the FlickrRssWidget class on the client and then fires its load function. Just like the RSS widget, it calls the client-side class's load function when the OnPreRender handler code executes so that after asynchronous postback, the JavaScript can refresh the UI based on new settings (shown in Example 5-15).

*Example 5-15. FastFlickrWidget web control's OnPreRender event*

```
protected override void OnPreRender(EventArgs e)
{
    base.OnPreRender(e);

    if( !this._Host.IsFirstLoad )
        ScriptManager.RegisterStartupScript(this,
        typeof(Widgets_FastFlickrWidget), "LoadFlickr",
        string.Format("
            flickrLoader{0}.url = '{1}';
            flickrLoader{0}.load( );",
            this.UniqueID,
            this.GetPhotoUrl( ),
            this.FlickrPhotoPanel.ClientID),
        true);
}
```

The following are some benefits of the client-side widget over the server-side version:

- ViewState is not delivered to client during the first load or asynchronous post-back because there's almost no UI element.
- The Flickr photo XML is cached on the browser and saves roundtrips to the network.
- The proxy's server-side caching (e.g., thousands of users requesting the same interesting photos will not make thousands of calls to Flickr).
- Paging through photos is instant because it is done entirely on the client side, which makes this version a lot faster.

# Summary

In this chapter, you learned how to make your pages load faster by using the delay loading approach. This can solve the immediate need for faster page loads. For even more speed and better utilization of the browser cache, you learned how to make client-side widgets that offer rich client-side interactivity without requiring asynchronous postback. Then you learned how to make one of the most important components of a Start page: a content proxy. In the next chapter, we will address some scalability challenges for Ajax web sites that depend too much on web services and communicate with a variety of external web services.

# CHAPTER 6

# Optimizing ASP.NET AJAX

Just like other frameworks, the ASP.NET AJAX Framework is not capable of serving all of the specific needs for every type of Ajax application. Frameworks are kept simple and generic enough to satisfy 70 percent of the Ajax application's requirements. But the remaining 30 percent of requirements require you to go deep into the framework to make the necessary modifications. Moreover, off-the-shelf Ajax frameworks don't solve all real-life problems, and new and unique challenges always come up every now and then. In this chapter, we will review several challenges posed by Ajax applications that must be resolved for high-volume Ajax web sites. There are also several design decisions that must be made if you release it as a mass consumer Ajax web site.

## Combining Multiple Ajax Calls into One Call

Network roundtrip is the most expensive part of Ajax applications. You need to do everything you can to reduce the number of calls made to the server. Because each call has the overhead of connecting to the server and then downloading the response, each call wastes some time on the network. When you have five calls going to the server within a short time for some particular operation, you are wasting about one second (assuming 200 ms network latency) on the network. So, a popular practice among Ajax developers is to batch multiple consecutive single calls into one large call. This saves the network roundtrip as there's only one network roundtrip to do, and thus the whole operation executes faster than making individual calls.

For example, say a user clicks on five different widgets from the widget gallery to add those widgets on the page. If the user is clicking quickly, instead of making one web service call per click and showing the newly added widget on the browser, the batch feature waits until the user has clicked several times and then makes a batch call to the server, sending all the widget names at once. All the widgets are downloaded and created in one shot. This saves a network roundtrip and condenses multiple single calls to the web service. Although the total time for a batch call will always be less than each individual call, it does not always make the user experience faster. The actual response time might be reduced, but the perceived delay is higher because the user will see nothing happen until multiple widgets are downloaded and created on the browser.

If three web service calls are batched into one call, the first single call doesn't finish first—all three calls finish at the same time. If you are doing some UI updates that wait for the completion of each web service call, all of the calls complete in one shot and then the UI is updated. As a result, you do not see incremental updates on the UI—instead, a long delay before the UI updates. If any of the calls download a lot of data, the user will see nothing happen until all three calls complete. So, the duration of the first call becomes nearly the duration of the sum of all three calls. Although the total duration is reduced, the perceived duration is higher. Batch calls are handy when each call is transmitting a small amount of data because the calls are executed in one roundtrip and the perceived speed is good.

Let's work on a scenario where three calls are made one at a time. Figure 6-1 shows how the calls are executed.

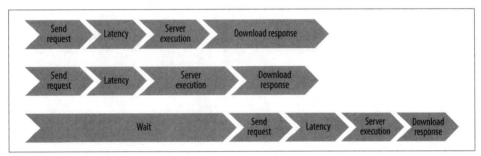

*Figure 6-1. The browser makes two calls at a time, so the third call needs to wait until one of the earlier calls completes*

The second call takes a bit more time to reach the server because the first call is eating up the bandwidth. For the same reason, it takes longer to download. Figure 6-2 shows these three calls batched into one.

*Figure 6-2. The batch call function combines multiple unit calls and executes them in one shot, which means there's only one request to server and one response to download*

The total download time is also reduced if the IIS response compression is enabled and if there is only one network latency. All three calls are executed on the server in one request, and the combined response is downloaded to one call. The total duration to complete the whole batch is always less than that for two calls.

# Timing and Ordering Ajax Calls to the Server

Browsers will always make a maximum of two concurrent Ajax calls to a domain. If five Ajax calls are made, the browser will first make two calls and queue the remaining three calls, wait for either one of them to complete, and then make another call until all queued calls are complete. However, the calls will not execute in the same order as you make them (see Figure 6-3).

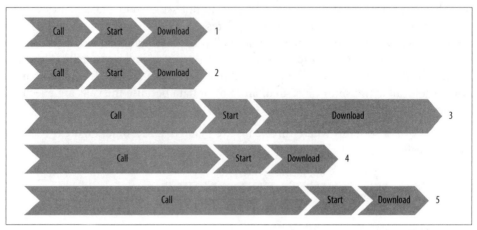

Figure 6-3. The browser makes two calls at a time to the server, so the smaller but later calls might finish before the larger calls that are made first

As Figure 6-3 shows, the third call is large and takes longer than the fifth call to download. So, the fourth and fifth calls are actually executed before the third call finishes.

## Bad Calls Make Good Calls Time Out

If two HTTP calls somehow get stuck for too long, they will make some good queued calls time out too (see Example 6-1).

Example 6-1. Testing bad calls that make good calls time out

```
function TestTimeout()
{
    debug.trace("--Start--");
    TestService.set_defaultFailedCallback(
            function(result, userContext, methodName)
    {
        var timedOut = result.get_timedOut();
        if( timedOut )
            debug.trace( "Timedout: " + methodName );
        else
            debug.trace( "Error: " + methodName );
    });
```

*Example 6-1. Testing bad calls that make good calls time out (continued)*

```
    TestService.set_defaultSucceededCallback( function(result)
    {
        debug.trace( result );
    });

    TestService.set_timeout(5000);

    TestService.HelloWorld("Call 1");
    TestService.Timeout("Call 2");
    TestService.Timeout("Call 3");
    TestService.HelloWorld("Call 4");
    TestService.HelloWorld("Call 5");
    TestService.HelloWorld(null); // This one will produce Error
}
```

Example 6-1 calls a TestService, which is a web service with two methods:
HelloWorld and Timeout. The idea is to find out which calls time out by hooking onto
the web service's default fail handler. If a call fails, that fail handler will be fired.

The web service's code is simple, as shown in Example 6-2.

*Example 6-2. The test web service calls timeout*

```
using System.Web;
using System.Web.Services;
using System.Web.Services.Protocols;
using System.Web.Script.Services;
using System.Threading;

[WebService(Namespace = "http://tempuri.org/")]
[WebServiceBinding(ConformsTo = WsiProfiles.BasicProfile1_1)]
[ScriptService]
public class TestService : System.Web.Services.WebService {

    public TestService () {

        //Uncomment the following line if using designed components
        //InitializeComponent( );
    }

    [WebMethod][ScriptMethod(UseHttpGet=true)]
    public string HelloWorld(string param) {
        Thread.Sleep(1000);
        return param;
    }

    [WebMethod][ScriptMethod(UseHttpGet=true)]
    public string Timeout(string param) {
        Thread.Sleep(10000);
        return param;
    }
}
```

Example 6-2 calls the Timeout method on the server, which does nothing but wait until the call is timed out. After that, you call a method that does not time out. Figure 6-4 shows the output.

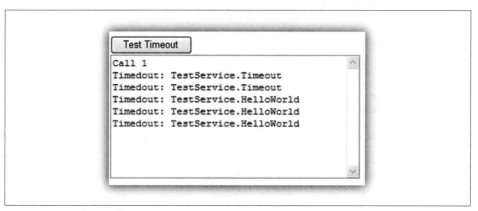

*Figure 6-4. Testing the Ajax call timeout*

Only the first call succeeded. So, if the browser's two connections get jammed, then other waiting calls will time out too.

## Real-Life: Resolving Timeout Error Reports

Problem: Bad web service calls get stuck causing excessive timeout errors.

Solution: Modify the ASP.NET AJAX runtime and introduce automatic retry.

At one community web portal company I worked at, we used to get 400 to 600 timeout error reports from users' browsers. We first suspected a slow Internet connection, but that couldn't happen for so many users. We then thought something was wrong with the hosting provider's network and did a lot of network analysis to find any problems on the network but there weren't. We used SQL Profiler to see if there were any long-running queries that timed out the ASP.NET request execution time, but that wasn't it either.

We finally discovered that it mostly happened when some bad web service calls got stuck and made the good calls time out while waiting in the browser's "maximum of two calls at a time" queue. So, we modified the ASP.NET AJAX runtime and introduced automatic retry on it. The problem disappeared almost completely. However, this auto retry requires sophisticated open-heart surgery on the ASP.NET AJAX Framework itself. The idea is to make each and every call retry once when it times out. To do that, we need to intercept all web method calls and implement a hook on the onFailed callback, which called the same web method again if the failure reason was a timeout.

## Common problems

Sometimes the first web service call gets an intermediate page or an invalid HTTP status instead of the expected result so the first call fails. Retrying it solves the problem (see the "Web Cache Problems" section in Chapter 3).

Another common problem is wireless Internet users and slow Internet users. Wireless connections drop randomly and sometimes wireless access points get stuck. And dial-up connection drops have an automated redial sequence. All these problems can make Ajax calls wait for too long and they eventually time out or fail. We can prevent a majority of these problems with an auto retry mechanism in place.

In the ASP.NET AJAX Framework, the Sys$Net$WebServiceProxy$invoke function is responsible for making all web service calls. So, we replace this function with a custom implementation that passes a custom onFailure callback. That custom callback gets fired whenever there's an error or timeout. When there's a timeout, it calls the invoke function again and thus a retry happens. Example 6-3 shows the code block that replaces the ASP.NET AJAX Framework's invoke function adds the auto retry capability to it. You do not need to open the Ajax runtime JavaScript files and modify the implementation—just put this block of JavaScript inside a <SCRIPT> tag on your page after the Ajax scripts download. It adds a retry capability on top of the original invoke function and eventually calls the original invoke function. It also does not break when newer version of the ASP.NET AJAX Framework is released. As long as Microsoft does not completely change the invoke function, it is safe to add this patch.

*Example 6-3. Implementing the auto retry at failure*

```
Sys.Net.WebServiceProxy.retryOnFailure =
    function(result, userContext, methodName, retryParams, onFailure)
{
    if( result.get_timedOut() )
    {
        if( typeof retryParams != "undefined" )
        {
            debug.trace("Retry: " + methodName);
            Sys.Net.WebServiceProxy.original_invoke.apply(this, retryParams );
        }
        else
        {
            if( onFailure ) onFailure(result, userContext, methodName);
        }
    }
    else
    {
        if( onFailure ) onFailure(result, userContext, methodName);
    }
}

Sys.Net.WebServiceProxy.original_invoke = Sys.Net.WebServiceProxy.invoke;
Sys.Net.WebServiceProxy.invoke =
```

*Example 6-3. Implementing the auto retry at failure (continued)*

```
function Sys$Net$WebServiceProxy$invoke(servicePath, methodName, useGet,
    params, onSuccess, onFailure, userContext, timeout)
{
var retryParams = [ servicePath, methodName, useGet, params,
    onSuccess, onFailure, userContext, timeout ];

    // Call original invoke but with a new onFailure
    // handler which does the auto retry
    var newOnFailure = Function.createDelegate( this,
        function(result, userContext, methodName)
        {
            Sys.Net.WebServiceProxy.retryOnFailure(result, userContext,
                methodName, retryParams, onFailure);
        } );

    Sys.Net.WebServiceProxy.original_invoke(servicePath, methodName, useGet,
        params, onSuccess, newOnFailure, userContext, timeout);
}
```

Each call is retried, as shown in Figure 6-5.

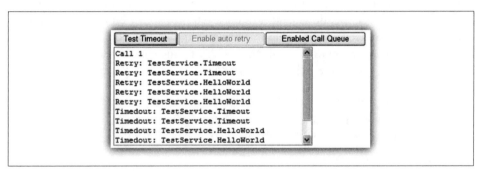

*Figure 6-5. Auto retry test*

The first method succeeded, and all the others timed out and were retried. Although you see them time out again because the TestService always times out, that won't happen in a real-world implementation because the second attempt will not time out unless there's a real problem on this call that makes the server time out on every attempt.

## Browsers Fail to Respond with Two or More Calls in Queue

Try this: go to any Start page that loads many RSS feeds or widgets on the first visit. While the page is loading, try clicking on a link that takes you to another web site, or try visiting another site by entering a URL on the browser address bar. The browser is stuck. Until all queued Ajax calls in the browser complete, the browser will not accept any other request. All browsers have this problem, but this problem is worse in Internet Explorer.

As discussed earlier, the browser keeps all calls in a queue and executes a maximum two of them in parallel. The browser has to wait for running calls to complete before it can take another call. The solution to this problem is to prevent more than two calls to be queued in the browser at a time. The solution is tricky: maintain a queue yourself and send the calls to the browser's queue from your own queue one at a time (see Example 6-4).

Example 6-4. *GlobalCallQueue prevents the browser from getting stuck*

```
var GlobalCallQueue = {
    _callQueue : [],      // Maintains the list of web methods to call
    _callInProgress : 0,     // Number of calls currently in progress by browser
    _maxConcurrentCall : 2, // Max number of calls to execute at a time
    _delayBetweenCalls : 50, // Delay in ms between execution of calls
    call : function(servicePath, methodName, useGet,
        params, onSuccess, onFailure, userContext, timeout)
    {
        var queuedCall = new QueuedCall(servicePath, methodName, useGet,
            params, onSuccess, onFailure, userContext, timeout);

        Array.add(GlobalCallQueue._callQueue,queuedCall);
        GlobalCallQueue.run();
    },
    run : function()
    {
        /// Execute a call from the call queue

        if( 0 == GlobalCallQueue._callQueue.length ) return;
        if( GlobalCallQueue._callInProgress <
            GlobalCallQueue._maxConcurrentCall )
        {
            GlobalCallQueue._callInProgress ++;
            // Get the first call queued
            var queuedCall = GlobalCallQueue._callQueue[0];
            Array.removeAt( GlobalCallQueue._callQueue, 0 );

            // Call the web method
            queuedCall.execute();
        }
        else
        {
            // cannot run another call. Maximum concurrent
            // web service method call in progress. Don't run
            // the call and wait until one call completes or fails
        }
    },
    callComplete : function()
    {
        GlobalCallQueue._callInProgress --;
        GlobalCallQueue.run();
    }
};

QueuedCall = function( servicePath, methodName, useGet, params,
```

```
    onSuccess, onFailure, userContext, timeout )
{
    this._servicePath = servicePath;
    this._methodName = methodName;
    this._useGet = useGet;
    this._params = params;

    this._onSuccess = onSuccess;
    this._onFailure = onFailure;
    this._userContext = userContext;
    this._timeout = timeout;
}

QueuedCall.prototype =
{
    execute : function( )
    {
        Sys.Net.WebServiceProxy.original_invoke(
            this._servicePath, this._methodName, this._useGet, this._params,
            Function.createDelegate(this, this.onSuccess), // Handle call complete
            Function.createDelegate(this, this.onFailure), // Handle call complete
            this._userContext, this._timeout );
    },
    onSuccess : function(result, userContext, methodName)
    {
        this._onSuccess(result, userContext, methodName);
        GlobalCallQueue.callComplete( );
    },
    onFailure : function(result, userContext, methodName)
    {
        this._onFailure(result, userContext, methodName);
        GlobalCallQueue.callComplete( );
    }
};
```

The QueuedCall class encapsulates one web method call. It takes all the parameters of
the actual web service call and overrides the onSuccess and onFailure callbacks. We
want to know when a call completes or fails so that we can issue another call from
our queue. The GlobalCallQueue maintains a list of all web service calls that get into
the queue. Whenever a web method is called, the call is queued in the
GlobalCallQueue, and calls are executed from the queue one at a time. This ensures
that the browser does not get more than two web service calls at a time, which means
the browser doesn't get stuck.

To enable the queue-based call, you have to override the ASP.NET AJAX web
method invocation again, as done in the "Bad Calls Make Good Calls Time Out"
section (see Example 6-5).

*Example 6-5. Override the default invoke function implementation and replace it with a queue implementation*

```
Sys.Net.WebServiceProxy.original_invoke = Sys.Net.WebServiceProxy.invoke;
Sys.Net.WebServiceProxy.invoke =
    function Sys$Net$WebServiceProxy$invoke(servicePath, methodName,
        useGet, params, onSuccess, onFailure, userContext, timeout)
{
    GlobalCallQueue.call(servicePath, methodName, useGet, params,
        onSuccess, onFailure, userContext, timeout);
}
```

The override in Example 6-5 ensures that all web service calls get into the queue instead of executing immediately. The GlobalCallQueue takes care of making the call at the right time. And just like the previous auto retry implementation, this is an add-on to the ASP.NET AJAX Framework. When you upgrade the framework, you don't need to change the GlobalCallQueue again as long as Microsoft does not change the invoke function approach completely.

## Caching Web Service Responses on the Browser

You already know browsers can cache images, JavaScript, and CSS files on a user's hard drive. They can also cache XML HTTP calls if the call is an HTTP GET and not an HTTP POST because the cache is based on the URL. If it's the same URL and it's cached on the computer, then the response is loaded from the cache, not from the server when it is requested again. Basically, the browser can cache any HTTP GET call and return cached data based on the URL. If you make an XML HTTP call as HTTP GET and the server returns a special header that informs the browser to cache the response, the response will be immediately returned from the cache on future calls and saves the delay of a network roundtrip and download time. Such client-side caching of XML HTTP can dramatically increase client-side performance as well as decrease server-side load.

You can also cache a user's state so that when the same user visits again the following day, the user gets a cached page that loads instantly from the browser cache, not from the server. This makes the second time load very fast. Other small actions can also be cached, such as clicking on the Start button, which shows you a list of widgets. When the user does the same action again, a cached result is loaded immediately from the local cache and thus saves the network roundtrip time. The user gets a responsive fast-loading site and the perceived speed increases dramatically.

The idea is to make HTTP GET calls while making ASP.NET AJAX web service calls and return some specific HTTP response headers that tell the browser to cache the response for some specified duration. If you return the Expires header during the response, the browser will cache the XML HTTP response.

There are two headers that you need to return with the response to instruct the browser to cache the response:

```
HTTP/1.1 200 OK
Expires: Fri, 1 Jan 2030
Cache-Control: public
```

This will instruct the browser to cache the responses until January 2030. As long as you make the same XML HTTP calls with the same parameters, you will get a cached response from the computer and no call will go to the server. There are more advanced ways to gain further control over response caching. For example, here is a header that will instruct the browser to cache for 60 seconds and get a fresh response after 60 seconds from the server. It will also prevent proxies from returning a cached response when the browser's local cache expires after 60 seconds. You can learn more about caching strategies for performance improvement in Chapter 9.

```
HTTP/1.1 200 OK
Cache-Control: private, must-revalidate, proxy-revalidate, max-age=60
```

Example 6-6 tries to produce such headers from the web service as per ASP.NET documentation.

*Example 6-6. Failed attempt to produce necessary response headers for caching on the client side*

```
[WebMethod][ScriptMethod(UseHttpGet=true)]
public string CachedGet()
{
    TimeSpan cacheDuration = TimeSpan.FromMinutes(1);
    Context.Response.Cache.SetCacheability(HttpCacheability.Public);
    Context.Response.Cache.SetExpires(DateTime.Now.Add(cacheDuration));
    Context.Response.Cache.SetMaxAge(cacheDuration);
    Context.Response.Cache.AppendCacheExtension(
            "must-revalidate, proxy-revalidate");

    return DateTime.Now.ToString();
}
```

However, the results are the HTTP response headers shown in Figure 6-6.

| | HTTP/1.1 200 OK |
|---|---|
| Server | ASP.NET Development Server/8.0.0.0 |
| Date | Thu, 21 Sep 2006 18:10:33 GMT |
| X-AspNet-Version | 2.0.50727 |
| Cache-Control | private, must-revalidate, proxy-revalidate, max-age=0 |
| Expires | Thu, 21 Sep 2006 18:11:33 GMT |
| Content-Type | application/json; charset=utf-8 |
| Content-Length | 23 |
| Connection | Close |

*Figure 6-6. Incorrect HTTP response headers are generated from the web method when you try to produce the headers as documented*

The Expires header is set properly, but the problem is with the Cache-Control header. It is showing that the max-age is set to zero, which will prevent the browser from doing any kind of caching. Looks like instead of caching the response, the exact opposite happened. The headers actually tell the browser to never cache the response, and always get fresh content from the server no matter what.

The output is incorrect and not cached. If you repeatedly call the web method, you will get a noncached response. Figure 6-7 shows the output of the web method call where it always produces a distinct timestamp. This means the browser is making a call to the server every time and no caching occurs.

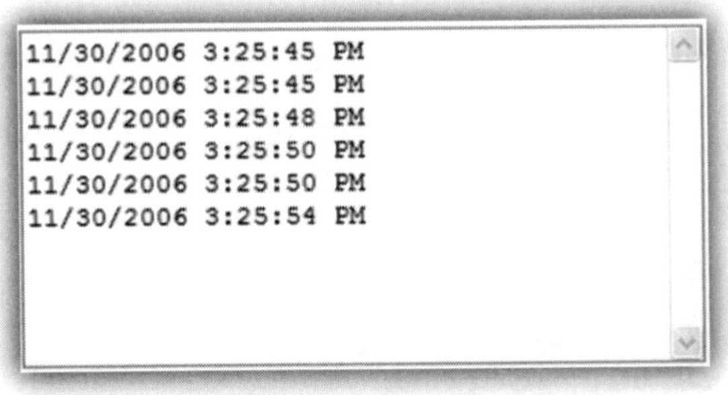

```
11/30/2006 3:25:45 PM
11/30/2006 3:25:45 PM
11/30/2006 3:25:48 PM
11/30/2006 3:25:50 PM
11/30/2006 3:25:50 PM
11/30/2006 3:25:54 PM
```

*Figure 6-7. Continuous calls to the web method return unique timestamps, which means the call is not being cached and the browser is requesting the server all the time*

There's a bug in ASP.NET 2.0 that does not let you change the max-age header once it is set. Because the max-age is set to zero by the ASP.NET AJAX Framework by default, ASP.NET 2.0 sets the Cache-Control to private because max-age = 0 means "Prevent caching at any cost." So, there's no way you can make ASP.NET 2.0 return proper headers that cache the response.

Time for a hack. I found the code after decompiling the `HttpCachePolicy` class's code (`Context.Response.Cache` object's class; see Figure 6-8).

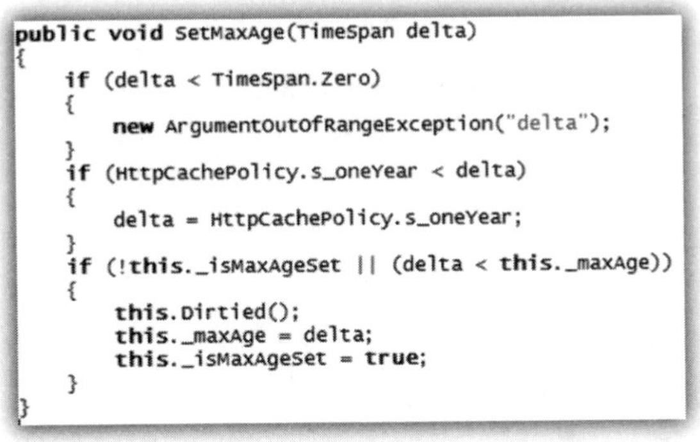

```
public void SetMaxAge(TimeSpan delta)
{
    if (delta < TimeSpan.Zero)
    {
        new ArgumentOutOfRangeException("delta");
    }
    if (HttpCachePolicy.s_oneYear < delta)
    {
        delta = HttpCachePolicy.s_oneYear;
    }
    if (!this._isMaxAgeSet || (delta < this._maxAge))
    {
        this.Dirtied();
        this._maxAge = delta;
        this._isMaxAgeSet = true;
    }
}
```

*Figure 6-8. The decompiled code in the HttpCachePolicy class in the ASP.NET 2.0 Framework that deals with the maxAge value*

From the ASP.NET AJAX Framework code, `this._maxAge` is being set to zero and `if (... || (delta < this._maxAge))` is preventing it from being set to a larger value.

We need to bypass the SetMaxAge function and set the value of the _maxAge field directly, using reflection (see Example 6-7).

*Example 6-7. Set _maxAge field's value directly by bypassing the SetMaxAge function*

```
[WebMethod][ScriptMethod(UseHttpGet=true)]
public string CachedGet2( )
{
    TimeSpan cacheDuration = TimeSpan.FromMinutes(1);

    FieldInfo maxAge = Context.Response.Cache.GetType( ).GetField("_maxAge",
        BindingFlags.Instance|BindingFlags.NonPublic);
    maxAge.SetValue(Context.Response.Cache, cacheDuration);

    Context.Response.Cache.SetCacheability(HttpCacheability.Public);
    Context.Response.Cache.SetExpires(DateTime.Now.Add(cacheDuration));
    Context.Response.Cache.AppendCacheExtension(
            "must-revalidate, proxy-revalidate");

    return DateTime.Now.ToString( );
}
```

This will return the headers in Figure 6-9.

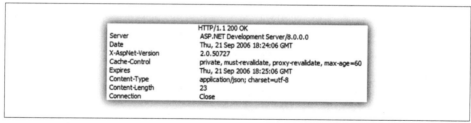

*Figure 6-9. The proper response headers for the cache*

Now max-age is set to 60, and the browser will cache the response for 60 seconds. If you make the same call again within 60 seconds, it will return the same response. Figure 6-10 shows a test output that shows the date time returned from the server.

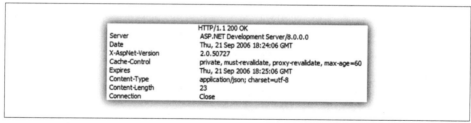

*Figure 6-10. Cache successful*

After one minute, the cache expires and the browser makes a call to the server again. The client-side code for this experiment is like this:

```
function testCache()
{
    TestService.CachedGet(function(result)
    {
        debug.trace(result);
    });
}
```

But there's another problem to solve. In *web.config*, ASP.NET AJAX will add:

```
<system.web>
        <trust level="Medium"/>
```

This prevents us from setting the _maxAge field of the Response object because it requires reflection, which requires full permission. So, you will have to change the trust level to Full:

```
<system.web>
        <trust level="Full"/>
```

You can create an HTTP module that intercepts all web service calls and returns the proper cache header for HTTP GET calls, which will save you from writing the same code in many web methods.

# Using HTTP GET Calls Instead of HTTP POST

ASP.NET AJAX, by default, uses HTTP POST for all web service calls, but HTTP POST is more "expensive" than HTTP GET. It transmits more bytes over the wire, which hogs precious network time, and makes ASP.NET AJAX do extra processing on the server end. So, you should use HTTP GET as much as possible. However, HTTP GET does not allow you to pass objects as parameters, only numerics, strings, and dates.

When you make an HTTP GET call, ASP.NET AJAX builds an encoded URL and hits that URL. So, you can't pass too much content that makes the URL larger than 2,048 characters. This is the maximum length for URLs in many browsers.

To enable HTTP GET on a web service method, you need to decorate the method with the [ScriptMethod(UseHttpGet=true)] attribute:

```
[WebMethod] [ScriptMethod(UseHttpGet=true)]
public string HelloWorld()
{
}
```

Another problem of POST versus GET is that POST makes two network transfers. When you first make a POST, the web server sends an "HTTP 100 Continue" message, which means that the web server is ready to accept the content. After that, the browser sends the actual data. So, initiation of a POST request takes more time than

GET. And network latency (the roundtrip time between your computer and the server) is the biggest concern with Ajax applications because Ajax makes many small calls that need to be done in milliseconds or the application won't feel smooth and the user is annoyed.

Ethereal (*http://www.ethereal.com*) is a nice tool that shows what happens under the hood on POST and GET calls (see Figure 6-11).

```
69.5.   127       192.168.0.158      ↑  HTTP   HTTP/1.1 100 Continue
192.168.0.158     69.5.  .127           HTTP   POST /CoreServices.asmx?mn=
69.5   .127       192.168.0.158   POST  TCP    http > 2789 [ACK] Seq=3992 Ack=447
69.5.  .127       192.168.0.158      ↓  HTTP   HTTP/1.1 200 OK (application/json)
192.168.0.158     69.5.  .127       GET TCP    2789 > http [ACK] Seq=4474 Ack=433
192.168.0.158     69.5.  .127           HTTP   GET /CoreServices.asmx?
69.5.  .127       192.168.0.158      ↑  TCP    [TCP segment of a reassembled PDU]
69.5.  .127       192.168.0.158      ↓  HTTP   HTTP/1.1 200 OK (application/json)
```

Figure 6-11. HTTP POST and GET calls viewed in a packet tracer

You can see that POST requires a confirmation from the web server—"HTTP/1.1 100 Continue"—before sending the actual data. After that, it transmits the data. However, GET transmits the data without waiting for any confirmation. So, you should use HTTP GET when downloading data from a server including parts of pages, contents in a grid, or a block of text, etc. But you should not use HTTP GET to send data, such as username submissions, passwords, or anything that will make the URL exceed the 2,000 character limit, to a server.

# Working with the this Function

XML HTTP callbacks are not executed on the same context where they are called. For example, if you are making a web method call from a JavaScript class:

```
function SampleClass()
{
    this.id = 1;
    this.call = function()
    {
        TestService.DoSomething( "Hi", function(result)
        {
            debug.dump( this.id );
        } );
    }
}
```

What happens when you call the call method? Do you get "1" on the debug console? No, you get null on the debug console because this is no longer the instance of the class, which is a common mistake everyone makes, especially because it is not yet documented in Ajax documentations.

We know whenever JavaScript events are raised that this refers to the HTML element that produces the event. So, if you run this code:

```
function SampleClass( )
{
    this.id = 1;
    this.call = function( )
    {
        TestService.DoSomething( "Hi", function(result)
        {
            debug.dump( this.id );
        } );
    }
}
var o = new SampleClass( );

<input type="button" id="ButtonID" onclick="o.onclick" />
```

and if you click the button, you see "ButtonID" instead of "1" because the button is making the call. So, the call is made within the button object's context and thus this refers to the button object, not the instance of the class.

Similarly, when XML HTTP raises the event onreadystatechanged and ASP.NET AJAX traps and fires the callback, the code execution is still on the XML HTTP's context. It's the XML HTTP object that raises the event. As a result, this refers to the XML HTTP object, not your own class where the callback is declared.

To make the callback fire in the context of the class's instance so that this refers to the instance of the class, you need to make the following change:

```
function SampleClass( )
{
    this.id = 1;
    this.call = function( )
    {
        TestService.DoSomething( "Hi",
            Function.createDelegate( this, function(result)
        {
            debug.dump( this.id );
        } ) );
    }
}
```

Here, the Function.createDelegate is used to create a delegate that calls the given function under the this context when passed as the first parameter. Function.createDelegate is defined in Ajax runtime as:

```
Function.createDelegate = function(instance, method) {
    return function( ) {
        return method.apply(instance, arguments);
    }
}
```

# Summary

The hacks and workarounds you've seen in this chapter will help you avoid many problems that you may never see in your development environment, but are likely to encounter in a large-scale deployment. Implementing these tricks right from the beginning will save you a lot of development and customer support effort.

# CHAPTER 7

# Creating Asynchronous, Transactional, Cache-Friendly Web Services

Web applications that expose a majority of their features via web services or depend on external web services for their functionality suffer from scalability problems at an early stage. When hundreds of users concurrently hit your site, long-running external web service calls start blocking ASP.NET worker threads, which makes your site slow and sometimes unresponsive. Sometimes requests fail from timeout errors and leave user data in an inconsistent state. Moreover, lack of response caching support in the ASP.NET AJAX Framework makes it even harder because servers serve the same requests again and again to the same browser. In this chapter, you will learn how to rewrite ASP.NET AJAX web service handlers to handle web method calls on your own and make your web methods asynchronous, transactional, and cache-friendly.

## Scalability Challenges with Web Services

Ajax web sites tend to be very chatty because they make frequent calls to web services, e.g., auto complete on text boxes, client-side paging on data grids, and client-side validations require frequent web service calls. Thus, Ajax web sites produce more ASP.NET requests than similar non-Ajax web sites. Moreover, it gets worse when the web service calls make another web service call to external services. Then you not only have an incoming request but also an outgoing request. This means double the load on ASP.NET. ASP.NET has a limited number of worker threads that serve the requests. When there's no threads left free, ASP.NET cannot execute requests. Requests are queued in a waiting queue, and only when a worker thread becomes free does a request from the queue gets the chance to execute. When web service calls perform long I/O operations, like calls to an external web service, long-running queries in the database, or long file operations, the thread that is executing the request is occupied until the I/O operation completes. So, if such long requests are made more frequently than they complete execution, the ASP.NET worker thread pool will be exhausted. Which means further requests will be queued in the application queue and your web site will become nonresponsive for some time.

Fetching Flickr photo widget's XML takes a couple of seconds. So, when hundreds of users load the Flickr photo widget concurrently, too many web service calls will get stuck while fetching the XML. If Flickr somehow becomes slow and takes 10 seconds to complete each request, all such proxy web service calls will get stuck for 10 seconds as well. If there's high traffic during these 10 seconds, ASP.NET will run out of worker threads, and it will not execute new requests and the site will appear very slow to users. Moreover, if requests in the application queue are stuck for more than 30 seconds, they will time out and the site will become nonresponsive to users.

In Figure 7-1, you can see a production server's state when it has exceeded its limit. External web service calls are taking too long to execute, which makes the request execution time too high. Some requests are taking more than 200 seconds to complete. As a result, 72 requests are stuck in calling external services, and additional incoming requests are getting queued in the application queue. The number of requests completing successfully per second is very low as shown in the Requests/Sec counter. Also, requests are waiting in the queue for more than 82 seconds to get a free worker thread.

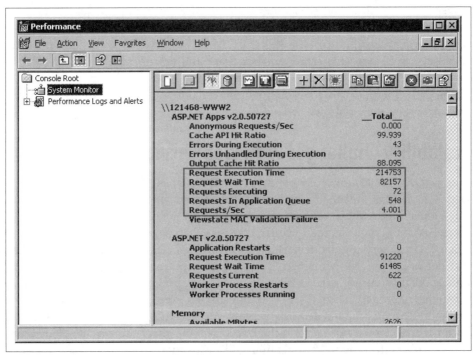

Figure 7-1. When there are too many requests for ASP.NET to handle, Requests In Application Queue starts to increase and Requests/Sec decreases. High Request Execution Time shows how long external web services requests are stuck.

## Real-Life: Fixing a Traffic Jam in the Request Pipeline

Problem: A popular widget took too long to execute, the web servers got stuck, and the web site was unusable.

Solution: Changed the proxy web service to an asynchronous HTTP handler.

One time at Pageflakes, the external stock quote service was taking too long to execute. Our web servers were all getting stuck. After they were restarted, the web servers would get stuck again within 10 minutes. The stock quote widget is very popular, and thousands of users have that widget on their page. So, as soon as they visited their page, the stock quote widget made a call via our proxy web service to fetch data from the external stock quote service. Requests to the proxy got stuck because the external web service was neither executing quickly nor timing out. Moreover, we had to use a high timeout because the external stock quote service is generally very slow. As a result, when we had a large traffic spike during the morning in the U.S., all our web servers repeatedly got stuck, and the web site became unusable. We had no choice but to disable the stock quote widget for an immediate solution. For a long-term solution, we had to change the stock quote proxy web service to an asynchronous HTTP handler because ASP.NET AJAX does not support asynchronous web methods.

Finding out what caused the web servers to get stuck was rather difficult. We went through the *HTTP.sys* error logs that are found under *C:\windows\system32\Logfiles\ HTTPERR*. The logfiles were full of timeout entries on many different URLs including the stock quote service URL. So, we had to turn off each URL one at a time to figure out which one was the real culprit.

# Asynchronous Web Methods

By default, all web methods declared on a web service are synchronous on the server side. However, the call from the browser via XML HTTP is asynchronous, but the actual execution of the web method at the server is synchronous. This means that from the moment a request comes in to the moment the response is generated from that web method call, it occupies a thread from the ASP.NET worker pool. If it takes a relatively long period of time for a request to complete, then the thread that is processing the request will be in use until the method call is done. Unfortunately, most lengthy calls are due to something like a long database query or perhaps a call to another web service. For instance, if you make a database call, the current thread waits for the database call to complete. The thread simply has to wait around doing nothing until it hears back from its query. Similar issues arise when a thread waits for a call to a TCP socket or a backend web service to complete.

When you write a typical ASP.NET web service using web methods, the compiler compiles your code to create the assembly that will be called when requests for its web methods are received. When your application is first launched, the ASMX handler reflects over the assembly to determine which web methods are exposed.

For normal synchronous requests, it is simply a matter of finding which methods have a [WebMethod] attribute associated with them.

To make asynchronous web methods, you need to ensure the following rules are met:

- There is a BeginXXX and EndXXX web method where XXX is any string that represents the name of the method you want to expose.
- The BeginXXX function returns an IAsyncResult interface and takes an AsyncCallback and an object as its last two input parameters, respectively.
- The EndXXX function takes an IAsyncResult interface as its only parameter.
- Both the BeginXXX and EndXXX methods must be flagged with the WebMethod attribute.

If the ASMX handler finds two methods that meet all these requirements, then it will expose the XXX method in its WSDL as if it were a normal web method.

Example 7-1 shows a typical synchronous web method and Example 7-2 shows how it is made asynchronous by introducing a Begin and End pair.

*Example 7-1. Example of a synchronous web method*

```
[WebMethod]
public string Sleep(int milliseconds)
{
    Thread.Sleep(milliseconds);
}
```

*Example 7-2. Asynchronous web methods*

```
[WebMethod]
public IAsyncResult BeginSleep(
                        int milliseconds,
                        AsyncCallback cb,
                        object s) {...}

[WebMethod]
public string EndSleep(IAsyncResult call) {...}
```

The ASMX handler will expose a web method named Sleep from the pair of web methods. The method will accept the parameters defined before the AsyncCallback parameter in the signature for BeginXXX as input and return with the EndXXX function.

After the ASMX handler reflects on the compiled assembly and detects an asynchronous web method, it must handle requests for that method differently than it handles synchronous requests. Instead of calling the Sleep method synchronously and producing responses from the return value, it calls the BeginSleep method. It deserializes the incoming request into the parameters to be passed to the function—as it does for synchronous requests—but it also passes the pointer to an internal callback function as the extra AsyncCallback parameter to the BeginSleep method.

After the ASMX handler calls the BeginSleep function, it will return the thread to the process thread pool so it can handle another request. The HttpContext for the request will not be released yet. The ASMX handler will wait until the callback function that it passed to the BeginSleep function is called to finish processing the request.

Once the callback function is called, a thread from the thread pool is taken out to execute the remaining work. The ASMX handler will call the EndSleep function so that it can complete any processing it needs to perform and return the data to be rendered as a response. Once the response is sent, the HttpContext is released (see Figure 7-2).

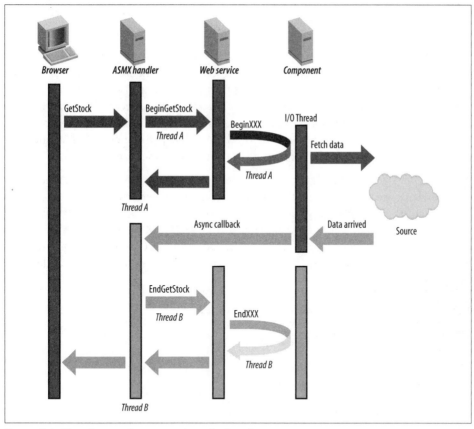

*Figure 7-2. How the asynchronous web method works*

The asynchronous web method concept is hard to grasp. It does not match with anything that we do in regular development. There are some fundamental differences and limitations to consider:

- You cannot use asynchronous web methods when you use a business layer to read or write data that's not asynchronous itself. For example, a web method calling some function on DashboardFacade will not benefit from an asynchronous approach.

- You cannot use the asynchronous method when you are calling an external web service synchronously. The external call must be asynchronous.

- You cannot use the asynchronous method when you perform database operations using regular synchronous methods. All database operations must be asynchronous.

- There's no benefit in making an asynchronous web method when there's no wait on some I/O operation such as HTTP requests, web service calls, remoting, asynchronous database operations, or asynchronous file operations. You won't benefit from simple Delegate.BeginInvoke calls, which run a function asynchronously, because asynchronous delegates take threads from the same thread pool as ASP.NET.

So, in Example 7-1, neither the simple sleep function nor any of the methods that we have used in our proxy web service can be real asynchronous functions (see Chapter 5). We need to rewrite them to support the asynchronous call nature. Before we do so, remember one principle—you can only benefit from the asynchronous method when the BeginXXX web method ends up calling a BeginYYY method on some other component, and your EndXXX method calls that component's EndYYY method. Otherwise, there's no benefit in making web methods asynchronous.

Example 7-3 shows the code for a simple stock quote proxy web service. The proxy web service's BeginGetStock method ends up calling the BeginGetStock method on a component that fetches the stock data from external source. When data arrives, the component calls back via the AsyncCallback cb. The ASMX handler passes down this callback to the web method. So, when it is called, ASP.NET's ASMX handler receives the callback, and it restores the HttpContext, calls EndGetStock, and renders the response.

*Example 7-3. Example of a stock quote proxy web service*

```
[WebService]
public class StockQuoteProxy : System.Web.Services.WebService
{
    [WebMethod]
    public IAsyncResult BeginGetStock(AsyncCallback cb, Object state)
    {
        net.stockquote.StockQuoteService proxy
            = new net.stockquote.StockQuoteService();
        return proxy.BeginGetStock("MSFT",
                                   cb,
                                   proxy);
    }
```

*Example 7-3. Example of a stock quote proxy web service (continued)*

```
[WebMethod]
public string EndGetStock(IAsyncResult res)
{
    net.stockquote.StockQuoteService proxy
        = (net.stockquote.StockQuoteService)res.AsyncState;
    string quotes = proxy.EndGetStock(res);
    return quotes;
}
}
```

The problem is ASP.NET's ASMX handler has the capability to call asynchronous web methods and return threads to the ASP.NET thread pool, but ASP.NET AJAX Framework's ASMX handler does not have that capability. It supports only synchronous calls. So, we need to rewrite the ASMX handler of ASP.NET AJAX to support asynchronous web method execution and then bypass ASP.NET AJAX's ASMX handler when web methods are called via XML HTTP. In the next section, you will see how the ASP.NET AJAX Framework's ASMX handler works and how you can rewrite such a handler yourself and introduce new features to it.

# Modifying the ASP.NET AJAX Framework to Handle Web Service Calls

When you make a web service call from the browser via the ASP.NET AJAX Framework, it uses XML HTTP to make a call to a server-side web service. Usually all calls to ASMX files are handled by ASP.NET's ASMX handler. But when you add ASP.NET AJAX to your web application, you need to make some changes in the *web.config* where you explicitly remove the default ASMX handler and add the ASP.NET AJAX Framework's own ScriptHandler as the ASMX handler (see Example 7-4).

*Example 7-4. ASP.NET AJAX handles all calls to ASMX*

```
<httpHandlers>
    <remove verb="*" path="*.asmx" />
    <add verb="*" path="*.asmx" validate="false" type="System.Web.Script.Services.
    ScriptHandlerFactory, System.Web.Extensions, Version=1.0.61025.0, Culture=neutral,
    PublicKeyToken=31bf3856ad364e35" />
```

You also add a ScriptModule in the HTTP modules pipeline. It intercepts each and every HTTP request and checks whether the call is to an ASPX page and is calling a page method. It intercepts only page method calls, not web service calls. So, you don't need to bypass it.

ScriptHandler is a regular HTTP handler that finds out which web service and web method is called by parsing the URL. It then executes the web method by reflecting on the web service type. The steps involved in calling a web method are as follows:

1. Confirm it's an Ajax web method call by checking Content-Type to see whether it has application/json. If not, raise an exception.

2. Find out which *.asmx* is called by parsing a requested URL and getting the assembly, which has the compiled code for the *.asmx*.

3. Reflect on the assembly and find the web service class and method that represents the web method being called.

4. Deserialize input parameters into the proper data type. In case of HTTP POST, deserialize the JSON graph.

5. See the parameters in the method and map each parameter to objects that have been deserialized from JSON.

6. Initialize the cache policy.

7. Invoke the method via reflection and pass the parameter values that match from JSON.

8. Get the return value. Serialize the return value into JSON/XML.

9. Emit the JSON/XML as the response.

To add asynchronous web method call support, you need to first change the way it reflects on the assembly and locates the web method. It needs to call the Begin and End pair, instead of the real web method. You also need to make the handler implement the IHttpAsyncHandler interface and execute the Begin and End pair in BeginProcessRequest and EndProcessRequest.

But there's no step that facilitates .NET 2.0 transactions. The only way to implement them is to use System.EnterpriseServices transactions or use your own .NET 2.0 TransactionScope class inside your web method code. .NET 2.0 introduced the new System.Transaction namespace, which has a much better way to handle transactions. It would be great if you could add a [Transaction] attribute in your web methods so they could work within a transaction managed by the ScriptHandler. But ScriptHandler does not deal with .NET 2.0 transactions.

## Initializing the Cache Policy

In the ASP.NET AJAX Framework, initialization of cache policy comes before invoking the web method. Example 7-5 shows the ASP.NET AJAX 1.0 code for the InitializeCachePolicy function that sets the cache policy before invoking the web method.

*Example 7-5. ScriptHandler's InitializeCachePolicy function initializes the cache settings before the web method is called*

```
private static void InitializeCachePolicy(WebServiceMethodData methodData, HttpContext
context) {
    int cacheDuration = methodData.CacheDuration;
    if (cacheDuration > 0) {
        context.Response.Cache.SetCacheability(HttpCacheability.Server);
        context.Response.Cache.SetExpires(DateTime.Now.AddSeconds(cacheDuration));
```

Example 7-5. ScriptHandler's InitializeCachePolicy function initializes the cache settings before the web method is called (continued)

```
            context.Response.Cache.SetSlidingExpiration(false);
            context.Response.Cache.SetValidUntilExpires(true);

            if (methodData.ParameterDatas.Count > 0) {
                context.Response.Cache.VaryByParams["*"] = true;
            }
            else {
                context.Response.Cache.VaryByParams.IgnoreParams = true;
            }
        }
        else {
            context.Response.Cache.SetNoServerCaching();
            context.Response.Cache.SetMaxAge(TimeSpan.Zero);
        }
    }
```

If you do not have cache duration set in the [WebMethod] attribute, it will set the MaxAge to zero. Once MaxAge is set to zero, it can no longer be increased; therefore, you cannot increase MaxAge from your web method code dynamically and thus make the browser cache the response.

# Developing Your Own Web Service Handler

In this section, you will learn how to develop your own web service handler and overcome the limitation of the ASP.NET AJAX Framework's built-in ASMX handler. The first step is to add asynchronous method invocation support to web methods. Then add .NET 2.0 transactions on the synchronous method calls. Unfortunately, I haven't found a way to make asynchronous functions transactional. The third step is to set the cache policies after invoking the web method (be careful not to overwrite the cache policies that the web method has already set for itself). Finally, some minor modifications are needed to generate responses with a proper Content-Length header, which helps browsers optimize a response's download time by using persisted connections and less strict exception handling to prevent event logs being flooded with errors.

## Basics of Asynchronous Web Service Handlers

First you need to create a HTTP handler that will intercept all calls to web services. You need to map that handler to the *.asmx extension in web.config's <httphandlers> section. By default, ASP.NET AJAX will map its ScriptHandler, which handles the *.asmx extension, so you will have to replace that with your own HTTP handler.

In the accompanying source code, the AJAXASMXHandler project is the new web service handler. ASMXHttpHandler.cs is the main HTTP handler class. The ASMXHttpHandler class implements IHttpAsyncHandler. When this handler is invoked during calls to web services, the ASP.NET Framework first calls `BeginProcessRequest`. In this function, the handler parses the requested URL and finds out which web service and web method to invoke (see Example 7-6).

*Example 7-6. The ASMXHttpHandler class BeginProcessRequest's function starts the execution of a request asynchronously*

```
IAsyncResult IHttpAsyncHandler.BeginProcessRequest(HttpContext context, AsyncCallback cb,
object extraData)
{
    // Proper content-type header must be present to make an Ajax call
    if (!IsRestMethodCall(context.Request)) return GenerateErrorResponse(context, "Not a
    valid AJAX call", extraData);

    string methodName = context.Request.PathInfo.Substring(1);

    WebServiceDef wsDef = WebServiceHelper.GetWebServiceType(context, context.Request.
    FilePath);
    WebMethodDef methodDef = wsDef.Methods[methodName];

    if (null == methodDef) return GenerateErrorResponse(context, "Web method not
    supported: " + methodName, extraData);

    // GET request will only be allowed if the method says so
    if (context.Request.HttpMethod == "GET" && !methodDef.IsGetAllowed)
        return GenerateErrorResponse(context, "Http Get method not supported",
        extraData);

    // If the method does not have a BeginXXX and EndXXX pair, execute it synchronously
    if (!methodDef.HasAsyncMethods)
    {
```

WebServiceDef is a class that wraps the Type class and contains information about a web service's type. It maintains a collection of WebMethodDef items where the item contains the definition of a web method. WebMethodDef has the name of each method, the attributes associated to the method, whether it supports HTTP GET or not, and a reference to the Begin and End function pair, if there's any. If there's no Begin and End pair, the function is executed synchronously, as in Example 7-7. Both of these classes are used to cache information about web services and web methods, so there's no need to repeatedly use reflection to discover the metadata.

*Example 7-7. BeginProcessRequest: synchronous execution of web methods when there's no Begin and End pair*

```
// If the method does not have a BeginXXX and EndXXX pair, execute it synchronously
if (!methodDef.HasAsyncMethod)
{
    // Do synchronous call
    ExecuteMethod(context, methodDef, wsDef);
```

```
    // Return a result that says method was executed synchronously
    return new AsmxHandlerSyncResult(extraData);
}
```

BeginProcessRequest returns immediately when the method is executed synchro-nously. It returns an AsmxHandlerSyncResult instance that indicates the request has executed synchronously and there's no need to fire EndProcessRequest. AsmxHandlerSyncResult implements the IAsyncResult interface. It returns true from the CompletedSynchronously property (see Example 7-8).

*Example 7-8. AsmxHandlerSyncResult implements IAsyncResult and returns true from the CompletedSynchronously property. It also returns a ManualReset event with state set to true indicating that the call has completed.*

```
public class AsmxHandlerSyncResult : IAsyncResult
{
    private object state;
    private WaitHandle handle = new ManualResetEvent(true);

    public AsmxHandlerSyncResult(object state)
    {
        this.state = state;
        this.handle = handle;
    }

    object IAsyncResult.AsyncState { get { return this.state; } }
    WaitHandle IAsyncResult.AsyncWaitHandle { get { return this.handle; } }
    bool IAsyncResult.CompletedSynchronously { get { return true; } }
    bool IAsyncResult.IsCompleted { get { return true; } }
}
```

Going back to BeginProcessRequest, when there is a Begin and End pair, it calls the BeginXXX method of the web method and returns from the function. Execution goes back to the ASP.NET Framework, and it returns the thread to the thread pool.

## Dynamically Instantiating a Web Service

Web services inherit from System.Web.Services.WebService, which implements the IDisposable interface. Activator.CreateInstance is a .NET Framework class that can dynamically instantiate any class from its type and return a reference to the object. In Example 7-9, a web service class instance is created, and the IDisposable interface ref-erence is used. IDisposable interface is used because we need to dispose of it when we are done.

Example 7-9 show the preparation step for calling the BeginXXX function on the web service. First, all the parameters are properly mapped from the request parameters except for the last two parameters, where one is the AsyncCallback and the other is the object state.

*Example 7-9. BeginProcessRequest: Preparing to invoke the BeginXXX web method on the web service*

```
else
{
    // Create an instance of the web service
    IDisposable target = Activator.CreateInstance(wsDef.WSType) as IDisposable;

    // Get the BeginXXX method and extract its input parameters
    WebMethodDef beginMethod = methodDef.BeginMethod;
    int allParameterCount = beginMethod.InputParametersWithAsyc.Count;

    // Map HttpRequest parameters to BeginXXX method parameters
    IDictionary<string, object> inputValues = GetRawParams(context, beginMethod.
    InputParameters);
    object[] parameterValues = StrongTypeParameters(inputValues, beginMethod.
    InputParameters);

    // Prepare the list of parameter values, which also includes the AsyncCallback and
    the state
    object[] parameterValuesWithAsync = new object[allParameterCount];
    Array.Copy(parameterValues, parameterValuesWithAsync, parameterValues.Length);

    // Populate the last two parameters with asynchonous callback and state
    AsyncWebMethodState webMethodState = new AsyncWebMethodState(methodName, target,
        wsDef, methodDef, context, extraData);

    parameterValuesWithAsync[allParameterCount - 2] = cb;
    parameterValuesWithAsync[allParameterCount - 1] = webMethodState;
```

Once the preparation is complete, the BeginXXX method is invoked. Now the BeginXXX method can execute synchronously and return immediately. In that case, you need to generate the response right out of BeginXXX and complete execution of the request. But if BeginXXX needs more time to execute asynchronously, then you need to return the execution to the ASP.NET Framework so that it can put the thread back into the thread pool. When the asynchronous operation completes, the EndProcessRequest function will be called back and you resume processing the request (see Example 7-10).

*Example 7-10. BeginProcessRequest: Invoke the BeginXXX function on the web service and return the IAsyncResult*

```
try
{
    // Invoke the BeginXXX method and ensure the return result has AsyncWebMethodState.
    // This state contains context and other information that we need to call
    // the EndXXX
```

*Example 7-10. BeginProcessRequest: Invoke the BeginXXX function on the web service and return the IAsyncResult (continued)*

```
        IAsyncResult result = beginMethod.MethodType.Invoke(target,
            parameterValuesWithAsync) as IAsyncResult;

        // If execution has completed synchronously within the BeginXXX function, then
        // generate response immediately. There's no need to call EndXXX
        if (result.CompletedSynchronously)
        {
            object returnValue = result.AsyncState;
            GenerateResponse(returnValue, context, methodDef);

            target.Dispose();
            return new AsmxHandlerSyncResult(extraData);
        }
        else
        {
            if (result.AsyncState is AsyncWebMethodState) return result;
            else throw new InvalidAsynchronousStateException("The state passed
            in the " + beginMethod.MethodName + " must inherit from "
            + typeof(AsyncWebMethodState).FullName);
        }
    }
    catch( Exception x )
    {
        target.Dispose();
        WebServiceHelper.WriteExceptionJsonString(context, x, _serializer);
        return new AsmxHandlerSyncResult(extraData);
    }
}
```

The `EndProcessRequest` function is fired when the asynchronous operation completes and the callback is fired. For example, if you call an external web service asynchronously inside the `BeginXXX` web method, you need to pass an `AsyncCallback` reference. This is the same callback that you receive on `BeginProcessRequest`. The ASP.NET Framework creates a callback reference for you that fires the `EndProcessRequest` on the HTTP handler. During the `EndProcessRequest`, you just need to call the `EndXXX` method of the web service, get the response, and generate output (see Example 7-11).

*Example 7-11. EndProcessRequest function of ASMXHttpHandler*

```
void IHttpAsyncHandler.EndProcessRequest(IAsyncResult result)
{
    if (result.CompletedSynchronously) return;

    AsyncWebMethodState state = result.AsyncState as AsyncWebMethodState;

    if (result.IsCompleted)
    {
        MethodInfo endMethod = state.MethodDef.EndMethod.MethodType;

        try
```

*Example 7-11. EndProcessRequest function of ASMXHttpHandler (continued)*

```
        {
            object returnValue = endMethod.Invoke(state.Target,
                new object[] { result });
            GenerateResponse(returnValue, state.Context, state.MethodDef);
        }
        catch (Exception x)
        {
            WebServiceHelper.WriteExceptionJsonString(state.Context, x, _serializer);
        }
        finally
        {
            state.Target.Dispose( );
        }

        state.Dispose( );
    }
}
```

When the EndXXX web method completes, you will get a return value if the function is not a void type function. In that case, you need to convert the return value to a JSON string and return to the browser. However, the method can return an XML string also instead of JSON. So, just write the string to the HttpResponse (see Example 7-12).

*Example 7-12. TheGenerateResponse function of ASMXHttpHandler prepares the response JSON or the XML string according to the web method definition*

```
private void GenerateResponse(object returnValue, HttpContext context, WebMethodDef
methodDef)
{
    string responseString = null;
    string contentType = "application/json";

    if (methodDef.ResponseFormat == System.Web.Script.Services.ResponseFormat.Json)
    {
        responseString = _serializer.Serialize(returnValue);
        contentType = "application/json";
    }
    else if (methodDef.ResponseFormat == System.Web.Script.Services.ResponseFormat.Xml)
    {
        responseString = returnValue as string;
        contentType = "text/xml";
    }

    context.Response.ContentType = contentType;

    // If we have a response and no redirection is happening and the client is
    // still connected, send response
    if (responseString != null
        && !context.Response.IsRequestBeingRedirected
        && context.Response.IsClientConnected)
```

```
{
    // Convert the return value to response encoding, e.g., UTF-8
    byte[] unicodeBytes = Encoding.Unicode.GetBytes(responseString);
    byte[] utf8Bytes = Encoding.Convert(Encoding.Unicode,
            context.Response.ContentEncoding, unicodeBytes);

    // Instead of Response.Write, which will convert the output to UTF-8,
    // use the internal stream
    // to directly write the UTF-8 bytes
    context.Response.OutputStream.Write(utf8Bytes, 0, utf8Bytes.Length);
}
else
{
    // Send no body as response and abort it
    context.Response.AppendHeader("Content-Length", "0");
    context.Response.ClearContent();
    context.Response.StatusCode = 204; // No Content
}
```

Basically this is how a web method is executed synchronously and asynchronously and response is prepared. Although there are more complicated steps in preparing the web service and web method definition, serialization/deserialization of JSON, and mapping deserialized objects to input parameters of web method, I will skip these areas. You can review the code of the HTTP handler and learn in detail how all these work. A lot of code has been reused from ASP.NET AJAX; I also used the JSON serializer that comes with the Framework.

## Adding Transaction Capability to Web Methods

Up to this point, the web method execution doesn't support transaction. The [TransactionalMethod] attribute defines the scope of transaction to use, as well as the isolation level and timeout period (see Example 7-13).

*Example 7-13. An example of implementing a transactional web method*

```
[WebMethod]
[TransactionalMethod(
    TransactionOption=TransactionScopeOption.RequiresNew,
    Timeout=10,
    IsolationLevel=IsolationLevel.Serializable)]
public void TestTransactionCommit()
{
    Debug.WriteLine(string.Format(
        "TestTransactionCommit: Status: {0},
        Isolation Level: {1}",
        Transaction.Current.TransactionInformation.Status,
        Transaction.Current.IsolationLevel));
```

*Example 7-13. An example of implementing a transactional web method (continued)*

```
    using (SqlConnection con = new SqlConnection(
        ConfigurationManager.ConnectionStrings["default"].ConnectionString))
    {
        con.Open( );
        using (SqlCommand cmdInsert = new SqlCommand("INSERT INTO Widget
            (Name, Url, Description, CreatedDate, LastUpdate,
            VersionNo, IsDefault, DefaultState, Icon)
            VALUES ( '', '', '', GETDATE( ), GETDATE( ), 0, 0, '', '');
            SELECT @@IDENTITY", con))
        {
            object id = cmdInsert.ExecuteScalar( );

            using (SqlCommand cmdDelete = new SqlCommand(
                "DELETE FROM Widget WHERE ID=" + id.ToString( ), con))
            {
                cmdDelete.ExecuteNonQuery( );
            }
        }
    }
}
```

A web method that has the `TransactionalMethod` attribute will automatically execute inside a transaction. We will use .NET 2.0 transactions here. The transaction management is done entirely in the HTTP handler and thus the web method doesn't have to do anything. The transaction is automatically rolled back when the web method raises an exception; otherwise, the transaction is committed automatically.

The `ExecuteMethod` function of the `ASMXHttpHandler` invokes web methods synchronously and provides transaction support. Currently, transaction support for asynchronous methods has not been implemented because execution switches from one thread to another, so the `TransactionScope` is lost from the thread local storage (see Example 7-14).

*Example 7-14. The ExecuteMethod of ASMXHttpHandler invokes a web method synchronously within a transaction scope*

```
private void ExecuteMethod(
    HttpContext context,
    WebMethodDef methodDef,
    WebServiceDef serviceDef)
{
IDictionary<string, object> inputValues =
    GetRawParams(context, methodDef.InputParameters);
object[] parameters =
    StrongTypeParameters(inputValues, methodDef.InputParameters);

object returnValue = null;
using (IDisposable target =
    Activator.CreateInstance(serviceDef.WSType) as IDisposable)
{
```

*Example 7-14. The ExecuteMethod of ASMXHttpHandler invokes a web method synchronously within a transaction scope (continued)*

```
TransactionScope ts = null;
try
{
    // If the method has a transaction attribute,
    // then call the method within a transaction scope
    if (methodDef.TransactionAtt != null)
    {
        TransactionOptions options = new TransactionOptions();
        options.IsolationLevel = methodDef.TransactionAtt.IsolationLevel;
        options.Timeout =
            TimeSpan.FromSeconds( methodDef.TransactionAtt.Timeout );

        ts = new TransactionScope(
            methodDef.TransactionAtt.TransactionOption, options);
    }

    returnValue = methodDef.MethodType.Invoke(target, parameters);

    // If transaction was used, then complete the transaction
    // because no exception was generated
    if( null != ts ) ts.Complete();

    GenerateResponse(returnValue, context, methodDef);
}
```

Example 7-14 shows a web method executing properly and generating a response. The web method executes within a transaction scope defined in the TransactionalMethod attribute. But when the web method raises an exception, it goes to the catch block where a exception message is produced. Finally, the TransactionScope is disposed and it checks whether it has been already committed. If not, TransactionScope rolls back the transaction (see Example 7-15).

*Example 7-15. ExecuteMethod: When a web method raises an exception, the transaction is rolled back*

```
catch (Exception x)
{
    WebServiceHelper.WriteExceptionJsonString(context, x, _serializer);
}
finally
{
    // If the transaction was started for the method, dispose the transaction.
    // This will roll back if not committed
    if( null != ts) ts.Dispose();

    // Dispose the web service
    target.Dispose();
}
```

The entire transaction management is inside the HTTP handler, so there's no need to worry about transactions in web services. Just add one attribute, and web methods become transaction enabled.

## Adding Cache Headers

The previous section "Modifying the ASP.NET AJAX Framework to Handle Web Service Calls" described how ASP.NET AJAX initializes the cache policy before invoking the web method. Due to a limitation in HttpCachePolicy, once the MaxAge is set to a value, it cannot be increased. Because ASP.NET AJAX sets the MaxAge to zero, there's no way to increase that value from within the web method code. Moreover, if you use Fiddler or any other HTTP inspection tool to see responses returned from web service calls, you will see the responses are missing Content-Length attribute. Without this attribute, browsers cannot use HTTP pipelining, which greatly improves the HTTP response download time.

Example 7-16 shows some additions made to the GenerateResponse function to deal with the cache policy. The idea is to confirm that the web method has already set some cache policy in the HttpResponse object so it will not change any cache setting. Otherwise, it will look at the WebMethod attribute for cache settings and then set the cache headers.

*Example 7-16. The GenerateResponse function handles cache headers properly by respecting the cache policy set by the web method*

```
// If we have a response and no redirection is happening and the client is still
//connected, send response
if (responseString != null
    && !context.Response.IsRequestBeingRedirected
    && context.Response.IsClientConnected)
{
    // Produces proper cache. If no cache information is specified on the method and
    // there's been no cache-related
    // changes done within the web method code, then the default cache will be private,
    // no cache.
    if (IsCacheSet(context.Response))
    {
      // Cache has been modified within the code; do not change any cache policy
    }
    else
    {
        // Cache is still private. Check to see if CacheDuration was set in WebMethod
        int cacheDuration = methodDef.WebMethodAtt.CacheDuration;
        if (cacheDuration > 0)
        {
            // If CacheDuration attribute is set, use server-side caching
            context.Response.Cache.SetCacheability(HttpCacheability.Server);
            context.Response.Cache.SetExpires(DateTime.Now.AddSeconds(cacheDuration));
            context.Response.Cache.SetSlidingExpiration(false);
            context.Response.Cache.SetValidUntilExpires(true);
```

*Example 7-16. The GenerateResponse function handles cache headers properly by respecting the cache policy set by the web method (continued)*

```
                if (methodDef.InputParameters.Count > 0)
                {
                    context.Response.Cache.VaryByParams["*"] = true;
                }
                else
                {
                    context.Response.Cache.VaryByParams.IgnoreParams = true;
                }
            }
            else
            {
                context.Response.Cache.SetNoServerCaching();
                context.Response.Cache.SetMaxAge(TimeSpan.Zero);
            }
        }

        // Convert the response to response encoding, e.g., UTF-8
        byte[] unicodeBytes = Encoding.Unicode.GetBytes(responseString);
        byte[] utf8Bytes = Encoding.Convert(Encoding.Unicode, context.Response.
        ContentEncoding, unicodeBytes);

        // Emit content length in UTF-8 encoding string
        context.Response.AppendHeader("Content-Length", utf8Bytes.Length.ToString());

        // Instead of Response.Write, which will convert the output to UTF-8, use the
        // internal stream
        // to directly write the UTF-8 bytes
        context.Response.OutputStream.Write(utf8Bytes, 0, utf8Bytes.Length);
}
```

The IsCacheSet function checks to see whether there's been any change in some of the common cache settings. If there has been a change, then the web method wants to deal with the cache itself, and GenerateResponse does not make any change to the cache policy (see Example 7-17).

*Example 7-17. The IsCacheSet function checks whether the cache policy has already been set by the web method*

```
private bool IsCacheSet(HttpResponse response)
{
    // Default is private. So, if it has been changed, then the web method
    // wants to handle cache itself
    if (response.CacheControl == "public") return true;

    // If maxAge has been set to a nondefault value, then the web method
    // wants to set maxAge itself.
    FieldInfo maxAgeField = response.Cache.GetType().GetField("_maxAge",
        BindingFlags.GetField | BindingFlags.Instance | BindingFlags.NonPublic);
    TimeSpan maxAgeValue = (TimeSpan)maxAgeField.GetValue(response.Cache);
```

```
    if (maxAgeValue != TimeSpan.Zero) return true;

    return false;
}
```

# Real-Life: Exception Handling

Problem: The ASMX handler kept firing exceptions.

Solution: Used the reflection-based `maxAge` hack in the "Caching Web Service Responses on the Browser" section in Chapter 6.

On an earlier portal project I worked on, our web servers' event logs were being flooded with this error:

```
Request format is unrecognized for URL unexpectedly ending in /SomeWebServiceMethod
```

In ASP.NET AJAX 1.0 version, Microsoft added a check for all web service calls to have `Content-Type: application/json` in the request headers. Unless this request header was present, ASMX handler fired an exception. This exception was raised directly from the `ScriptHandler`, which handled all web service calls made via ASP.NET AJAX. This resulted in an `UnhandledException` and was written in the event log.

This is done for security reasons; it prevents someone from feeding off your web services. For example, you might have a web service that returns some useful information that others want. So, anyone could just add a `<script>` tag pointing to that web service URL and get the JSON. If that web service is a very expensive web service in terms of I/O and/or CPU, then other web sites feeding off your web service could easily bog down your server.

Now, this backfires when you have HTTP GET supported web service calls that produce response headers to cache the response in the browser and proxy. For example, you might have a web method that returns stock quotes. You have used response caching so the browser caches the response of that web method, and repeated visits do not produce repeated calls to that costly I/O web service. Because it has a cache header, proxy gateways or proxy servers will see that their client users are requesting this frequently and it can be cached. So, they will make periodic calls to that web service and try to precache the headers on behalf of their client users. However, during the precache process, the proxy gateways or proxy servers will not send the `Content-Type: application/json` header. As a result, an exception is thrown and your event log is flooded.

The reason why this went undetected is because there's no way to make a HTTP GET response cacheable on the browser from web service calls unless you do the reflection-based `maxAge` hack in the "Caching Web Service Responses on the Browser" section in Chapter 6.

---

So, the `ASMXHttpHandler` just returns HTTP 405 saying the call is not allowed if it does not have the application/json content type. This solves the event log flood problem and prevents browsers from getting a valid response when someone uses a <script> tag on your web method.

## Using the Attributes

You have seen that the `BeginXXX` and `EndXXX` functions don't have the `[WebMethod]` attribute, but instead only have the `[ScriptMethod]` attribute. If you add `WebMethod` attribute, the Ajax JavaScript proxy generator will unnecessarily generate function wrappers for those methods in the JavaScript proxy for the web service. So, for the JavaScript proxy generator, you need only to put the `WebMethod` attribute on the XXX web method. Moreover, you cannot have a `WebMethod` attribute on `BeginXXX`, `EndXXX`, and the XXX functions at the same time because the WSDL generator will fail to generate. So, the idea is to add the `WebMethod` attribute only to the XXX function, and the JavaScript proxy generator will generate a JavaScript function for the web method and add only the `ScriptMethod` attribute on the `BeginXXX` and `EndXXX` functions.

## Handling the State Object

The last parameter passed in the `BeginXXX` function, the object state parameter, needs to be preserved. It contains a reference to the `HttpContext`, which is needed by the ASMX handler to call the `EndXXX` function on proper context. So, if you create a custom state object and pass that to a `BeginYYY` function of some component, e.g., `File.BeginRead`, then you need to inherit that custom state object from the `AsyncWebMethodState` class. You must pass the state parameter in the constructor. This way, your custom state object will carry the original state object that is passed down to your `BeginXXX` function.

# Making an Asynchronous and Cache-Friendly Proxy

You can make proxy methods asynchronous by using the new Ajax ASMX handler. This will solve a majority of the proxy web service's scalability problems. Moreover, the proxy service will become cache-friendly for browsers, and they will be able to download responses faster from the proxy by using the `Content-Length` header.

The `GetString` and `GetXml` method can become asynchronous very easily by using the `HttpWebRequest` class and its asynchronous methods. `HttpWebRequest` has the `BeginGetResponse` function, which works asynchronously. So, you just need to call `BeginResponse` in the `BeginGetString` class of the proxy (see Example 7-18).

*Example 7-18. A proxy's BeginGetString function asynchronously downloads responses from an external source*

```
private class GetStringState : AsyncWebMethodState
{
    public HttpWebRequest Request;
    public string Url;
    public int CacheDuration;
    public GetStringState(object state) : base(state) {}
}

[ScriptMethod]
public IAsyncResult BeginGetString(string url, int cacheDuration, AsyncCallback cb, object
state)
{
    // See if the response from the URL is already cached on server
    string cachedContent = Context.Cache[url] as string;
    if (!string.IsNullOrEmpty(cachedContent))
    {
        this.CacheResponse(Context, cacheDuration);
        return new AsmxHandlerSyncResult(cachedContent);
    }

    HttpWebRequest request = WebRequest.Create(url) as HttpWebRequest;

    GetStringState myState = new GetStringState(state);
    myState.Request = request;
    myState.Url = url;
    myState.CacheDuration = cacheDuration;

    return request.BeginGetResponse(cb, myState);
}
```

The `BeginGetString` method has two modes. It executes them synchronously when the content is cached in the ASP.NET cache. Then there's no need to return the thread to the thread pool because the method can complete right away. If there isn't any content in the cache, it makes a `BeginGetResponse` call and returns execution to the ASMX handler. The custom state object, `GetStringState`, inherits from the `AsyncWebMethodState` defined in the `AJAXASMXHandler` project. In its constructor, it takes the original state object passed down to the `BeginGetString` function. The `ASMXHttpHandler` needs the original state so that it can fire the `EndGetString` function on proper context.

When `HttpWebRequest` gets the response, it fires the ASMX handler's callback. The ASMX handler, in turn, calls `EndGetString` to complete the response. `EndGetString` downloads the response, caches it, and returns it as a return value (see Example 7-19).

*Example 7-19. The EndGetString method of a proxy web service*

```
[ScriptMethod]
public string EndGetString(IAsyncResult result)
```

*Example 7-19. The EndGetString method of a proxy web service (continued)*

```
{
    GetStringState state = result.AsyncState as GetStringState;

    HttpWebRequest request = state.Request;
    using( HttpWebResponse response =
        request.EndGetResponse(result) as HttpWebResponse )
    {
        using( StreamReader reader = new
            StreamReader(response.GetResponseStream()) )
        {
            string content = reader.ReadToEnd();
            state.Context.Cache.Insert(state.Url, content, null,
                Cache.NoAbsoluteExpiration,
                TimeSpan.FromMinutes(state.CacheDuration),
                CacheItemPriority.Normal, null);

            // produce cache headers for response caching
            this.CacheResponse(state.Context, state.CacheDuration);

            return content;
        }
    }
}
```

Keep in mind that the Context object is unavailable in the EndGetString function because this function is fired on a different thread that is no longer tied to the original thread that initiated the HTTP request. So, you need to get a reference to the original Context from the state object.

Similarly, you can make GetRss asynchronous by introducing a BeginGetRss and EndGetRss pair.

# Scaling and Securing the Content Proxy

As widgets start using the proxy service, described in Chapter 5, more and more, this single component will become the greatest scalability bottleneck of your entire web portal project. It's not unusual to spend a significant amount of development resources to improve scalability, reliability, availability, and performance on the content proxy. This section describes some of the challenges you will face when going live to millions of users with such a proxy component.

## Maintaining Speed

Widgets call a proxy service to fetch content from an external source. The proxy service makes the call, downloads the response on server, and then transmits the response back to the browser. There are two latencies involved here: between the browser and your server, and your server and the destination. If the response's payload is high, say 500 KB, then there's almost 1 MB of transfer that takes place during the call. So, you need to put a limit on how much data transfer you allow from the proxy (see Example 7-20). HttpWebResponse class has a ContentLength property that tells you how much data is being served by the destination. You can check whether it exceeds the maximum limit that you can take in. If widgets are requesting a large amount of data, it not only slows that specific request, but also other requests on the same server, since the server's bandwidth is occupied during the megabyte transfer. Servers generally have 4 Mbps, 10 Mbps, or, if you can afford it, 100 Mbps connectivity to the Internet. At 10 Mbps, you can transfer about 1 MB per second. So, if one proxy call is occupied transferring megabytes, there's no bandwidth left for other calls to happen and bandwidth cost goes sky high. Moreover, during the large transfer, one precious HTTP worker thread is occupied streaming megabytes of data over a slow Internet connection to the browser. If a user is using a 56 Kbps ISDN line, a 1 MB transfer will occupy a worker thread for about 150 seconds.

*Example 7-20. Putting a limit on how much data you will download from external sources via a HttpWebRequest*

```
HttpWebResponse response = request.GetResponse( ) as HttpWebResponse;

if (response.StatusCode == HttpStatusCode.OK)
{
    int maxBytesAllowed = 512 * 1024; // 512 K
    if (response.ContentLength > maxBytesAllowed)
    {
        response.Close( );
        throw new ApplicationException("Response too big.
            Max bytes allowed to download is: " + maxBytesAllowed);
    }
}
```

Sometimes external sources do not generate the content length header, so there's no way to know how much data you are receiving unless you download the entire byte stream from the server until the server closes the connection. This is a worst-case scenario for a proxy service because you have to download up to your maximum limit and then abort the connection. Example 7-21 shows a general algorithm for dealing with this problem.

*Example 7-21. An algorithm for downloading external content safely*

```
Get content length from the response header.

If the content length is present, then
    Check if content length is within the maximum limit
    If content length exceeds maximum limit, abort

If the content length is not present
    And there are more bytes available to download
        Read a chunk of bytes, e.g., 512 bytes,
        Count the total number of bytes read so far
        If the count exceeds the maximum limit, abort
```

## Connection management

Every call to the proxy makes it open an HTTP connection to the destination, download data, and then close it. Setting up an HTTP connection is expensive because there's network latency involved in establishing a connection between the browser and the server. If you are making frequent calls to the same domain, like Flickr.com, it will help to maintain an HTTP connection pool, just like an ADO.NET connection pool. You should keep connections open and reuse open connections when you have frequent requests going to the same external server. However, the HTTP connection pool is very complicated to make because, unlike SQL Servers in fast private networks, external servers are on the Internet, loaded with thousands of connection from all over the world, and are grumpy about holding a connection open for long period. They are always eager to close down an inactive connection as soon as possible. So, it becomes quite challenging to keep HTTP connections open to frequently requested servers that are quite busy with other clients.

## DNS resolution

DNS resolution is another performance obstacle. If your server is in the U.S., and a web site that you want to connect to has a DNS in Australia, it's going to take about 1 second just to resolve the web site's IP. DNS resolution happens in each and every HttpWebRequest. There's no built-in cache in .NET that remembers the host's IP for some time. You can benefit from DNS caching if there's a DNS server in your data center. But that also flushes out the IP in an hour. So, you can benefit from maintaining your own DNS cache. Just a static thread-safe dictionary with the key as the domain name and the value as the IP will do. When you open HttpWebRequest, instead of using the URI that is passed to you, replace the domain name with the cached IP on the URI and then make the call. But remember to send the original domain as the host header's value.

The HttpWebRequest class has some parameters that can be tweaked for performance and scalability for a proxy service. For example, the proxy does not need any keep-alive connections. It can close connections as soon as a call is finished. In fact, it must do that or a server will run out of TCP sockets under a heavy load. A server can handle a maximum of 65,535 TCP connections that connect one a time. However, your application's limit is smaller than that because there are other applications running on the server that need free TCP sockets. Besides closing a connection as soon as you are finished, you need to set a much lower Timeout value for HttpWebRequest. The default is 100 seconds, which is too high for a proxy that needs content to be served to a client in seconds. So, if an external service does not respond within 3 to 5 seconds, you can give up on it. Every second the timeout value increases, the risk of worker threads being jammed is increased as well. ReadWriteTimeout is another property that is used when reading data from the response stream. The default is 300 seconds, which is too high; it should be as low as 1 second. If a Read call on the response stream gets stuck, not only is an open HTTP connection stuck but so is a worker thread on the ASP.NET pool. Moreover, if a response to a Read request takes more than a second, that source is just too slow and you should probably stop sending future requests to that source (see Example 7-22).

*Example 7-22. Optimizing the HttpWebRequest connection for a proxy*

```
HttpWebRequest request = WebRequest.Create("http://... ") as HttpWebRequest;
request.Headers.Add("Accept-Encoding", "gzip");
request.AutomaticDecompression = DecompressionMethods.GZip;
request.AllowAutoRedirect = true;
request.MaximumAutomaticRedirections = 1;
request.Timeout = 15000;
request.Expect = string.Empty;
request.KeepAlive = false;
request.ReadWriteTimeout = 1000;
```

Most of the web servers now support gzip compression on response. Gzip compression significantly reduces the response size, and you should always use it. To receive a compressed stream, you need to send the Accept-Encoding: gzip header and enable AutomaticDecompression. The header will tell the source to send the compressed response, and the property will direct HttpWebRequest to decompress the compressed content. Although this will add some overhead to the CPU, it will significantly reduce bandwidth usage and the content's fetch time from external sources. For text content, like JSON or XML where there are repeated texts, you will get a 10 to 50 times speed gain while downloading such responses.

## Avoiding Proxy Abuse

When someone uses your proxy to anonymously download data from external sources, it's called *proxy abuse*. Just like widgets, any malicious agent can download content from external sources via your proxy. Someone can also use your proxy to produce malicious hits on external servers. For example, a web site can download external content using your proxy instead of downloading it itself, because it knows it will benefit from all the optimization and server-side caching techniques you have done. So, anyone can use your site as their own external content cache server to save on DNS lookup time, benefit from connection pooling to your proxy servers, and bring down your server with additional load.

This is a really hard problem to solve. One easy way is to limit number of connections per minute or day from a specific IP to your proxy service. Another idea is to check cookies for some secure token that you generate and send to the client side. The client will send back that secure token to the proxy server to identify it as a legitimate user. But that can easily be misused if someone knows how to get the secure token. Putting a limit on the maximum content length is another way to prevent a large amount of data transfer. A combination of all these approaches can save your proxy from being overused by external web sites or malicious clients. However, you still remain vulnerable to some misuse all the time. You just have to pay for the additional hardware and bandwidth cost that goes into misuse and make sure you always have extra processing power and bandwidth to serve your own need.

## Defending Against Denial-of-Service Attacks

The proxy service is the single most vulnerable service on the whole project. It's so easy to bring down a site by maliciously hitting a proxy that most hackers will just ignore you, because you aren't worth the challenge.

Here's one way to bring down any site that has a proxy service:

1. Create a web page that accepts an HTTP GET call.
2. Make that page sleep for as long as possible.
3. Create a small client that will hit the proxy to make requests to that web page. Every call to that web page will make the proxy wait for a long time.
4. Find the timeout of the proxy and sleep it so that proxy will always time out on each call (this may take some trial and error).
5. Spawn 100 threads from your small client and make a call to the proxy from each thread to fetch content from that slow page. You will have 100 worker threads stuck on the proxy server. If the server has two processors, it will run out of worker threads and the site will become nonresponsive.

You can take this one step further by sleeping until timeout minus 1 second. After that sleep, start sending a small number of bytes to the response as slowly as possible. Find the `ReadWriteTimeout` value of the proxy on the network stream. This will prevent the proxy from timing out on the connection. When it's just about to give up, it will start getting some bytes and not abort the connection. Because it is receiving bytes within the `ReadWriteTimeout`, it will not time out on the `Read` calls. This way, you can make each call to the proxy go on for hundreds of seconds until the ASP.NET request times out. Spawn 100 threads and you will have 100 requests stuck on the server until they time out. This is the worst-case scenario for any web server.

To prevent such attacks, you need to restrict the number of requests allowed from a specific IP per minute, hour, and day. Moreover, you need to decrease the ASP.NET request timeout value on `machine.config`, e.g., you can set it to 15 seconds so that no request is stuck for more than 15 seconds, including calls to the proxy (see Example 7-23).

*Example 7-23. The machine.config setting for ASP.NET request timeout; set it as low as you can*

```
<system.web>
...
...
<httpRuntime executionTimeout="15/>
...
...
</system.web>
```

Another way to bog down your server is to produce unique URLs and make your proxy cache those URLs. For example, anyone can make your proxy hit *http://msdn. microsoft.com/rss.xml?1* and keep adding some numbers in the query string to make the URL unique. No matter what you add on the query string, it will return the same feed. But because you are using an URL as the key for cache, it will cache the large response returned from MSDN against each key. So, if you hit the proxy with 1 to 1,000 query strings, there will be 1,000 identical copies of the MSDN feed on the ASP.NET cache. This will put pressure on the server's memory, and other items from the cache will purge out. As a result, the proxy will start making repeated requests for those lost items and become significantly slower.

One way to prevent this is to set `CacheItemPriority` as `Low` for such items in the cache. It will prevent more important items in the cache from purging out. Moreover, you can maintain another dictionary where you store the content's MD5 hash as key and the URL as value. Before storing an item in the cache, calculate the content's MD5 hash and check if it's already in the dictionary. If it is, then this item is already cached, regardless of the URL. So, you can get the original cached URL from the hash dictionary and then use that URL as the key to get the cached content from the ASP.NET cache.

# Summary

In this chapter, you learned how to rewrite the Ajax ASMX handler to add asynchronous, transactional, cache-friendly, and faster web service response download capabilities than those provided by the ASP.NET AJAX 1.0 Framework. You also learned the scalability challenges of a proxy service and how to overcome them. The principles introduced here apply to many types of web services, and knowing these in advance will help you eliminate common bottlenecks.

# CHAPTER 8

# Improving Server-Side Performance and Scalability

Running a large consumer web application for a mass audience is challenging, to say the least. You will face many scalability, maintainability, extensibility, and performance challenges as you grow from hundreds to thousands to, eventually, millions of users. As the number of concurrent users grows, you will face challenges in software that will require significant re-engineering and sometimes a rewrite of major components. Any type of re-engineering or rewrite of components becomes very expensive in the later stages of the project when you have a production site running and performing poorly. You have to go through rigorous impact analysis, careful coding while maintaining backward-compatibility, and many rounds of regression testing. So, acknowledging such challenges up front while the project is small, and provisioning for them will help mitigate complexity later in the project and save a lot of time and money.

Before you address scalability, maintainability, and performance issues, the first thing you need is very good instrumentation, which includes logging, performance metrics, and exception handling. You will first have to log key areas of your application before you can identify where the bottleneck is and what kind of problems your users are facing on the production site. Remember, there's no way to attach a Visual Studio debugger on a production site, set the breakpoint, and debug the application while thousands of users are hitting the site. The only way you can identify problems is by thoroughly logging what key components are doing. After that, you will have to record performance metrics that isolate areas that need improvement. These metrics will help you benchmark your application and see what areas become slow during peak load. The most important thing to remember is to record exception logs in such a way that you can easily analyze them; they contain sufficient context to help you identify the problem areas quickly.

Once you have identified and fixed key problem areas of the application, the next step is to re-engineer some framework components such as the HTTP pipeline, implement intelligent caching, and optimize the business and data access layers. I will also share with you some best and proven practices that I have implemented at previous companies, as well as Pageflakes, to mitigate scalability and performance issues.

# Instrumenting Your Code to Identify Performance Problems

You need to record the execution time of web service calls, page loads, and expensive code blocks before you can identify scalability issues. Example 8-1 shows a way to calculate the execution time of a code block.

*Example 8-1. Record executing time of code block for instrumentation*

```
private void SomeFunction()
{
    using (new TimedLog(Profile.UserName, "Some Function"))
    {
        ...
        ...
    }
}
```

You can measure the execution time of a function and a smaller block of code. Whatever is inside the using block is timed and logged, and you get an output like Example 8-2.

*Example 8-2. Output from TimedLog class*

```
6/14/2006 10:58:26 AM omar@pageflakes.com    SomeFunction  9.578125
```

The `TimedLog` class measures execution time of code blocks as shown in Example 8-3.

*Example 8-3. The TimedLog class records the time of its creation and disposal. The execution time is the difference between these two timestamps.*

```
public class TimedLog : IDisposable
{
    private string _Message;
    private long _StartTicks;
    public TimedLog(string userName, string message)
    {
        this._Message = userName + '\t' + message;
        this._StartTicks = DateTime.Now.Ticks;
    }
    #region IDisposable Members
    void IDisposable.Dispose()
    {
        Debug.WriteLine(this._Message + '\t' + TimeSpan.FromTicks(DateTime.Now.Ticks -
        this._StartTicks).TotalSeconds.ToString());
    }
    #endregion
}
```

The benefit of such a log is you get a tab-delimited output, which you can use to do many types of analysis using Microsoft Excel. For example, you can generate graphs to see how the performance goes up and down during peak and nonpeak hours. You can also see whether there are high response times and determine the pattern. All these give you valuable indications of where the bottleneck is. You can also find out which calls take the most time by doing a sort on the duration column.

You can use logging utilities, such as Log4net or the Enterprise Library Logging Application Block, to log text files. Logging has a very small overhead and won't have a significant effect on the timing of execution.

Logging the code block execution time is an invaluable tool for debugging performance issues. When you have problems with an action being timed out or taking a noticeably long time, open up the logs and analyze the average delay in the code blocks. You can then further narrow the problem down to smaller blocks of code and pinpoint which block is the culprit. It is a good idea to have a timed log added to all web service calls and business layer functions. A timed log has been added to all DashboardFacade public functions. So, whenever there's any performance issue, you can isolate the slow Facade method.

## Optimizing the HTTP Pipeline

There are some HTTP Modules that sit in the ASP.NET request pipeline by default that you may not need. You can remove those modules and eliminate some extra processing. For example, in *web.config*, these modules can be removed as shown in Example 8-4. This is a very easy way to get a small boost on request processing.

*Example 8-4. Remove unnecessary HTTP Modules from the ASP.NET request pipeline for faster request processing*

```
<httpModules>
    <remove name="Session" />
    <remove name="WindowsAuthentication" />
    <remove name="PassportAuthentication" />
    <remove name="UrlAuthorization" />
    <remove name="FileAuthorization" />
```

In this example, Session has been removed from the modules. ASP.NET Membership uses a cookie to store the current username, and Profile provider loads its data from SQL Server continually. So, there's no need to store the user state in Session. Moreover, you need Session to be on a web farm or web garden (multiple processes per application pool) with SQL Server. So, there's no need for ASP.NET default Session support when you are using Profile provider. Windows and Passport authentication is not needed because ASP.NET Membership provider is being used.

UrlAuthorization might be useful to protect administrative folders by defining roles in *web.config*.

FileAuthorization uses Windows Access Control List (ACL) on files. There's no need for using Windows file access permissions to authenticate or authorize here because we aren't using Windows authentication.

# Optimizing ASP.NET 2.0/3.5 Before Going Live

The following are some tweaks that should be made to *web.config* before you go live on your production server, if you are using the ASP.NET 2.0/3.5 Membership provider.

1. Add the applicationname attribute in Profile provider. If you do not add a specific name here, Profile provider will use a GUID. So, on your local machine you will have one GUID and on the production server you will have another GUID. If you copy your local database to the production server, you won't be able to reuse the records available in your local database, and ASP.NET will create a new application on the production server (see Example 8-5).

*Example 8-5. Add a fixed application name in the Profile provider configuration section so that when you move a prepopulated database from the development server to production, the application ID does not change*

```
<profile enabled="true">
<providers>
<clear />
<add name="..." type="System.Web.Profile.SqlProfileProvider"
connectionStringName="..." applicationName="YourApplicationName"
description="..." />
</providers>
```

2. Turn off auto profile save. Profile provider will automatically save the profile whenever a page request completes, even if you have already saved the profile or you don't want it to save anything. So, this might result in an unnecessary UPDATE on your database, which is a significant performance penalty. So, turn off automatic save and do it explicitly from your code using Profile.Save( ); (see Example 8-6).

*Example 8-6. Turning off automatic save in Profile provider configuration*

```
<profile enabled="true" automaticSaveEnabled="false" >
```

3. Configure RoleManager to use cookies. RoleManager always queries the database to get the user roles, which has a significant performance penalty. You can avoid this by letting RoleManager cache role information on cookies. However, this will work only for users that don't have many assigned roles that exceed Cookie's 2 KB limit. It's unlikely you would have many roles with a kilobyte of storage after encryption. So, you can safely store role info on a cookie and save one database roundtrip on every request to *.aspx* and *.asmx* whenever you check for a user's role. The cookie is encrypted using Triple DES algorithm and is safe enough to store such information (see Example 8-7).

*Example 8-7. Configure the role manager to use Cookie to store the user's roles instead of doing a database lookup on every request*

```
<roleManager enabled="true" cacheRolesInCookie="true" >
```

These small changes in *web.config* will protect you from significant scalability problems when site traffic increases, such as 50 to 100 requests per second per server. These changes will save 2 to 3 database calls per request, and you will save about 100 to 300 database calls per second on such a load, which puts much less stress on your database server and lets you grow more on the same hardware.

# Optimizing Queries in the ASP.NET Membership Tables

With ASP.NET Membership provider, you can find a user with UserName or get profile information with the user's ID. You can also change a user's email address by locating the user with UserName. Example 8-8 shows an example of such queries.

*Example 8-8. Some common queries in ASP.NET Membership tables*

```
Select * from aspnet_users where UserName = 'john@hotmail.com'
Select * from aspnet_profile where userID = '......'

Update aspnet_membership
SET Email = 'newemailaddress@somewhere.com'
Where Email = '...'
```

But when you have a giant database on your production server, running any of these queries will bring your server down. Although they look obvious, and you might need to run them frequently, these queries don't use an index, which results in a "table scan" on millions of rows on respective tables, which is the worst-case scenario for any query.

---

## Real-Life: Querying ASP.NET Membership Tables

---

Problem: Generating reports slowed the server and increased CPU usage.

Solution: Put the ApplicationID in the WHERE clause.

In a previous portal project that I worked on, we used fields, such as UserName, Email, UserID, and IsAnonymous, on many marketing reports, which were used only by the marketing team. Now, the site ran fine, but we would get calls several times a day from marketing and customer support telling us that the site was slow, users were reporting extremely slow performance, and that some pages were timing out. Usually when they called we would check SQL profiler for a long-running query. But we couldn't find any problem on the profiler, and the CPU load was within parameters. The site ran nice and smooth while we investigated the problem. So, why was the site really slow several times during the day but not while we were investigating the problem?

The marketing team used to generate reports several times every day, which meant running a query that worked on large number of rows. Those queries made the server's disk I/O and CPU spike, like you see on Figure 8-1.

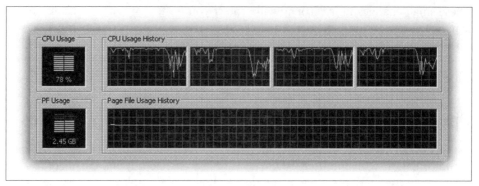

Figure 8-1. The CPU sees a spike when an index is not used on tables with many rows

We had SAS drives that spun at 15,000 RPM—very expensive, very fast—and the CPU was Dual-Core Dual Xeon 64 bit. Still, those queries brought us down due to the huge database, which was about 70 GB at that time. However, the problem occurred only when the marketing team tried to generate any of the reports.

Let's look at the indexes and see whether our queries really match any index on the ASP.NET Membership tables. Table 8-1 shows the default index available on ASP.NET Membership tables.

Table 8-1. ASP.NET Membership table index plan

| Table | Index type | Indexed fields |
| --- | --- | --- |
| aspnet_users | Clustered | ApplicationID, LoweredUserName |
| aspnet_users | NonClustered | ApplicationID, LastActivityDate |
| aspnet_users | NonClustered | UserID |
| aspnet_membership | Clustered | ApplicationID, LoweredEmail |
| aspnet_membership | NonClustered | UserID |
| aspnet_Profile | Clustered | UserID |

Most of the indexes have `ApplicationID`. This means that unless you put `ApplicationID='...'` in the WHERE clause, it's not going to use any of the indexes. As a result, all the queries were suffering from table scan. So, if I put `ApplicationId` in the queries, they should become blazingly fast, but in reality, they didn't. This was because `Email` and `UserName` fields were not part of the indexes, but instead `LoweredUserName` and `LoweredEmail` were in the fields in conjunction with `ApplicationID` in those indexes.

ApplicationID is used in these tables to support multiple applications running on the same database tables. ASP.NET allows you to run several applications on the same database and on the same aspnet_users tables. If you are running only one application in a single database, then you don't need the ApplicationID at all. But because it is part of the index, you need to put the ApplicationID in the WHERE clause.

Our admin site had many such reports, and each had lots of queries on the aspnet_users, aspnet_membership, and aspnet_Profile tables. As a result, whenever the marketing team tried to generate reports, they took all the power from the CPU and HDD and the rest of the site became very slow and sometimes nonresponsive.

However, the solution was not just using the right index. Sometimes the marketing reports ran queries that required a table scan no matter how many indexes were on a table. Imagine if you ran a query that makes SQL Server go through thousands of index entries and lookup rows one by one. SQL Server would be better off doing a clustered index scan. Example 8-9 shows such a query where a large number of rows can be returned.

*Example 8-9. Running queries that run through a lot of rows*

```
SELECT * FROM aspnet_users WHERE LastActivityDate < '1/1/2007'
```

If you have 10,000 users in your aspnet_users table that were active before 2007, then even if you put a nonclustered index on LastActivityDate, it won't hit the index if there are 20,000 rows in the table. In fact, it is better not to use the index because it will then go through 10,000 index entries and look up table rows for each entry, which means it will need 10,000 row lookups from the table. In this scenario, it's better to just do a table scan, which means you can never run such queries on a production server. You must move data to a staging server and then run these queries.

# Optimizing the ASP.NET 2.0/3.5 Profile Provider Before You Go Live

Did you know there are two important stored procedures in ASP.NET 2.0/3.5 Profile provider that can be significantly optimized? If you use them without doing the necessary optimization, your servers will sink and take your business down with them during a heavy load.

## Real-Life: Optimizing Stored Procedures

Problem: An ASP.NET Membership stored procedure caused the server to fail.

Solution: Eliminate use of temporary tables from SP.

Pageflakes was demoed at Microsoft's MIX06 conference when we were in early beta stage. We were featured on Microsoft's ASP.NET AJAX, site and the number of visits per day skyrocketed. Then one day we noticed that the server was gone; we restarted it, brought it back, and it died within an hour. After doing a lot of postmortem analysis on the server's remaining body parts, we found that it had 100 percent CPU, super-high I/O usage, and that the hard drives were overheated and had turned themselves off. So, we went through hundreds of megabytes of logs hoping to find a web service function that was killing our server. We suspected one web service in particular—the first function that loads a user's page setup. So, we broke it up into smaller parts to see which part was taking most of the time (see Example 8-10).

*Example 8-10. Pageflake's most complicated function*

```
private GetPageflake(string source, string pageID, string userUniqueName)
{
  if( Profile.IsAnonymous )
  {
    using (new TimedLog(Profile.UserName,"GetPageflake"))
    {
```

We also timed smaller parts that we suspected could be taking most of the resources. But we could not find a single place in our code that was taking any significant time. Meanwhile, the users were shouting, management was screaming, the support staff was complaining, and the developers were furiously sweating.

Now, you are saying, "You could have used SQL Profiler!" However, we were using the SQL Server workgroup edition back then, which did not have SQL Profiler. So, we had to hack our way through to get SQL Profiler running on a server somehow (don't ask how). And after running the SQL Profiler, boy, were we surprised! The settings property that was giving us so much trouble was aspnet_Profile_GetProfiles. Let's analyze aspnet_Profile_GetProfiles in detail. First, it looks up the ApplicationID (see Example 8-11).

*Example 8-11. Part of aspnet_profile_GetProfiles, which looks up the application ID from the application name*

```
DECLARE @ApplicationId
                    uniqueidentifier
   SELECT @ApplicationId = NULL
   SELECT @ApplicationId = ApplicationId
          FROM aspnet_Applications


            WHERE LOWER(@ApplicationName)
                    = LoweredApplicationName
   IF (@ApplicationId IS NULL)

   RETURN
```

It then creates a temporary table to store profiles of users (see Example 8-12).

*Example 8-12. Part of aspnet_profile_GetProfiles that creates a temporary table to store results*

```
-- Create a temp table to store the select results
CREATE TABLE #PageIndexForUsers
(
    IndexId
    int IDENTITY (0, 1) NOT NULL,
    UserId
    uniqueidentifier
)

-- Insert into
    our temp table
INSERT INTO #PageIndexForUsers (UserId)
```

If it is frequently called, the I/O will be too high due to the temporary table creation. It also runs through two very big tables—aspnet_Users and aspnet_Profile. The settings property is written in such a way that if one user has multiple profiles, it will return all of the user's profiles. But because we normally store one profile per user, there's no need to create a temporary table. Moreover, there's no need for doing LIKE LOWER(@UserNameToMatch), which was always being called with a full username that can be matched directly using the equal operator.

So, we opened up the stored procedure and operated (see Example 8-13).

*Example 8-13. aspnet_profile_GetProfiles gets a bypass code for running faster*

```
IF @UserNameToMatch IS NOT NULL

        BEGIN

        SELECT u.UserName, u.IsAnonymous, u.LastActivityDate, p.LastUpdatedDate,

                DATALENGTH(p.PropertyNames)
                + DATALENGTH(p.PropertyValuesString) + DATALENGTH(p.
                PropertyValuesBinary)

        FROM    dbo.aspnet_Users u

        INNER JOIN dbo.aspnet_Profile p ON u.UserId = p.UserId

        WHERE

            u.LoweredUserName = LOWER(@UserNameToMatch)

        SELECT @@ROWCOUNT

        END

        ELSE
BEGIN -- Do the original bad things
```

It ran fine locally. Now it was time to run it on the server. If we do something wrong here, we might not be able to see the problem immediately, but later realize the users profiles are messed up and there is no way to get them back. So, a tough decision had to be made: do we run this on a live production server directly without testing? We didn't have time for testing anyway; we were already down. So, we gathered around, said a prayer, and hit the execute button on SQL Server Management Studio.

The settings property ran fine. The server decreased from 100 percent CPU usage to 30 percent. The I/O usage also came down to 40 percent. We went live again. We were saved that day!

## Accessing the Use of Profile Provider

aspnet_Profile_GetProperties is another settings property that is called on every page load and web service call because we use Profile provider extensively. It is called whenever you access properties on Profile object (see Example 8-14).

*Example 8-14. aspnet_Profile_GetProperties is called whenever you try to access Profile object in Context*

```
CREATE PROCEDURE [dbo].[aspnet_Profile_GetProperties]
    @ApplicationName        nvarchar(256),
    @UserName
nvarchar(256),
    @CurrentTimeUtc         datetime
AS
BEGIN
    DECLARE @ApplicationId uniqueidentifier
    SELECT @ApplicationId = NULL
    SELECT @ApplicationId = ApplicationId
            FROM dbo.aspnet_Applications
                    WHERE LOWER(@ApplicationName) = LoweredApplicationName
    IF (@ApplicationId IS NULL)

        RETURN

    DECLARE @UserId uniqueidentifier
    SELECT @UserId = NULL

    SELECT @UserId = UserId
    FROM   dbo.aspnet_Users
    WHERE ApplicationId = @ApplicationId
            AND LoweredUserName =
                    LOWER(@UserName)

    IF (@UserId IS NULL)

        RETURN
    SELECT TOP 1 PropertyNames, PropertyValuesString, PropertyValuesBinary
    FROM        dbo.aspnet_Profile
```

*Example 8-14. aspnet_Profile_GetProperties is called whenever you try to access Profile object in Context (continued)*

```
    WHERE        UserId = @UserId

    IF (@@ROWCOUNT > 0)
    BEGIN

        UPDATE dbo.aspnet_Users

        SET    LastActivityDate=@CurrentTimeUtc

        WHERE UserId = @UserId
    END
END
```

Example 8-15 shows aspnet_Profile_GetProperties's statistics.

*Example 8-15. aspnet_Profile_GetProperties's statistics*

```
Table 'aspnet_Applications'. Scan count 1, logical reads 2, physical reads 0,
                     read-ahead reads 0, lob logical reads 0, lob physical
                         reads 0, lob read-ahead reads
                                 0.

(1 row(s) affected)
Table 'aspnet_Users'. Scan count 1, logical reads 4, physical reads 0,
                     read-ahead reads 0, lob logical reads 0, lob physical
                         reads 0, lob read-ahead reads
                                 0.

(1 row(s) affected)

(1 row(s) affected)
Table 'aspnet_Profile'. Scan count 0, logical reads 3, physical reads 0,
                     read-ahead reads 0, lob logical reads 0, lob physical
                         reads 0, lob read-ahead reads
                                 0.

(1 row(s) affected)
Table 'aspnet_Users'. Scan count 0, logical reads 27, physical reads 0,
                     read-ahead reads 0, lob logical reads 0, lob physical
                         reads 0, lob read-ahead reads
                                 0.

(1 row(s) affected)

(1 row(s) affected)
```

First it does a SELECT on aspnet_application to find the application ID from the application name. You can easily replace this with a hardcoded application ID inside the settings property and save one SELECT that happens on every call. Usually we run only one application on our production server, so there's no need to look up the application ID on every single call. ASP.NET Membership provider is built to support multiple applications on the same database, and as a result, all the tables and settings properties try to first identify the application and then do their job. It's a real waste of processing power and space when you have only one application on your database.

The I/O statistics may not look that bad, but from client statistics you can see how expensive it is (see Figure 8-2).

| Client Execution Time | 23:17:50 | | 23:17:41 | | |
|---|---|---|---|---|---|
| Query Profile Statistics | | | | | |
| Number of INSERT, DELETE and UPDATE statements | 2 | ↑ | 0 | → | 1.0000 |
| Rows affected by INSERT, DELETE, or UPDATE statem... | 1 | ↑ | 0 | → | 0.5000 |
| Number of SELECT statements | 10 | ↑ | 0 | → | 5.0000 |
| Rows returned by SELECT statements | 9 | ↑ | 0 | → | 4.5000 |
| Number of transactions | 2 | ↑ | 0 | → | 1.0000 |
| Network Statistics | | | | | |
| Number of server roundtrips | 4 | → | 4 | → | 4.0000 |
| TDS packets sent from client | 4 | → | 4 | → | 4.0000 |
| TDS packets received from server | 14 | ↑ | 4 | → | 9.0000 |
| Bytes sent from client | 574 | ↓ | 578 | → | 576.0000 |
| Bytes received from server | 43236 | ↑ | 169 | → | 21702.5000 |
| Time Statistics | | | | | |
| Client processing time | 15 | → | 15 | → | 15.0000 |
| Total execution time | 15 | → | 15 | → | 15.0000 |
| Wait time on server replies | 0 | → | 0 | → | 0.0000 |

Figure 8-2. GetProperties's client statistics taken from SQL Server Management Studio—you can turn on Include Client Statistics from the Query menu

Now look at the last block where the aspnet_users table is updated with LastActivityDate. This is the most expensive block. Figure 8-3 shows the cost of that line is 82 percent compared to the cost of the whole settings property.

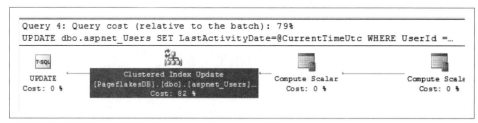

Figure 8-3. The cost of a single UPDATE statement is 82 percent of the whole setting property's cost. The query plan is generated from SQL Server Management Studio by turning on Include Actual Execution Plan from Query menu.

The update is done to ensure Profile provider remembers when the last time a user's profile was accessed. We do not need to do this on every single page load and web service call, perhaps just when a user first logs in or logs out. In our case, many web services are called while user is still on the page (the only page—the Start page). So, we can easily remove the UPDATE statement to save a costly update on the giant aspnet_users table on every single web service call that needs the Profile object.

## Using Email for a Username

The Membership class has a method—CreateUser—that can be used to create user accounts. You can specify anything in the username and password fields as long as it satisfies the password policy defined in *web.config*. This function creates an entry in both aspnet_users and aspnet_membership tables.

---

## Real-Life: Troubleshooting Using Email for a Username

Problem: Using email as a username broke the password recovery option.

Solution: Include the email address during account creation.

In Dropthings, we use an email address as the username in the ASP.NET 2.0/3.5 Membership provider. During signup, a user account is created using the Membership.CreateUser function (see Example 8-16).

*Example 8-16. Creating user using Membership class*

```
Membership.CreateUser( email, password );
```

However, users started complaining:

> Hi,
>
> I got the email invitation. I went to your site and tried login, and it said the username or password is wrong. So, I tried Signup. Signup said my username was already taken. Then I went to forgot password to retrieve the password. It shows something is wrong and the password email cannot be sent.
>
> I am stuck. Please help!

Here's the problem. When we use the code in Example 8-16, it creates a row in aspnet_users table using the email address as the username. But in the aspnet_membership table, the row it creates contains null in the email column. Therefore, the user cannot use the "forgot password" option to request the password because the email address is null. So, we had to run the SQL shown in Example 8-17 to fix it. This code sets the user's email address in the aspnet_membership table from the username field in aspnet_users table.

*Example 8-17. Cleaning up users' invalid email addresses*

```
update aspnet_membership
set email = (select username from aspnet_users
            where applicationID = '...'
            and userID = aspnet_membership.userID)
,loweredemail = (select loweredusername from aspnet_users
            where applicationid = '...'
            and userid = aspnet_membership.userID)
```

*Example 8-17. Cleaning up users' invalid email addresses (continued)*

```
where loweredemail is null and
applicationID = '...'
```

However, the `applicationID` is something that you need to specify for your own application. You can find the ID from `aspnet_application` table.

To fix this problem we then added the email address as the third parameter to the `CreateUser` function. See Example 8-18.

*Example 8-18. The Proper way of creating user account using Membership class*

```
Membership.CreateUser( email, password, email );
```

We had not noticed that this overloaded function had created users accounts in the `aspnet_membership` table, which had the email address set to `null`. Unless you specify the email address while creating new user accounts, a user cannot use the "forgot password" option to get his password emailed to him.

## Changing a Username in the ASP.NET 2.0/3.5 Membership Provider

`Profile.UserName` is a read-only field. So, how do you change a username? This is an important capability when a user wants to change his email address, which, in turn, changes his username. Although there is no way with Membership provider to change the username of a user, there is a workaround (see Example 8-19):

1. Create a new user using the new email address.
2. Get the password of the old account and set it to the new account. If you can't get the old password via Membership provider (the password is hashed), then ask the user for the password.
3. Create a new profile for the new user account.
4. Copy all the properties from the old profile to the new profile object.
5. Log out the user from the old account.
6. Auto log in to the new account.

*Example 8-19. Changing a username from code*

```
if (Profile.UserName != newUserName)
{
  // Changing email address of user. Delete current user account and create
  // a new one using the new email address but the same password
  if (null != Membership.GetUser(newUserName))
    throw new ApplicationException("There's another user with the same email. Please enter
    a different email.");

  MembershipUser newUser = Membership.CreateUser(newUserName, currentPassword);
```

*Example 8-19. Changing a username from code (continued)*

```
// Create profile for the new user and copy all values from current profile
// to new profile

ProfileCommon newProfile = ProfileCommon.Create(newUserName, true) as ProfileCommon;
newProfile.IsInvited = Profile.IsInvited;
newProfile.IsRealUser = Profile.IsRealUser;
newProfile.Name = newUserName;
newProfile.Save( );

if (Membership.ValidateUser(newUserName, currentPassword))
{
  FormsAuthentication.SignOut( );
  Session.Abandon( );
  // Delete the old profile and user
  ProfileManager.DeleteProfile(Profile.UserName);
  Membership.DeleteUser(user.UserName);

  FormsAuthentication.RedirectFromLoginPage(newUserName, true);
}
}
```

You can also go directly to the aspnet_membership and aspnet_users tables and change the LoweredUserName, UserName, Email, and LoweredEmail fields if you want. But that's an unsupported way of doing it. If the table schema changes in a later version of Membership provider, your code will break. The best way to do it is to use Membership provider's own functions.

## Rendering Page Parts As JavaScript

A giant page full of HTML works best if the whole page can be cached on the browser. You can do this by using HTTP response caching headers, either by injecting them manually or by using the @OutputCache tag directive on ASPX pages:

```
<%@ OutputCache Location="Client" Duration="86400" VaryByParam="*" VaryByHeader="*"
%>
```

But this caches the entire page on the browser for one day. If you have a page with static and dynamic parts, you cannot use this output caching at page level. Generally, the header, logo, left-side navigation menu, and footer are static parts. Sometimes there are many static sections in the body part that do not change frequently. All these, when combined, take up a significant amount of download time. Users have to download the entire page again and again when a significant part never changes. If you could cache those static parts on the browser, you could save a lot of bytes every time the page downloads. If the whole page size is 50 KB, at least 20 KB is static and 30 KB might be dynamic. If you can use the page fragment's client-side caching (not ASP.NET's server-side page output cache), you can save 40 percent in download time easily. Moreover, no request is sent to the server for those static parts because they are already cached on the browser. Thus, the server doesn't have to process the giant page at every load.

ASP.NET offers page fragment caching using @Outputcache, which is good, but that caching is on the server side. It caches the output of user controls and serves them from the server-side cache. But you cannot eliminate the download of those costly bytes. It just saves some CPU power on the server, which doesn't have much benefit for users.

The only way to cache part of the page is to allow the browser to download those parts separately and make those parts cacheable just like images, CSS, or JavaScript. So, we need to download page fragments separately and cache them on the browser's cache. IFrame is an easy way to do this, but it makes the page heavy and does not follow the parent's page CSS. Inside IFrame, you need to download Ajax frameworks again along with any other JavaScript that you might need. Although the download can be fast because files are coming from the cache, downloading the whole framework and lots of JavaScript again will put significant stress on the browser.

There is a better way: use JavaScript to render the content of the page; that JavaScript will get cached on the browser's cache. Here's the idea:

1. Split the whole page into multiple parts.
2. Generate page content using JavaScript. Each cacheable part is JavaScript, which is then rendered to HTML.
3. Cache the cacheable parts with the browser so they aren't downloaded again (until the user does a hard refresh or clear cache). The parts that are non-cachable and change frequently do not get cached by the browser. Consider the page layout shown in Figure 8-4.

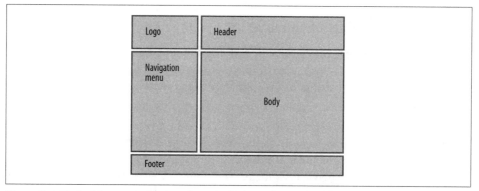

Figure 8-4. Typical homepage layout where the body section is dynamic and the header, footer, left menu, and logo are static

Because only the body section is dynamic, the rest of the page is fully cacheable. So, the *Default.aspx* that renders this whole page looks like Example 8-20.

Example 8-20. Default.aspx with cacheable parts

```
<%@ Page Language="VB" AutoEventWireup="false" %>
<%@ OutputCache NoStore="true" Location="None" %>
```

*Example 8-20. Default.aspx with cacheable parts (continued)*

```
<!DOCTYPE html PUBLIC "-//W3C//DTD XHTML 1.0 Transitional//EN" "http://www.w3.org/TR/
xhtml1/DTD/xhtml1-transitional.dtd">
<html xmlns="http://www.w3.org/1999/xhtml" >
<head runat="server">
<title>My Big Fat Page</title>
</head>
<body>
<form id="form1" runat="server">
<table width="100%" border="1">
  <tr>
  <td>Some logo here</td>
  <td><script id="Script1" src="Header.aspx" type="text/javascript"></script></td>
  </tr>
  <tr>
  <td><script id="LeftMenu" src="LeftMenu.aspx" type="text/javascript"></script></td>
  <td bgcolor="lightgrey">
  <div>This is the dynamic part which gets changed on every load.
  Check out the time whenit was generated: <%= DateTime.Now %></div></td>
  </tr>
  <tr>
  <td colspan="2">
  <script id="Footer" src="Footer.aspx" type="text/javascript"></script>
  </td>
  </tr>
</table>
</form>
</body>
</html>
```

The output looks like Figure 8-5.

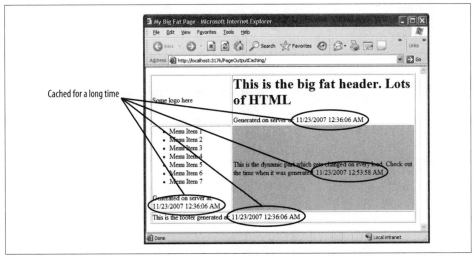

*Figure 8-5. Caching parts of a page on a browser eliminates downloading static blocks. For example, the header, left menu, and footer do not change much, so they are cached on repeat visit, but the body part is delivered fresh from the server on every visit.*

The cached parts are 30 minutes older because the browser has not downloaded them at all and saved a significant amount of data transfer. Only the body part was downloaded from the server.

On the first visit, the page parts are downloaded one after another, as you see on Figure 8-6.

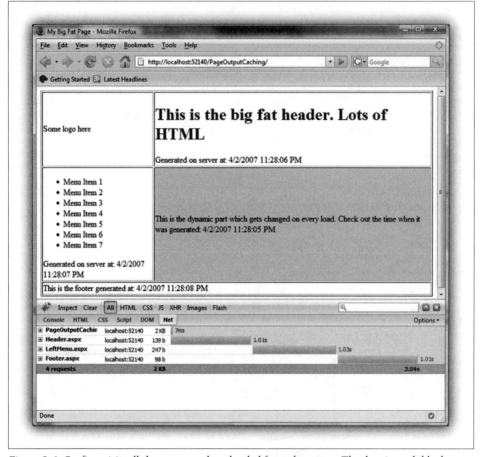

*Figure 8-6. On first visit, all the parts are downloaded from the server. The date in each block shows the same date time, which means it was just delivered from the server. Look at the time it took to download each block; the total page download time was three seconds.*

But on second visit, only the *Default.aspx* downloads and the parts are instantly loaded from cache. Figure 8-7 shows the instant loading of different cached parts of the page.

The download time for the parts is between 5 and 7 ms the second time, compared to the first time where each of them took more than 1 second to download. This shows you how fast the second visit is with cached page parts.

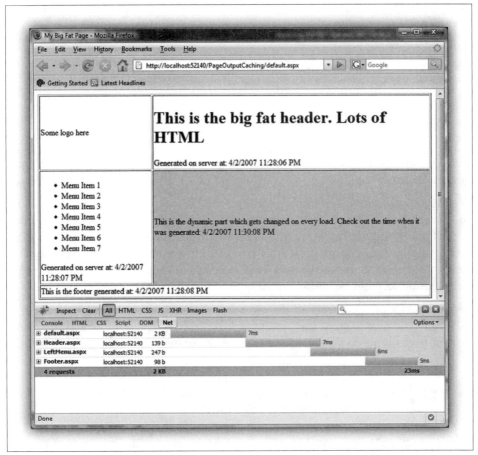

*Figure 8-7. On second visit, the cached parts are served from browser cache instantly. So, the total downloaded bytes are only for the Default.aspx, not for the smaller parts of the page. Therefore, the download time is reduced significantly and the second visit becomes blazingly fast.*

Let's look at one of the files named *Header.aspx* in Example 8-21, which gets cached.

*Example 8-21. The cached Header.aspx; notice the ContentType is the only change compared to a standard ASPX page*

```
<%@ Page Language="C#" AutoEventWireup="false" ContentType="text/html/javascript" %>
<%@ OutputCache Location="Client" Duration="86400" VaryByParam="*" VaryByHeader="*" %>
<!DOCTYPE html PUBLIC "-//W3C//DTD XHTML 1.0 Transitional//EN" "http://www.w3.org/TR/
xhtml1/DTD/xhtml1-transitional.dtd">
<html xmlns="http://www.w3.org/1999/xhtml" >
<head runat="server">
    <title>This is the big fat header</title>
</head>
<body>
```

*Example 8-21. The cached Header.aspx; notice the ContentType is the only change compared to a standard ASPX page (continued)*

```
    <form id="form1" runat="server">
    <div>
    <h1>This is the big fat header. Lots of HTML</h1>
    Generated on server at: <%= DateTime.Now %>
    </div>
    </form>
</body>
</html>
```

The content type has been set to *text/html/javascript*, which is something that must be done by hand.

When you put an ASPX inside a `Script` tag, it doesn't work because `<script id="Script1" src="Header.aspx" type="text/javascript">` expects JavaScript output, not HTML output. If HTML output is provided, the browser simply ignores it. So, first of all, the *Header.aspx* must emit JavaScript instead of HTML in order to work on a `<script>` tag. Second, the JavaScript needs to render the *Header.aspx*'s HTML output using `document.writeln`.

An HTTP Module intercepts all the *.aspx* calls. When a page is ready to be sent to the browser, check to see if the content type is *text/html/javascript*. If it is, then convert the page output to a similar JavaScript representation.

 For details about HTTP Module and how to use the response filter to modify page output, please read this wonderful article: *http://www. aspnetresources.com/articles/HttpFilters.aspx.*

Create a response filter named *Html2JSPageFilter.cs* to override the response stream's `Write` method and convert the page's HTML to a JavaScript representation. So, ASP. NET gives you generated HTML, and you convert it to a JavaScript representation that renders the original HTML on the browser.

### Using HttpModule

You might wonder if you can use an HTTP handler to do this. For example, you need to intercept calls going to an *\*.aspx* extension that is handled by ASP.NET's default page handler, but you can't register another handler to the same extension. In this situation, you need to use `HttpModule`, which intercepts any incoming request to the ASP.NET pipeline. To do this, you:

1. Get the entire page output as HTML.
2. Filter out what is inside the `<form>` tag. ASP.NET always generates a `<form>` tag, and the content of the page is available inside of that (see Example 8-22).

*Example 8-22. Getting the generated HTML from the ASPX page and parsing out the content inside the <form> tag*

```
public override void Write(byte[] buffer, int offset, int count)
{
  string strBuffer = System.Text.UTF8Encoding.UTF8.GetString (buffer, offset, count);

  // ---------------------------------
  // Wait for the closing </html> tag
  // ---------------------------------
  Regex eof = new Regex ("</html>", RegexOptions.IgnoreCase);

  if (!eof.IsMatch (strBuffer))
  {
    responseHtml.Append (strBuffer);
  }
  else
  {
    responseHtml.Append (strBuffer);
    string  finalHtml = responseHtml.ToString ();

    // extract only the content inside the form tag tag ASP.NET generates in all .aspx
    int formTagStart = finalHtml.IndexOf("<form");
    int formTagStartEnd = finalHtml.IndexOf('>', formTagStart);
    int formTagEnd = finalHtml.LastIndexOf("</form>");

    string pageContentInsideFormTag = finalHtml.Substring(formTagStartEnd + 1, formTagEnd
    - formTagStartEnd - 1);
```

3. Remove the ViewState hidden field, otherwise it will conflict with the ViewState on the *Default.aspx* (the default page already has its own ViewState). So, the ViewState <input> tag cannot be sent again to the browser. This means you cannot use Control, which uses ViewState and is one shortcoming of this approach. Generally, cached parts are static content, so there should not be much need for ViewState anyway (see Example 8-23).

*Example 8-23. Removing the ViewState <input> field so that it does not conflict with Default.aspx page's ViewState*

```
Regex re = new Regex("(<input.*?__VIEWSTATE.*?/>)",RegexOptions.IgnoreCase);
pageContentInsideFormTag = re.Replace(pageContentInsideFormTag, string.Empty);
```

4. Convert the entire HTML output to a JavaScript string format. The string contains an escaped HTML that can be set as innerHTML or can be used inside the document.write('') statement (see Example 8-24).

*Example 8-24. Convert the HTML output to a JavaScript string representation and eliminate new lines, spaces, apostrophes, etc. The resulting string can be set to an element's innerHTML or it can be passed to document.write.*

```
string javascript2Html =
  pageContentInsideFormTag.Replace("\r", "")
  .Replace("\n", "")
```

*Example 8-24. Convert the HTML output to a JavaScript string representation and eliminate new lines, spaces, apostrophes, etc. The resulting string can be set to an element's innerHTML or it can be passed to document.write. (continued)*

```
.Replace("      ", " ")
.Replace("   ", " ")
.Replace("    ", " ")
.Replace("\\", "\\\\")
.Replace("'", "\\'");
```

5. Emit document.write, which writes the JavaScript string to the browser. The HTML is added to the page content (see Example 8-25).

*Example 8-25. Generate a document.write statement that will write the HTML on the browser*

```
string pageOutput = "document.write('" + javascript2Html + "');";
byte[] data = System.Text.UTF8Encoding.UTF8.GetBytes (pageOutput);
responseStream.Write (data, 0, data.Length);
```

That's pretty much the trick. Use a response filter to get the *.aspx* output, then convert it to a JavaScript representation. Use document.write to render the HTML on the browser DOM and get that JavaScript cached. For convenience, an HttpModule is used here to hook into the ASP.NET pipeline and wait for *.aspx* files to emit *text/html/javascript* content. Then hook the response filter into the ASP.NET request pipeline.

### The HttpModule in detail

The HttpModule is very simple. It hooks the context's ReleaseRequestState event, which is fired when the page output is ready to be sent to the browser. Inside the event handler, the response filter is called to convert the HTML to a JavaScript representation (see Example 8-26).

*Example 8-26. HttpModule hooks the response filter and intercepts the page render*

```
void IHttpModule.Init(HttpApplication context)
{
  context.ReleaseRequestState += new EventHandler(InstallResponseFilter);
}

private void InstallResponseFilter(object sender, EventArgs e)
{
 HttpResponse response = HttpContext.Current.Response;

 if (response.ContentType == "text/html/javascript")
 {
   response.ContentType = "text/javascript";
   response.Filter = new Html2JSPageFilter(response.Filter);
 }
}
```

Finally, the module is registered in *web.config* by adding an entry in the
`<httpModules>` section (see Example 8-27).

*Example 8-27. Registering the web.config entry*

```
<httpModules>
  <add name="Html2JSModule" type="Html2JavascriptModule" />
</httpModules>
```

You can use this approach in your *.aspx* files and save a significant amount of download time on the user's end. Although it slightly increases the first-time visit download—it takes an average of 200 ms for each script tag on network roundtrip—it makes the second-time visit a breeze. See the performance difference yourself: visit *www.pageflakes.com* and let the site load fully. Then close your browser, open it, and enter the URL again. See how fast it loads second time. If you use a HTTP debugger to monitor how much data is transferred, you will see that it takes only 10 to 12 KBs the second time, compared to about 400 KB on first time. All the page fragments are cached on the browser's cache and require no download time on subsequent visits as long as the cache doesn't expire.

# ASP.NET Production Challenges

Now we will look at two ASP.NET-related production challenges: solving the authentication cookie problem on web farms and changing hosting providers while your site is publicly available.

## Fixing Cookie Authentication Problems

When you turn on a web garden or create a multiserver load balance deployment where many servers are serving the same web site, you will have forms authentication problems. Users will frequently be automatically logged out or see the "yellow screen of death" (the ASP.NET error page). This happens because ASP.NET encrypts the login information in a cookie, but the encryption key is unique for each machine and process in the web garden. If a user hits server No. 1 and gets an encrypted key, and the next hit goes to server No. 2, it will fail to decrypt the cookie and log the user out or throw the user an ASP.NET general error message.

This is what Stefan Schackow on the Microsoft ASP.NET AJAX team said:

> In order to prevent this on your production server, you need to remember this before you go live:

> The reasons for a forms auth ticket failing are normally that either the validation key or the decryption key are not in sync across all servers in a web farm. Another potential reason can be if both ASP.NET 1.1 and ASP.NET 2.0 applications are issuing forms auth tickets with the same domain and path.

For the first case, setting the validationKey and decryptionKey attributes explicitly on <machineKey /> on each web server will solve the problem.

For the second case, setting the validationKey and decryptionKey attributes explicitly in <machineKey /> for *both* the ASP.NET 1.1 and ASP.NET 2.0 applications is necessary. Additionally on the ASP.NET 2.0 apps, the "decryption" attribute in <machineKey /> should be set to "3DES".

Example 8-28 shows how the *machine.config* should look.

*Example 8-28. Configuring machine.config with fixed validation keys in all servers*

```
<system.web>
<processModel autoConfig="true"/>
<machineKey validationKey="..." decryptionKey="..." validation="SHA1"/>
```

You need to introduce the <machineKey> in the <system.web> node if it doesn't already exist. Be sure to back up *machine.config* before making such change. If you make any mistake here, none of the web applications on the server will run properly.

### Generating the key

How do you generate the machine key? You need to use a utility to produce the key for your PC. I have made a tool that can generate such keys for you. Example 8-29 shows how you run it.

*Example 8-29. Running the security key generator*

```
SecurityKey.exe 24 64
```

Download the tool from *http://omar.mvps.org/pics/SecurityKey.exe*.

The two parameters in the download are the length of the security keys—the validation key and decryption key, respectively. They need to be exactly the same as specified in the example.

### Each machine requires a key

You have put the same machine keys in all the web servers in your production environment, but event logs show users are still having a problem. You've restarted IIS and all your servers, but you still see lots of event log error entries that show users are getting the dreaded "Forms authentication failed for the request. Reason: The ticket supplied was invalid." So, what did you do wrong? You call Microsoft support and go to the forums looking for solutions, but everyone says what you did was correct.

Here's what you need to do: wait. Wait for two or three days until all those users come back to your web site at least once. Many users will have a cookie encrypted with the previously assigned encryption key pair. Naturally, it will fail to decrypt with the new key pair you have just specified in *machine.config*. Until all those users get a new key, you will keep having the error message. So, every returning user will get the error once after the *machine.config* change. Don't be alarmed if you see this randomly happening even after one week or a month. This just means some user visited you after a long time.

# Redirecting Traffic from an Old Web Site to a New One

When you change hosting providers, you get new a IP for your servers. If you change your DNS configuration for your site to the new IP, it takes about four days to propagate through all the ISPs. During this time, users will hit the old IP, get no response, and assume the site is down. So, we need a way to redirect users to the new IP when they go to the old one.

## Real-Life: Avoiding Downtime When Switching Hosting Providers

Problem: Changing hosting providers threatens the user experience and costs you money.

Solution: Redirect traffic to an intermittent subdomain.

At Pageflakes, we had all sorts of problems with our hosting providers and, at one point, had changed hosting providers almost once every four months. So, we had to come up with a solution that works transparently and without any downtime. Here's what we do:

1. Map a new subdomain, such as *new.pageflakes.com*, to the new server IP. Then we create a new web site (not virtual directory) on the old web server called *Redirector*. It maps to a folder that has nothing but *global.asax* and *web.config* (see Figure 8-8).

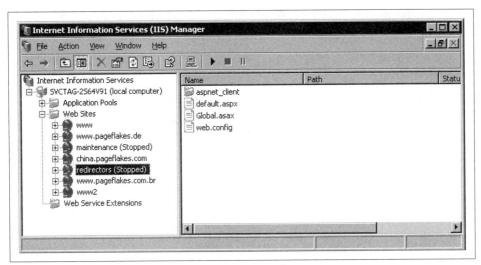

*Figure 8-8. Setup a Redirector web site on an old server that forwards users to the new server*

2. Go to *Redirector*, navigate to Web site Properties → Home Directory → Configuration, and map ASP.NET to receive all web requests. This includes all URLs, including *.html*, *.gif*, *.css*, and *.js*, etc. (see Figure 8-9).

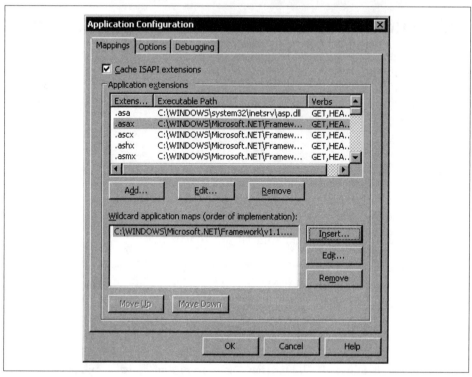

*Figure 8-9. Configure ASP.NET to receive all requests including requests for .html files*

3. Write the code in Example 8-30 to *Global.asax*, which redirects all traffic to the new server.

*Example 8-30. In Global.asax, theApplication_BeginRequest intercepts all calls and redirects users to the new server*

```
protected void Application_BeginRequest(Object sender, EventArgs e)
{
    string url = HttpContext.Current.Request.Url.AbsolutePath;
    string QueryParams = HttpContext.Current.Request.QueryString.ToString( );
    if (QueryParams != "") {
      Response.Redirect("http://new.pageflakes.com" + url + "?"+ QueryParams);
    } else {
        Response.Redirect("http://new.pageflakes.com" + url );
    }
}
```

Now, anyone trying to go to *www.pageflakes.com/aboutus.html* is redirected to *new.pageflakes.com/aboutus.html*. The Redirector keeps the query string and logical path intact. So, complicated URLs like *www.pageflakes.com/something/somefile.html?someparam=somevalue* are converted nicely.

4. Stop the default web site that is listening to port 80 and turn the Redirector web site on. Before you turn off the default web site, ensure the new server is already up and running on the new subdomain. Change the DNS and map the new server's IP to your main domain site (e.g., www.pageflakes.com).

So, users that still have the old IP in their DNS cache go to the old server and are redirected to the new server. But after a while, when their DNS cache is refreshed and they get the new IP, their requests go to the new server and no redirection is required. After four or five days, you can safely bring down the old server.

# Summary

In this chapter, you have learned about some best practices for working with ASP. NET 2.0/3.5 Membership and Profile providers. You have seen how some tweaking of their configurations can greatly improve request throughput. Moreover, you have learned how to optimize some of the key stored procedures for ASP.NET Membership and Profile providers and tailor them to your specific needs. We reviewed some caching strategies to break pages into smaller parts and eliminate the repeated download of static parts. Finally, you have learned two production challenges that can be solved with ASP.NET. In the next chapter, we will focus more on client-side performance and talk about many advanced caching strategies that can add a significant boost to Ajax web sites.

# CHAPTER 9

# Improving Client-Side Performance

There are three major reasons for an Ajax site to slow down: large amount of content loaded in one single page, frequent web service calls, and repeated web service calls. Unless these three reasons are handled effectively, the site becomes slow to load and feels sluggish to use. However, intelligent caching can solve both problems. Besides caching, there are some browser-specific issues and design decisions that need to be made for a smoother user experience after the whole page is loaded. In this chapter, you will learn some advanced caching techniques, how to load pages progressively, and how to give the browser a chance to render content in a fast and smooth way.

## Understanding Web Caching

Let's get into the details of the various ways to make web caching work in your favor. Web caching needs careful thinking and planning. Sometimes it requires architectural changes to make various parts of the site cacheable. In this section, we will discuss in detail how web caching works and how it can be used for a faster download experience. If you plan your site well, caches can help your web site load faster and reduce the load on your server and Internet link. The difference can be dramatic—a site that is difficult to cache may take several seconds to load, while one that takes advantage of caching can seem instantaneous in comparison. Users will appreciate a fast-loading site and will visit more often.

## Basics of Web Caching

Web caches preserve a local version of responses served from origin servers to the client browser. The web cache keeps track of responses served for specific URL requests, and if there are instructions to store the response in the cache, it remembers them for a certain period. Next time when the same URL is requested, the web cache intercepts the request and returns the stored response from its storage (cached response) to the client browser.

Web caching has three benefits:

*Reduces latency between request and response*
> Because content is served from the local store, there's no need to go to the origin server to fetch the response. The delay between the request and response is always lower than making a call to the origin server.

*Saves network bandwidth*
> The response is served from the web cache, not from the origin server. If your proxy acts as the web cache, then there's no data transfer between your proxy and origin server. If your browser acts as the web cache, then there's no network activity at all.

*Reduces server load*
> The origin server doesn't have to execute the request and produce the response for the same request repeatedly.

## Types of Web Caches

There are a number of web caches.

*Browser caches*
> The browser cache is the fastest cache of all because the response is stored right on your computer. All modern browsers have finite storage dedicated for cache, usually about 100 MB. This means the browser can store 100 MB worth of data locally on a user's computer and not request it again from the origin server. However, this 100 MB is shared among all the web sites user visits. So, you need to only store critical information that is accessed frequently and takes the most download time, e.g., ASP.NET AJAX Framework JavaScript files.

*Proxy caches*
> Proxies serve hundreds or thousands of users in the same way and large corporations and ISPs often set them up behind their firewalls or as standalone devices (also known as intermediaries).
>
> Proxy caches are a type of shared cache. This means if you have five users coming from the same proxy, the content is delivered to the proxy from the origin server just once for the first user hitting the site. For the other users, the content is served directly from the proxy server although it may be their very first visit to your site.

*Gateway caches*
> Gateway caches are deployed by webmasters in the user's network and the origin server. They are not part of your production environment nor are they part of end user's network. They work as intermediaries between user (or proxy servers) and origin server. Requests are routed to gateway caches by a number of methods, but typically some form of load balancer is used to make one or more of them look like the origin server to clients.

Content delivery networks (CDNs) have cache servers in many different locations. Whenever a client requests a resource that is cached by a CDN, the request goes to nearest server, which saves network roundtrip time and delivers the resource faster. Moreover, CDNs have very high-speed networks optimized to deliver content as fast as possible. So, storing content on the CDN significantly increases site load time.

## Web Cache Problems

When you implement effective caching, users don't hit your site like they used to. This means you are being hit less than you should be, so you get an inaccurate traffic report.

Another concern is that caches can serve out-of-date or stale content. Caching requires very careful planning or your users will see old content instead of what you want to serve them. You will learn how to control caching and make sure this does not happen in the upcoming section "Controlling Response Cache."

## How Web Caches Work

Web caches work based on the following conditions:

- If the response's headers tell the cache not to keep it, it won't. The "no cache" mode is the default. But sometimes proxies and browsers cache content if there's no explicit cache header present.
- If the request is authenticated or secure, it won't be cached. HTTPS content is never cached.
- A cached representation is considered fresh (that is, able to be sent to a client without checking with the origin server) if:
  — It has an expiry time or other age-controlling header set but is still within the fresh period.
  — If a browser cache has recently cached the content but does not need to check it until the next launch.
  — If a proxy cache has seen the content recently but it was modified a relatively long time ago.
- Cached content is directly served from the web cache. There's no communication between origin and client.
- If a cached content has become stale, the web cache will forward the request to the origin server transparently and serve fresh content from origin server. The client browser will not notice what the web cache is doing. It will only experience a delay.

Details about how HTTP 1.1 caching works can be found in RFC 2616: Hypertext Transfer Protocol Section 14.9 (*http://www.w3.org/Protocols/rfc2616/rfc2616-sec14.html#sec14.9*).

## Controlling Response Cache

You can define caching at the server level (through IIS Administration) or at the page level using some special tags in the HTML files. With dynamic content, you have complete control on how and when to cache a particular response.

### HTML metatags and HTTP headers

HTML authors can put *metatags* in a document's <HEAD> section that describe its attributes. Besides describing what's in the content, metatags can be used to cache pages or prevent pages from being cached.

Metatags are easy to use, but aren't very effective because they're only honored by a few browser caches (which actually read the HTML), not proxy caches (which almost never read the HTML in the document). You can put a Pragma: no-cache metatag into a web page, but it won't necessarily prevent it from being cached because an intermediate proxy might be caching the page.

 If your site is hosted at an ISP or hosting farm but they don't give you the ability to set arbitrary HTTP headers (like Expires and Cache-Control), you will not be able to implement caching effectively.

### Cache control in response header

*HTTP headers* give you a lot more control over how browser caches and proxies handle your representations compared to metatags. HTTP headers are not part of the response body and thus not available in the HTML and are usually automatically generated by the web server. However, you can control them to some degree, depending on the server you use.

HTTP headers are sent by the server before the HTML and are only seen by the browser and any intermediate caches. Typical HTTP 1.1 response headers might look like Example 9-1.

*Example 9-1. Example of response header that says the response should be cached*

```
HTTP/1.1 200 OK
Date: Fri, 30 Oct 1998 13:19:41 GMT
Server: IIS 6.0Cache-Control: max-age=3600, must-revalidate
Expires: Fri, 30 Oct 1998 14:19:41 GMT
Last-Modified: Mon, 29 Jun 1998 02:28:12 GMT
ETag: "3e86-410-3596fbbc"
Content-Length: 1040
Content-Type: text/html
```

The Cache-Control, Expires, Last-Modified, and ETag headers are responsible for controlling how to cache the entire response.

### Pragma HTTP headers

Many people believe that assigning a Pragma: no-cache HTTP header to a HTTP response will make it uncacheable. This is not necessarily true, because the HTTP specification does not set guidelines for Pragma response headers, but instead Pragma request headers (the headers that a browser sends to a server). Although a few caches may honor this header, the majority won't, and it won't have any effect.

### Controlling caches with the Expires HTTP header

The Expires HTTP header is a basic way to control caches; it tells all caches how long the response can be stored in cache. After the expiry date, browsers will ignore what's on the cache and make a call to the origin server to get the fresh content. Expires headers are supported by practically every cache.

Most web servers allow you to set the expiration in a number of ways. Commonly, they will allow setting an absolute time to expire, the last time that the client saw the representation (last *access time*), or the last time a document changed on your server (last *modification time*).

---

### Using the Expires Header for Static Content

The Expires header is especially good for making static images (like navigation bars and buttons) cacheable. Because it doesn't change much, you can set an extremely long expiration time on it, making your site appear much more responsive to your users. It is also useful for controlling the caching of a page that is regularly changed. For instance, if you update a news page once a day at 6 a.m., you can set the representation to expire at that time so caches will know when to get a fresh copy, without users having to hit reload.

---

The only value valid in an Expires header is a HTTP date—anything else will most likely be interpreted as "in the past," so that the response is uncacheable. Also, remember that the time in a HTTP date is Greenwich Mean Time (GMT), not local time.

For example:

```
Expires: Fri, 30 Oct 1998 14:19:41 GMT
```

Although the Expires header is useful, it has some limitations. First, because there's a date involved, the clocks on the web server and the cache must be synchronized. If they aren't, the intended results won't be achieved and the caches might wrongly consider stale content as fresh.

---

If you use the Expires header, it's important to make sure that your web server's clock is accurate. One way is to use the Network Time Protocol (NTP, *http://www.ntp.org/*)—talk to your system administrator to find out more. On Windows servers, you can configure the server to check the time synchronization services on the Web and update its clock.

Another problem with absolute Expires is that it's easy to forget that you've set some content to expire at a particular time. Although you change the expiration date to some other date, some browser are still going to request the content on a previously set date because they have already received the response with the previous expiration date.

## Cache-control HTTP headers

HTTP 1.1 introduced a new class of headers, Cache-Control response headers, to give web publishers more control over their content and to address the limitations of Expires.

Useful Cache-Control response headers include:

max-age=[seconds]
> Specifies the maximum amount of time that a response will be considered fresh. Similar to Expires, this directive is relative to the time of the request, rather than absolute. [seconds] is the number of seconds from the time of the request you wish the response to be cached for.

s-maxage=[seconds]
> Similar to max-age, except that it applies only to shared (e.g., proxy) caches.

public
> Indicates that the response *may* be cached by any cache (if max-age is not specified), even if it normally would be noncacheable or cacheable only within a non-shared cache.

private
> Indicates that all or part of the response message is intended for a single user and *must not* be cached by a shared cache. This allows an origin server to state that the specified parts of the response are intended for only one user and are not a valid response for requests by other users. A private (nonshared) cache *may* cache the response unless max-age is defined.

no-cache
> Forces caches to submit the request to the origin server for validation before releasing a cached copy, every time. This is useful to ensure that authentication is respected (in combination with public) or to maintain rigid freshness, without sacrificing all of the benefits of caching.

`no-store`

Instructs caches not to keep a copy of the representation under any conditions.

`must-revalidate`

If this header is not present, the browser sometimes return cached responses that have already expired on some special occasion, e.g., when the browser's back button is pressed. When the response has expired, this header instructs the browser to fetch fresh content no matter what.

`proxy-revalidate`

Similar to `must-revalidate`, except that it applies only to proxy caches.

For example:

```
Cache-Control: public, max-age=3600, must-revalidate, proxy-revalidate
```

This header tells the browser and proxy servers to cache the content for one hour. After one hour, both the browser and proxy must fetch fresh content from the origin no matter what.

### ETag, last-modified headers

The `Cache-control` header allows you to set the duration of the cache. Once the browser or proxy caches the content for that duration, they won't make a call to the origin regardless of whether the content has changed or not. So, if you have set a piece of JavaScript to be cached for seven days, no matter how many times you change that JavaScript, the browser and proxies that have already cached it for seven days will not ask for the latest JavaScript. This could be exactly what you want to do in some cases because you want content to be delivered from the cache instantly, but it isn't always a desired result.

Say you are delivering an RSS feed from your server to the browser. You have set the cache control to cache the feed for one day. However, the feed has already changed and users cannot see it because they are getting cached content no matter how many times they visit the site. So, you want to verify whether there's a new RSS feed available by hitting the server. If it is available, then fresh content should be downloaded. If not, then the response is served from the cache.

One way to do this is to use the `Last-Modified` header. When a cache has stored content that includes a `Last-Modified` header, it can use the `Last-Modified` header to ask the server if the content has changed since the last time it was fetched with an `If-Modified-Since` request. However, the `Last-Modified` header is applicable to content that is date-dependent. You cannot use the `Last-Modified` header unless you have timestamped your content.

HTTP 1.1 introduced a new tag called the *ETag* for better control over cache validations. ETags are unique identifiers that are generated by the server and changed every time the content is updated. Because the server controls how the ETag is generated, the server can check if the *ETag* matches when a `If-None-Match` request is made.

Browsers will send the *ETag* for a cached response to the server, and the server can check whether the content has changed or not. The server does this by using an algorithm to generate an *ETag* out of available content and seeing whether the *ETag* is the same as what the browser has sent. Some hashing of content can be used to generate the *ETag*. If the generated *ETag* does not match with the *ETag* that the browser sent, then the content has changed in between. The server can then decide to send the latest content to the browser.

In our previous example of caching an RSS feed, we can use the hash of the last item in the feed as an *ETag*. So, when the user requests the same feed again, the browser will make a call to the server and pass the last known *ETag*. On the server, you can download the RSS from the feed source (or generate it), check the hash of the last item, and compare it with *ETag*. If they match, then there's no change in the RSS feed, and you can return HTTP 304 to inform the browser to use cached content. Otherwise, you can return the freshly downloaded feeds to the browser.

## Principles for Making the Best Use of Cache

Now that you know how caching works and how to control it, here are some tips on how to make best use of cache.

*Use URLs consistently*

Browsers cache content based on the URL. When the URL changes, the browser fetches a new version from the origin server. The URL can be changed by changing the query string parameters. For example, if */default.aspx* is cached on the browser and you request */default.aspx?123*, it will fetch new content from the server. The response from the new URL can also be cached in the browser if you return the proper caching headers. In that case, changing the query parameter to something else like */default.aspx?456* will return new content from the server.

So, you need to make sure you use the URL consistently everywhere when you want to get the cached response. From the homepage, if you have requested a file with the URL */welcome.gif*, make sure you request the same file from another page using the same URL. One common mistake is to sometimes omit the "www" subdomain from the URL. *www.pageflakes.com/default.aspx* is not the same as *pageflakes.com/default.aspx*. Both will be cached separately.

*Cache static content for longer period*

Static files can be cached for longer period, like a month. If you are thinking that you could cache for couple of days and then change the file so users will pick it up sooner, you're mistaken. If you update a file that was cached by the Expires header, new users will immediately get the new file while old users will see the old content until it expires on their browser. So, as long as you are using the Expires header to cache static files, you should use as a high value as possible to cache the files for as long as possible.

For example, if you have set the Expires header to cache a file for three days, one user will get the file today and store it in cache for next three days. Another user will get the file tomorrow and cache it for three days after tomorrow. If you change the file on the day after tomorrow, the first user will see it on the fourth day and the second user will see it on he fifth day. So, different users will see different versions of the file. As a result, it does not help to set a lower value and assume all users will pick up the latest file soon. You will have to change the file's URL to ensure everyone gets the same exact file immediately.

You can set up the Expires header from static files in IIS Manager. You'll learn how to do this in the "How to Configure Static Content Caching in IIS" section later in this chapter.

*Use a cache-friendly folder structure*

Store cached content in a common folder. For example, store all images of your site in the */static* folder instead of storing images separately under different subfolders. This will help you use consistent URLs throughout the site because you can use */static/images/somefile.gif* from anywhere. It's easier to move to a CDN when you have static cacheable files under a common root folder (see the "Different Types of CDNs" section later in this chapter).

*Reuse common graphics files*

Sometimes we put common graphics files under several virtual directories to write smaller paths. For example, say you have *indicator.gif* in the root folder, in some subfolders, and in a CSS folder. You did it because you don't want to worry about paths from different places and can use the filename as a relative URL. This does not help with caching. Each copy of the file is cached in the browser separately. So, eliminate the duplicates, collect all of the graphics files in the whole solution, put them under the same root static folder, and use the same URL from all the pages and CSS files.

*Change filename when you want to expire a cache*

When you want to change a static file, don't just update the file because it's already cached in the user's browser. You need to change the filename and update all references everywhere so that the browser downloads the new file. You can also store the filenames in database or configuration files and use data binding to generate the URL dynamically. This way you can change the URL from one place and have the whole site receive the change immediately.

*Use a version number when accessing static files*

If you don't want to clutter your static folder with multiple copies of the same file, use a query string to differentiate versions of same file. For example, a GIF can be accessed with a dummy query string like */static/images/indicator.gif?v=1*. When you change the *indicator.gif*, you can overwrite the same file and update all references to the file to direct to */static/images/indicator.gif?v=2*. This way you can keep changing the same file again but just update the references to access the graphics using the new version number.

*Store cacheable files in a different domain*

It's always a good idea to put static contents into a different domain. First of all, the browser can open two additional concurrent connections to download the static files. Another benefit is that you don't need to send the cookies to the static files. When you put the static files on the same domain as your web application, the browser sends both the ASP.NET cookies and all other cookies that your web application is producing. This makes the request headers unnecessarily large and wastes bandwidth. You don't need to send these cookies to access the static files. So, if you put the static files in a different domain, those cookies will not be sent. For example, you could put your static files in the *www.static-content.com* domain while your web site is running on *www.dropthings.com*. The other domain doesn't need to be a completely different web site. It can just be an alias and share the same web application path.

*SSL is not cached, so minimize SSL use*

Any content that is served over SSL is not cached. So, you need to put static content outside SSL. Moreover, you should try limiting SSL to only secure pages like the login or payment page. The rest of the site should be outside SSL over regular HTTP. Because SSL encrypts requests and responses, it puts an extra load on the server. Encrypted content is also larger than the original content and takes more bandwidth.

*HTTP POST requests are never cached*

Cache happens only for HTTP GET requests. HTTP POST requests are never cached. So, any kind of Ajax call you want to make cacheable needs to be HTTP GET-enabled.

*Generate Content-Length response header*

When you are dynamically serving content via web service calls or HTTP handlers, make sure you emit a Content-Length header. A browser has several optimizations for downloading contents faster when it knows how many bytes to download from the response by looking at the Content-Length header. Browsers can use persisted connections more effectively when this header is present. This saves the browser from opening a new connection for each request. When there's no Content-Length header, the browser doesn't know how many bytes it's going to receive from the server and keeps the connection open (as long as bytes are delivered from the server) until the connection closes. So, you miss the benefit of persisted connections that can greatly reduce the download time of several small files.

## How to Configure Static Content Caching in IIS

In IIS Manager, the web site properties dialog box has an HTTP headers tab where you can define the Expires header for all requests that IIS handles (see Figure 9-1). You can set the content to expire immediately, after a certain number of days, or on a specific date. The option to Expire after uses sliding expiration, not absolute expi-ration, which is useful because it works per request. When someone requests a static file, IIS will calculate the expiration date based on the number of days/months from the Expire after.

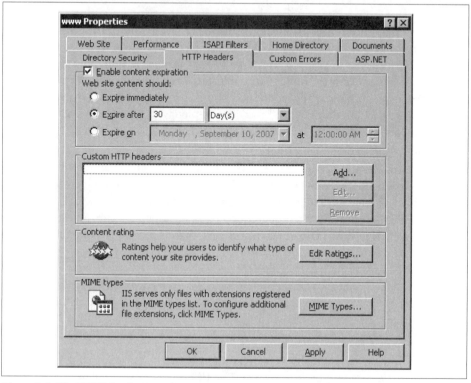

*Figure 9-1. The HTTP header is set for static content to expire in 30 days*

For dynamic pages that are served by ASP.NET, a handler can modify the expiration header and override the IIS default setting.

## Content Delivery Networks

A CDN (Content Delivery Network) is a system of computers networked together across the Internet. The computers cooperate transparently to deliver content (espe-cially large media content) to end users. CDN nodes (clusters of servers at a specific location) are deployed in multiple locations, often over multiple backbones. These nodes cooperate with each other to serve requests for content by end users. They also transparently move content behind the scenes to optimize the delivery process. A CDN serves a request by intelligently choosing the nearest server. It looks for the fastest connectivity between your computer to the nearest node that has the content you are looking for. A CDN measures its strength by the number of nodes in different countries and the amount of redundant backbone connectivity. Some of the most popular CDNs are Akamai, Limelight, and EdgeCast. Akamai is used by large companies like Microsoft, Yahoo!, and AOL. Comparatively, it is an expensive solution but has the best performance throughout the world because it has servers in almost every prominent city in the world.

## Examining Web Site Performance Without a CDN

Every request from a browser goes to your server and travels through the Internet backbones that span the world. The more countries, continents, and oceans a request passes through to reach your server, the slower it is. For example, if you have your servers in the U.S. and someone from Australia is browsing your site, each request is crossing the planet from one end to the other to reach your server and then come back again to the browser. If your site has a large number of static files, including images, CSS, and JavaScript, that are sending requests, then downloading them across the world takes a significant amount of time.

If you could set up a server in Australia and redirect users to your Australian server, then each request would take fraction of the time it takes from reach U.S. The network latency would be lower and the data transfer rate would be faster, so static content will download a lot faster. It will significantly improve the user's performance if your web site is rich in static content. Moreover, ISPs provide far greater speed for a country-wide network compared to the Internet because each country generally has a handful of connections to the Internet backbone that are shared by all ISPs within the country. As a result, users with a 4 Mbps broadband connection will get the full 4 Mbps speed from servers that are in the same country, but the speed could drop to 512 kbps from servers that are outside the country. So, having a server in the same country or city significantly improves site speed.

Figure 9-2 shows the average response time for *www.pageflakes.com* from Washington, D.C., where the servers are in Dallas, Texas. The average response time is about 0.4 seconds. This response includes server-side execution time as well. Generally, it takes 0.3 to 0.35 seconds to execute the page on the server. So, time spent on the network is 0.05 seconds or 50 ms. This connectivity is really fast because it takes only four to six hops to reach Dallas from Washington D.C.

The average response time from Australia is 1.5 seconds, which is significantly higher than Washington D.C., as you see from Figure 9-3. Moreover, it takes 17 to 23 hops to reach Sydney from Dallas. So, the site downloads at least four times slower in Australia than from anywhere in the U.S.

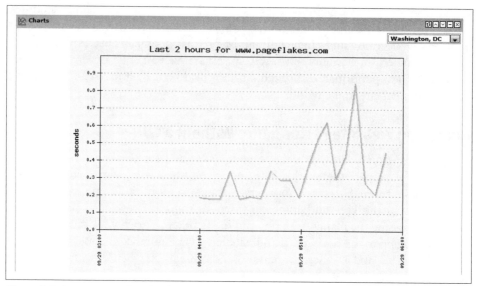

*Figure 9-2. Average page download time from Washington D.C. (taken from www.websitepulse.com)*

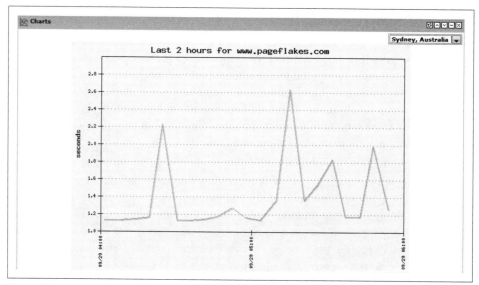

*Figure 9-3. Average response time from Sydney, Australia is significantly higher than it is from Washington D.C.*

## Different Types of CDNs

There are generally two types of CDNs:

*Upload content to the CDN's servers via FTP*

By doing this you will get a subdomain in the CDN's domain, e.g., *dropthings.somecdn.net*. You then change all of the static content URLs on your site to download content from the CDN domain instead of from the relative URL on your own domain. For example, a URL like */logo.gif* will be renamed to *http://dropthings.somecdn.net/logo.gif*. This is easy to configure, but there are maintenance problems. You have to keep the CDN's store synchronized with the files all the time. Deployment becomes complicated because you need to update both your web site and the CDN store at the same time. CacheFly is an example of such a CDN (it is also very inexpensive).

*Store static content on your own site but use domain aliasing*

You can store your content in a subdomain that points to your own domain, e.g., *static.dropthings.com*. Then you use CNAME to map that subdomain to a CDN's nameserver, such as *cache.somecdn.net*. When a browser tries to resolve *static.dropthings.com*, the DNS lookup request goes to the CDN nameserver. The nameserver then returns the CDN node's IP that is closest to you to give you the best download performance. The browser next sends requests for files to that CDN node. When the CDN node sees the request, it checks whether it has the content already cached. If it is cached, it delivers the content directly from its local store. If not, it makes a request to your server and then looks at the cache header generated in response. Based on the cache header, the CDN node decides how long to cache the response in its own cache. In the meantime, the browser does not wait for the CDN node to get content and return to it (see Figure 9-4).

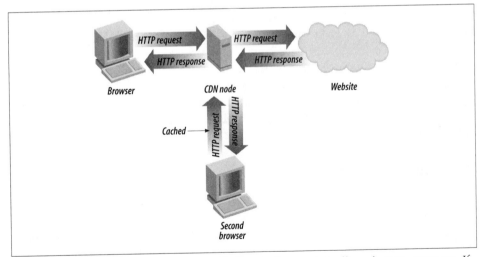

Figure 9-4. The CDN node that is closest to the browser intercepts traffic and serves a response. If it does not have the response in the cache, it fetches it from the origin server using a faster route and more optimized connectivity than the browser's ISP can provide. If the content is already cached, then it's served directly from the node.

The CDN does an interesting trick on the Internet backbone to actually route the request to the origin server so that the browser gets the response directly served from origin server while the CDN is updating its cache. Sometimes the CDN acts as a proxy, intercepting each request and then fetching uncached content from the origin using a faster route and optimized connectivity to the origin server.

# Optimizing Internet Explorer JavaScript Performance

Ajax web portals require a lot of JavaScript to be loaded in the browser. Because there's only one page, the more features on the user's Start page, the more JavaScript needed to deliver to the page. ASP.NET AJAX Framework, extenders, and scripts from widgets make the browser slower to run JavaScript and respond to user actions. If the JavaScript doesn't follow best practices, such as keeping careful consideration on performance and memory allocation, then the browser starts to crawl after some time. Old browsers, like Internet Explorer 6, are not made to run the large amount of JavaScript that Ajax web portals require. This means sometimes re-engineering is needed on your client-side framework, and sometimes several major components will need to be rewritten to overcome the performance limitation of browsers.

Re-engineering and rewriting is always expensive in the later stage of a project. So, knowing performance- and memory-related issues with old browsers upfront will save you lot of time and money.

Internet Explorer 6 has the worst performance when it comes to JavaScript execution speed and memory leaks; Internet Explorer 7 is much better. Firefox and Opera provide the best performance on a large amount of JavaScript and have almost no memory leak. Unfortunately, IE 6 is still the most used browser in the world. So, the majority of your users will still be using IE 6, which makes it a challenge to deliver a rich user interface to the browser while maintaining speed and reliability. In next sections, we will look at some JavaScript performance issues in IE 6 and some major memory leak problems and their solutions.

## Reducing IE Symbolic Lookups

A primary source of IE JavaScript performance issues is the constant symbolic lookup. *Symbolic lookup* occurs whenever the JavaScript engine tries to pair a name or identifier in the script with an actual object, method call, or property running in the context of the engine. For example, document.write will result in symbolic lookup on document object for the write function. Symbolic lookups are expensive, especially on DOM elements, because IE has to do a lookup on the DOM element's interface and find the function/property that you need. To improve JavaScript performance in IE, the first step is to reduce the number of symbolic lookups and help IE limit lookups to as small scope as possible.

## Evaluating local variables

A variable is accessed based on a scope chain that resolves backward from the most specific scope to the least specific. Sometimes these symbolic lookups can pass through multiple levels of scope and eventually wind up in generic queries to the IE DOM, which can be quite expensive. The worst-case scenario is that your variable doesn't yet exist and every level of scope in the chain is investigated, only to find that an *expando* variable (a dynamically defined property attached to a DOM element) needs to be created.

Example 9-2 shows a classic example of a local variable lookup that results in creating an expando on the window object. When you try to access some_variable, IE needs to see whether it is defined in the test( ) function; if not, it checks the parent function, then its grandparent until it reaches the window object. It then finds that there's no property named some_variable to window object. So, it creates an expando and assigns the value to it. Next time you try to access that variable, it moves up the same lookup chain, but this time it finds the variable on window object.

*Example 9-2. Symbolic lookup on local variables*

```
function test( )
{
    some_variable = some_function( );
    return some_variable + 1;
}
```

The solution to this is to use the var keyword to ensure the variable is created in the local scope only. Example 9-3 shows how you can force a local variable and thus limit symbolic lookup efforts for IE.

*Example 9-3. Solution to local variable lookup*

```
function test( )
{
    var local_variable = some_function( );
    return local_variable + 1;
}
```

Declaring local variables with the var keyword will create fast execution and greatly improve your JavaScript performance if you have mistakenly created a lot of variables without using the var keyword. You can easily see the difference by running both versions of the test( ) function from Examples 9-2 and 9-3 inside a loop in a low-end computer and see the difference in their execution times.

This optimization is not IE-specific—other browsers will benefit from optimized code as well if they can do shorter symbolic lookups.

### Reducing symbolic lookup on DOM elements

All binding in JavaScript is late binding, not early binding like in compiled languages such as C#. Moreover, because JavaScript is interpreted and not compiled, the JavaScript engine has no idea what will be next in line to do any compiler optimization. This means that each time you access a property, variable, or method, a lookup is performed. Within the DOM, this could mean an extensive search of the element to find the same property over and over again, only to return to the JavaScript engine unchanged from the previous request.

In Example 9-4, the innerHTML property on a div is accessed several times. Each time, the JavaScript engine does a symbolic lookup on the div. The first statement is a plain assignment. But the following statements actually require two lookups each: to get the existing value and to set the combined value.

*Example 9-4. Example of performance degradation from repeated DOM lookups*

```
function slow_function()
{
    var div = document.getElementById('someDiv');
    div.innerHTML = "";
    div.innerHTML += build_part1();
    div.innerHTML += build_part2();
    div.innerHTML += build_part3();
}
```

In Example 9-5, the solution is to build a combined string first and then assign the string to the innerHTML property in a single assignment. This will clear the previous content and set the new HTML.

*Example 9-5. Faster code by eliminating repeated lookups*

```
function faster_function()
{
    var div = document.getElementById('someDiv');
    div.innerHTML = build_part1() + build_part2() + build_part3();
}
```

### Speeding symbolic lookup by caching DOM elements, properties, and functions

Because local variables lookups are the fastest, you can benefit from performance improvement by caching DOM element properties and function references in local variables to access them easily. Local variables maintain a direct reference to the original item (by reference) and do not create or duplicate any item.

In Example 9-6, document.body is looked up over and over, which creates repeated lookups for the body property on the document object. Storing the document.body in a local variable can optimize this performance.

*Example 9-6. Slow code on repeated DOM lookup*

```
function slow_code()
{
    document.body.innerHTML = document.body.div1.innerHTML + document.body.div2.
    innerHTML;
}
```

In Example 9-7, we have eliminated repeated lookups on the document object, which is a big object. Caching the body object's `childNodes` property in a local variable will further optimize the code.

*Example 9-7. Caching the DOM element reference will make the code faster*

```
function faster_code()
{
    var body = document.body;
    body.innerHTML = body.childNodes[0].innerHTML + body.childNodes[1].innerHTML;
}
```

Example 9-8 shows the fastest implementation of this code.

*Example 9-8. Fastest implementation*

```
function fastest_code()
{
    var body = document.body;
    var childNodes = body.childNodes;
    body.innerHTML = childNodes[0].innerHTML + childNodes[1].innerHTML;
}
```

Not only can you cache the DOM properties but also the functions. Functions are also looked up on every call. If it's not a local function, then there is an expensive scan for it in the ancestor scopes. You can benefit from caching JavaScript functions as well as DOM element functions like `appendChild`. Example 9-9 shows how repeated calls to functions can be optimized.

*Example 9-9. Repeated calls to functions result in slow performance*

```
function repeated_function(items)
{
    var node = document.getElementById('someDiv');
    for( var i = 0; i < items.length; i ++ )
    {
        node.appendChild( my_function( items[i] ) );
    }
}
```

Example 9-10 shows how we can optimize two functions by caching node. appendChild and my_function.

*Example 9-10. Cache functions in local variables*

```
function faster_repeated_function(items)
{
    var node = document.getElementById('someDiv');
    var appendChild = node.appendChild;
    var cache_function = my_function;

    for( var i = 0; i < items.length; i ++ )
    {
        appendChild( cache_function( items[i] ) );
    }
}
```

You will benefit from caching DOM properties, as well as your own JavaScript functions, especially the ones that are defined at global scope, which is the JavaScript engine's last step in the symbolic lookup to find them. Generally, you will have some utility functions defined at global scope and use those utility functions repeatedly in many places. Caching those heavily used utility functions in local variables will give you some performance boost.

## Mitigating Internet Explorer Memory Leak

A *circular reference* results when a DOM object contains a reference to a JavaScript object (such as an event handling function) and that JavaScript object contains a reference back to that DOM object. The garbage collector, which is a memory manager, collects objects that are not referenced by anything and reclaims their memory. The JavaScript garbage collector understands circular references and is not confused by them. Unfortunately, IE's DOM is not managed by JavaScript. It has its own memory manager that does not understand circular references. As a result, when a circular references occurs, the garbage collector cannot reclaim the memory because it does not know whether the JavaScript object needs the DOM object. The memory that is not reclaimed is said to have leaked. Over time, this can result in memory starvation. The more IE runs and leaks memory, the slower it becomes. Lack of memory makes other programs page to disk and become slower also. The operating system has too much paging to do between RAM and the page file on disk, so the computer gets slower. You have to close the browser to free up the RAM that IE has allocated and to return to normal operational speed.

### Avoid using event handlers as closures

Cyclic reference can happen if global variables holding references to DOM objects or event handlers are defined as closures. *Closures* are functions that refer to free variables in their lexical context. When closures reference DOM objects, there's no way to know when that object will be needed, so the object is never freed.

In Example 9-11, a closure is formed in the event handler where it references two variables outside its local scope. For example, the closure_test execution function completes and the local variables (img and div) are ready to be released, but the event handler on img needs both img and div to be alive when it is fired. Therefore, the JavaScript engine cannot release the reference to the DOM objects. So, there are active references on both an image and a DIV. The IE garbage collector will not be able to reclaim these elements' memories even if explicitly removed from the DOM element by calling removeChild. They will remain in the memory forever and never be released, and IE will leak memory.

*Example 9-11. Example of a closure leaking memory*

```
function closure_test()
{
    var img = document.getElementById('someImage');
    var div = document.getElementById('somediv');
    img.onclick = function(event) { div.innerText = "Image loaded: " + img.src"; }
}
```

The first step to avoid closure leaking is to use the this keyword to refer to the element that fires the event. Example 9-12 shows improvement in one step.

*Example 9-12. Preventing the image from leaking*

```
function closure_step1()
{
    var img = document.getElementById('someImage');
    var div = document.getElementById('somediv');
    img.onclick = function(event) { div.innerText = "Image loaded: " + this.src"; }
}
```

Now IE can release someImage but not someDiv as the closure still holds the reference to the DIV. There are two workarounds to this problem:

- Get the DIV inside the event handler using its ID (if the ID is known at this stage)
- Store enough information to resolve the DIV from within the event handler if ID is not known (see Example 9-13)

*Example 9-13. Leak-free event handling*

```
function closure_step2()
{
    var img = document.getElementById('someImage');
    img.onclick = function(event)
    {
        var div = document.getElementById('somediv');
        div.innerText = "Image loaded: " + this.src;
    }
}
```

## Use out-of-scope functions

However, there's an even safer and better approach to event handling—out-of-scope functions. This ensures the callback function will never be able to hold onto any reference to local variables within the main function.

Example 9-14 shows that by declaring the event handler function out of the scope, there's no way the function can hold onto any variable reference inside the closure_step3 function.

*Example 9-14. Using out-of-scope functions for event callback*

```
function closure_step3()
{
    var img = document.getElementById('someImage');
    img.onclick = image_onclick;
}

function image_onclick(event)
{
    var div = document.getElementById('somediv');
    div.innerText = "Image loaded: " + this.src";
}
```

A .NET developer might think that Example 9-14 is how C# code is written for event handling. But closures are the norm for event handling in JavaScript. Most popular frameworks, such as Prototype, Dojo, and jQuery, and utility libraries like Script.aculo.us, are full of closures. Closure gives JavaScript developers a powerful syntax to reduce code size significantly, so they are familiar with using closure for many purposes including event handling.

The best way, however, is to use ASP.NET AJAX Framework's $addHandler and $removeHandler functions to subscribe/unsubscribe to events on DOM elements because they provide cross-browser implementation to work safely with events:

$addHandler

> Subscribes to a specific event multiple times; when the event is raised, it fires the event handlers one after another. You generally call it using an out-of-scope function and avoid the closure problem.

$removeHandler

> Removes a specific handler from an event but leaves other handlers intact.

$clearHandlers

> Removes all event handlers from an element, marking it safe to be reclaimed by the garbage collector (see Example 9-15).

*Example 9-15. Using $addHandler and $removeHandler*

```
function closure_safer()
{
    var img = document.getElementById('someImage');
```

*Example 9-15. Using $addHandler and $removeHandler (continued)*

```
    $addhandler( img 'click', image_onclick );
}

function image_onclick(event)
{
    var div = document.getElementById('somediv');
    div.innerText = "Image loaded: " + this.src";
    $removeHandler( this, 'click', image_onclick );
}
```

It is a good practice to remove all event handlers when you are done with an element. This ensures IE can collect the item properly. One thing to note: you can use `$removeHandler` and `$clearHandler` only when you have used `$addHandler` on an element. These functions are useless if you have used the `element.event = function() { }` approach of subscribing to events. In that case, you need to set `element.event = null` to release the event handler.

Example 9-16 shows a new function—`$clearEvents`—that calls the ASP.NET AJAX Framework's `$clearHandlers` function to clear any event attached by `$addHandler` and then sets the common event handler properties to `null`. This ensures that all event handlers are cleared.

*Example 9-16. Backward-compatible $clearEvents*

```
var $clearEvents = function(e)
{
    $clearHandlers(e);

    // Clear common events
    e.onmouseup = null; e.onmousedown = null; e.onmousemove = null; e.onclick = null;
    e.onkeypress = null; e.onkeyup = null;
    e.onmouseover = null; e.onmouseout = null;
    e.onreadystatechange = null;
}
```

## Remove DOM elements

To reduce memory leaks, you will have to remove unused events from DOM elements. However, it's always difficult to keep track of DOM elements and ensure they are released properly. So, one handy way to clean up DOM elements and make them ready for the garbage collector is to remove all event handlers during the `window.onunload` event. There are some common elements where events are generally attached, e.g., DIV, input, select, and hyperlinks. So, if you call `$clearEvents` on all such nodes, you can get rid of the majority of event handlers and make them safe for removal (see Example 9-17).

*Example 9-17. Safe way to release DOM elements during window.onunload*

```
$disposeElements = function(tagName)
{
    var elements = document.getElementsByTagName(tagName);
    for( var i = 0; i < elements.length; i ++ )
        $clearEvents(elements[i]);
}

window.onunload = function( )
{
    $clearEvents(document.body);
    $disposeElements("DIV");
    $disposeElements("INPUT");
    $disposeElements("A");
    $disposeElements("SELECT");
}
```

The `window.onunload` event is fired right before browser is closed or the user navigates away to a different page. During this time, cleaning up a majority of the event handlers will ensure you have removed as much of the memory leak as possible. However, expandos attached to DOM elements need to be released. It is difficult to find these expandos because you have to run through each and every property of a DOM element and set it to null. Browsers will get stuck for several seconds if you do this for all DIV tags or all hyperlinks. There's not much you can do about this, except hope most of the memory leak was resolved by removing the event handlers.

# Reducing the Web Service Call Payload

Generally, we exchange entity classes between the browser and a web service via JSON, e.g., returns an array of `Widget` objects from a web service call. But having the ability to exchange entity classes between the browser and server side makes Ajax programming a lot easier. However, sometime the `Entity` class contains data that is not safe or must be sent to the browser. You should exclude those sensitive properties for security reasons or to avoid sending large amount of data to the browser.

The `Widget` class contains the `State` property, which stores large amounts XML data. So, if you store the Flickr response XML in `State`, it will take up about 25 to 50 KB. The idea is not to prevent sending `Entity` classes, but instead create a shallow version of `Entity` classes that are sent to browser. If you send such giant XML data to the browser via a web service call when it isn't needed, you waste bandwidth and the response takes longer to download. Unfortunately, there's no way to exclude a property from JSON serialization. So, the only way to do it is to make another class that contains only the properties that you want to send to the browser as a web service call's response. For example, you can create a `Widget2` class that contains only `Row`, `Column`, and `Title` properties. On the server-side web service code, you convert the `Widget` class to `Widget2` and return that to the browser. This reduces the response size.

There are also some data types that you should never send to browser via JSON, such as byte arrays, streams, trees, etc. If any of your Entity classes contains such properties, you must make a lightweight copy of that Entity class and exclude such properties. Such lightweight classes will not only save download time but also save request time if the browser wants to send such objects to the web service. Moreover, the lightweight objects will save JSON serialization and deserialization overhead because they are both entirely reflection-based.

# Loading the UI on Demand

Ajax web sites are all about having as much functionality on one page as possible. But you can't deliver the entire UI of the whole web site along with all the functionality in one shot. The Start page needs to fetch the UI from the server on demand as the user explores different areas. For example, there's a Help link on the top-right corner of Dropthings.com. Clicking on that link pops up a gigantic help section (see Figure 9-5).

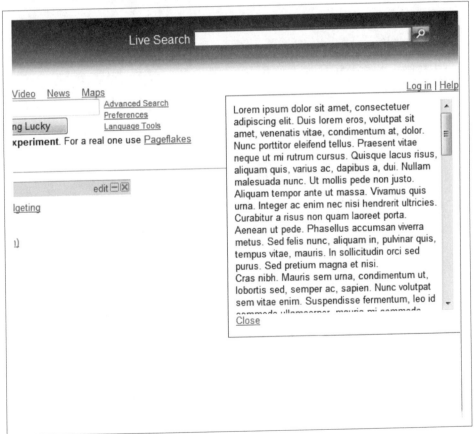

*Figure 9-5. Loading UI on demand via XML HTTP calls*

If you make it a hidden DIV on *Default.aspx*, it will waste bandwidth because it downloads on every visit to the homepage. You can, of course, use an IFrame, but IFrame makes browser rendering slower and has a high-memory footprint on IE 6. Moreover, IFrame does not inherit the parent page's stylesheet. So, the most effective way to load the UI on demand is to make XML HTTP calls to some *.aspx* files, get the response, and add the response to a DIV container via innerHTML.

The ASP.NET AJAX Framework has a Sys.Net.WebRequest class that you can use to make regular HTTP calls. You can define the HTTP method, URI, headers, and the body of the call. It's kind of a low-level function for making direct calls via XML HTTP. Once you construct a web request, you can execute it using Sys.Net.XMLHttpExecutor.

Example 9-18 shows how the help section is loaded by hitting *help.aspx* and injecting its response inside the HelpDiv. The response can be cached by the output cache directive set on *help.aspx*. So, next time the user clicks on the link, the UI pops up immediately. The *help.aspx* file has no <html> block, only the content that is set inside the DIV.

*Example 9-18. Making XML HTTP calls directly*

```
function showHelp()
{
    var request = new Sys.Net.WebRequest();
    request.set_httpVerb("GET");
    request.set_url('help.aspx');
    request.add_completed( function( executor )
    {
        if (executor.get_responseAvailable())
        {
            var helpDiv = $get('HelpDiv');
            var helpLink = $get('HelpLink');

            var helpLinkBounds = Sys.UI.DomElement.getBounds(helpLink);

            helpDiv.style.top = (helpLinkBounds.y + helpLinkBounds.height) + "px";

            var content = executor.get_responseData();
            helpDiv.innerHTML = content;
            helpDiv.style.display = "block";
        }
    });

    var executor = new Sys.Net.XMLHttpExecutor();
    request.set_executor(executor);
    executor.executeRequest();
}
```

Example 9-19 partially shows the *help.aspx*.

*Example 9-19. Help.aspx partial content*

```
<%@ Page Language="C#" AutoEventWireup="true" CodeFile="Help.aspx.cs" Inherits="Help" %>
<%@ OutputCache Location="ServerAndClient" Duration="604800" VaryByParam="none" %>
```

*Example 9-19. Help.aspx partial content (continued)*

```
<div class="helpContent">
<div id="lipsum">
<p>
Lorem ipsum dolor sit amet, consectetuer adipiscing elit. Duis lorem
eros, volutpat sit amet, venenatis vitae, condimentum at, dolor. Nunc
porttitor eleifend tellus. Praesent vitae neque ut mi rutrum cursus.
```

Using this approach, you can break the UI into smaller *.aspx* files. Although these *.aspx* files cannot have JavaScript or stylesheet blocks, they can contain large amounts of HTML that you need to show on the UI.

---

### @OutputCache Directive

ASP.NET gives you the @OutputCache directive to control caching for ASP.NET Page or WebControl. By using this directive, you can specify *where* (server or client or both) and *how long* to cache the response. The proper response header is generated when the response is sent—basically, it sets the HttpCachePolicy in the Response. Cache property. Moreover, @OutputCache can also cache responses on the server by using ASP.NET Cache. If you mention Location="Server", the output of the page is stored in ASP.NET Cache. When the same page is hit again within the cache expiration time, ASP.NET does not execute the page at all, and instead returns the cached response, thus saving processing time on the web server.

---

Pageflakes uses a similar approach to load the large 200 KB onsite menu on demand (see Figure 9-6).

*Figure 9-6. Loading large UI blocks on demand using XML HTTP. The black gradient box appears when you click the big round button on the top right; this whole area is loaded on demand.*

By using this approach, you can keep the initial download to an absolute minimum for loading the widgets. When the user explores new features on the site, load those areas incrementally.

# Using Read-Ahead Caching for Ajax Calls

Ajax applications are quite chatty—they make frequent web service calls. During first load, several web service calls are made to load the initial data. And each widget on a Start page might need one web service call to get its initial data. Sometimes such calls return the same data over and over again.

For example, a blog feed where new blog posts appear once a week will repeatedly return the same content. If you could know in advance that the feed is not going to return new data, you could avoid making a web service call during page load and thus save precious loading time. One way to avoid making calls to the server during page load is to make those calls ahead of time in the background so that a fresh result remains in browser cache. So, while the user is reading some feeds on the Start page, calls to the RSS feed web service can happen behind the scene and cache the result in the browser. So, if the user goes away to some other site and comes back, the web service calls will get the cached data from the browser and render immediately, which will give the user a fast-loading experience.

Read-ahead caching basically means you make some HTTP GET calls behind the scene that you will need in future. Those calls get cached in the browser so when you really need them, they execute instantly and return content from the cache. You can use read-ahead caching to load content on other tabs behind the scene so that when the user switches to another tab, the content is already available in the browser cache and the tabs will load instantly. Similarly, widgets on your page can precache content by making behind-the-scene calls when the user is idle and keep fresh content in cache. On the next visit, they will get content directly from the cache and the user won't have to wait for the calls to complete.

# Hiding HTML Inside <textarea>

As soon as browser gets some HTML, it parses it and starts downloading external resources like images, stylesheets, and JavaScript immediately. Sometimes this results in unwanted resources downloading. For example, you might have a pop-up dialog box hidden inside the *Default.aspx* that you show only on certain actions. However, the browser will get the HTML for the pop-up dialog and download the graphics files associated with the content, which wastes a precious HTTP connection during site load. Of course, you can defer loading such UI elements by using the on-demand UI loading approach, but sometimes you need to deliver some essential UI elements instantly when the user performs some action and cannot wait for an XML HTTP call to complete, e.g., confirmation dialog boxes.

When the user deletes a widget, she sees a warning dialog box (see Figure 9-7). The HTML for the warning dialog box is embedded inside *Default.aspx*.

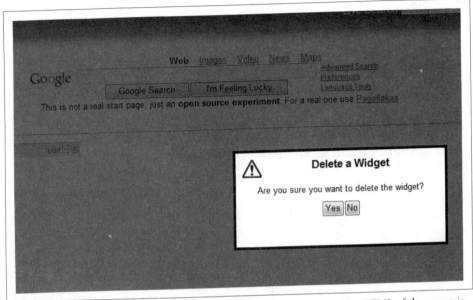

Figure 9-7. *When a widget is deleted, a confirmation window pops up. The HTML of the popup is inside Default.aspx.*

When you put the HTML for the pop-up dialog box inside *Default.aspx*, the image used in the stylesheet is downloaded even though the popup is not visible on the screen. If the popup has multiple decorative images, such as a background picture, icons, and button shades, they will be downloaded during page load, wasting several HTTP calls and bandwidth (see Example 9-20).

Example 9-20. *Pop-up HTML embedded inside Default.aspx makes the browser download associated images during page load*

```
</form>

    <div id="DeleteConfirmPopup">
        <h1>Delete a Widget</h1>
        <p>Are you sure you want to delete the widget?</p>
        <input id="DeleteConfirmPopup_Yes" type="button" value="Yes" /><input
        id="DeleteConfirmPopup_No" type="button" value="No" />
    </div>

</body>
</html>
```

The HTML snippet is at the end of the document to force the images to download as late as possible. But it still does not eliminate CSS images (Example 9-21), even though the popup is not visible on screen until the user clicks on a widget's close button.

*Example 9-21. CSS defined for the popup*

```
#DeleteConfirmPopup
{
    display:none;
    z-index: 60000;
    position: absolute;
    left: 50%;
    top: 50%;
    margin-left: -150;
    margin-top: -60;
    width: 300px;
    height: 120px;
    border: solid 4px black;
    padding: 10px;
    background: white url('warning.jpg') no-repeat 10px 10px;
    text-align: center
}
```

By using an HTTP analyzer like Nikhil's web development helper (*http://www. nikhilk.net*), you can see the image is downloaded during page load, as shown in Figure 9-8.

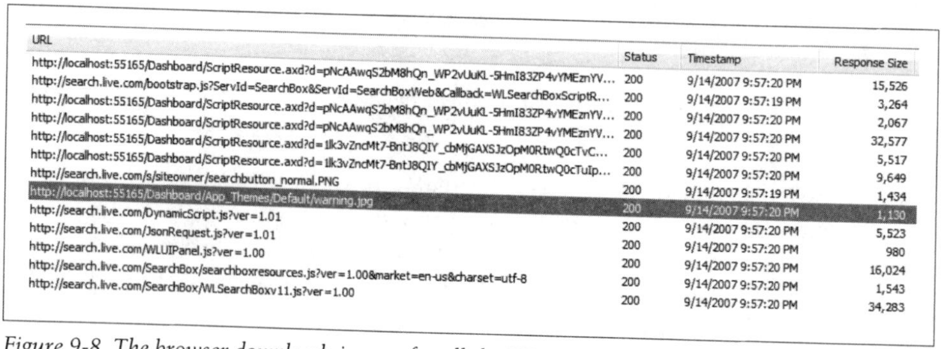

| URL | Status | Timestamp | Response Size |
| --- | --- | --- | --- |
| http://localhost:55165/Dashboard/ScriptResource.axd?d=pNcAAwqSZbM8hQn_WP2vUuKL-5HmI83ZP4vYMEznYV... | 200 | 9/14/2007 9:57:20 PM | 15,526 |
| http://search.live.com/bootstrap.js?ServId=SearchBox&ServId=SearchBoxWeb&Callback=WLSearchBoxScriptR... | 200 | 9/14/2007 9:57:19 PM | 3,264 |
| http://localhost:55165/Dashboard/ScriptResource.axd?d=pNcAAwqSZbM8hQn_WP2vUuKL-5HmI83ZP4vYMEznYV... | 200 | 9/14/2007 9:57:20 PM | 2,067 |
| http://localhost:55165/Dashboard/ScriptResource.axd?d=pNcAAwqSZbM8hQn_WP2vUuKL-5HmI83ZP4vYMEznYV... | 200 | 9/14/2007 9:57:20 PM | 32,577 |
| http://localhost:55165/Dashboard/ScriptResource.axd?d=1lk3vZncMt7-8ntJ8QIY_cbMjGAXSJzOpM0RtwQ0cTvC... | 200 | 9/14/2007 9:57:20 PM | 5,517 |
| http://search.live.com/s/siteowner/searchbutton_normal.PNG | 200 | 9/14/2007 9:57:20 PM | 9,649 |
| http://localhost:55165/Dashboard/App_Themes/Default/warning.jpg | 200 | 9/14/2007 9:57:19 PM | 1,434 |
| http://search.live.com/DynamicScript.js?ver=1.01 | 200 | 9/14/2007 9:57:20 PM | 1,130 |
| http://search.live.com/JsonRequest.js?ver=1.01 | 200 | 9/14/2007 9:57:20 PM | 5,523 |
| http://search.live.com/WLUIPanel.js?ver=1.00 | 200 | 9/14/2007 9:57:20 PM | 980 |
| http://search.live.com/SearchBox/searchboxresources.js?ver=1.00&market=en-us&charset=utf-8 | 200 | 9/14/2007 9:57:20 PM | 16,024 |
| http://search.live.com/SearchBox/WLSearchBoxv11.js?ver=1.00 | 200 | 9/14/2007 9:57:20 PM | 1,543 |
| | 200 | 9/14/2007 9:57:20 PM | 34,283 |

*Figure 9-8. The browser downloads images for all the HTML, regardless of whether it is visible on the UI*

Popups occupy a significant amount of bandwidth during page load, but the solution is to deliver the HTML without letting the browser parse it. You pass a large amount of HTML inside a <textarea> tag. The browser will get encoded HTML inside a <textarea> tag and not parse the content. Because it will not see the HTML, it will not download the associated images. When you need to get the HTML, extract the value of the <textarea>, decode the content to get the HTML, and inject the HTML inside DOM.

In Example 9-22, the HTML is encoded inside a <textarea> tag, so the browser cannot parse the HTML and apply it to the DOM. An easy way to convert a block of HTML to its encoded form is to copy the HTML inside Visual Studio HTML editor and then select Edit → Paste Alternative.

*Example 9-22. Delivering HTML for the popup inside <textarea> tags*

```
    </form>

    <textarea id="DeleteConfirmPopupPlaceholder">
    &lt;div id="DeleteConfirmPopup"&gt;
        &lt;h1&gt;Delete a Widget&lt;/h1&gt;
        &lt;p&gt;Are you sure you want to delete the widget?&lt;/p&gt;
        &lt;input id="DeleteConfirmPopup_Yes" type="button" value="Yes" /&gt;&lt;input
        id="DeleteConfirmPopup_No" type="button" value="No" /&gt;
    &lt;/div&gt;
    </textarea>

</body>
</html>
```

Example 9-23 shows how the HTML is extracted from the <textarea> and injected into the DOM.

*Example 9-23. Extracting HTML from <textarea> and injecting it into the DOM*

```
var hiddenHtmlTextArea = $get('DeleteConfirmPopupPlaceholder');
var html = hiddenHtmlTextArea.value;
var div = document.createElement('div');
div.innerHTML = html;
document.body.appendChild(div);
```

You can create checks to make sure you do this only once because if you repeatedly add the same elements to the DOM, you'll duplicate the ID and won't be able to access the elements via the $get call.

One drawback of this approach is that resources referenced by the HTML block will get downloaded only after they are added in the DOM. So, the HTML will appear without graphics for a moment until the browser downloads the resources.

# Summary

In this chapter, you learned how to improve client-side performance by implementing an effective caching policy. Proper caching techniques maximizes browser cacheability and reduces network roundtrip. For both cached and noncached content, a CDN can save roundtrip time and increase content's download speed. Due to heavy JavaScript usage in Ajax sites, browsers suffer from performance degradation and memory leaks. Writing optimized JavaScript and keeping memory leaks in check ensures good responsiveness and long-term use for your site. Finally, you learned how to load UI blocks on-demand and thus make initial loading even faster. In the next chapter, you will learn about some real-life problems and the solutions to build, deploy, and run a production web site.

# CHAPTER 10

# Solving Common Deployment, Hosting, and Production Challenges

This chapter details several under-the-hood secrets for ASP.NET that you will rarely find documented on the Internet. You will also learn about deploying web farms and solving common production challenges. These real-world lessons will help you avoid repeating the same mistakes and save time and money in the long run.

## Deploying Your Web Site in a Web Farm

A web farm is a cluster of multiple web servers running the same copy of code, serving the same web site, and distributing traffic among them in a load-balanced environment. Generally, you use a hardware load balancer or implement Network Load Balancing (NLB) for Windows to make multiple web servers respond to a fixed IP. The outside world sees only one IP; when traffic comes to that IP, it is distributed among the web servers in the web farm.

Figure 10-1 shows a web farm configuration where a load balancer serves a public IP 69.15.89.1.

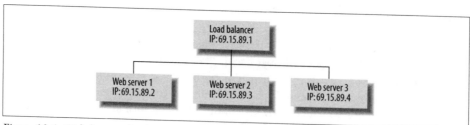

*Figure 10-1. Web farm with a load balancer*

Let's say this IP is mapped to the domain *www.dropthings.com*. When users go to *www.dropthings.com*, traffic is sent to 69.15.89.1. The load balancer gets the incoming requests, and then, based on its load table and load balancing algorithm, it decides which of the web servers to send traffic to. Traffic never goes directly to the web servers from the Internet.

# Web Farm Pros and Cons

A web farm environment is critical for successful web site operations, but there are some things that you must keep in mind.

Pros:

*Easy to load balance*
> If a web server reaches its limit on the CPU or disk I/O, just add another server to balance the load. There's no need to change code as long as your code can support the web farm scenario. Unless there's some really bad code, you can always add more servers to a web farm and support the higher load.

*Easy to replace a malfunctioning server*
> If one web server is malfunctioning, take it out of the web farm, fix it, and put it back in. Users will notice nothing. There'll only be a temporary increase on other servers running in the web farm.

*Directs traffic away from a nonresponsive server*
> If one web server crashes, your site still runs fine. The load balancer can detect nonresponsive servers and automatically divert traffic to responsive servers.

*Removes slow servers from the web farm*
> If one server has become too slow for some reason, the load balancers can automatically remove it from the web farm.

*Avoids a single point of failure*
> There's really no way you can run a production web site on one web server and ensure 99 percent uptime. That web server becomes a single point of failure, and when it goes down, your site goes down as well.

Cons:

*Session cannot be used unless it is stored in a centralized database*
> An ASP.NET session won't work in the in-process or out-of-process modes because they make each server maintain its own copy of the session. So, Session will only work in SQL Server mode when there's one SQL Server storing the sessions, and all of the web servers participating in the web farm have access to that centralized SQL Server store. However, one good thing is that the ASP.NET Profile provider acts almost like Session because you can store a user's properties, and it can be used instead of an ASP.NET session in a web farm.

*Not all requests from a particular user will go to the same web server*
> It is possible that a user's first hit to *Default.aspx* will go to Web Server 1, the JavaScript files will be downloaded from Web Server 2, and subsequent web service calls or asynchronous postback will go to Web Server 3. So, you need to make completely stateless web applications when you deploy a web farm. There are some very expensive load balancers that can look at a cookie, identify the user, and send all requests containing the same cookie to same web server all the time.

*Web application logs will be distributed in web servers*

If you want to analyze traffic logs or generate reports from logs, you will have to combine logs from all web servers and then do a log analysis. Looking at one web server's log will not reveal any meaningful data.

*The ASP.NET cache is not always available or up-to-date*

One request could store something in the ASP.NET cache on Web Server 1, and the following request might try to get it from Web Server 2. So, you can only store static data in a cache that does not change frequently, and if it doesn't matter whether old data is added from the cache or not. Such data includes configuration cache, a cache of images from a database, or content from external sources that do not change frequently. You cannot store entities like User object in the ASP.NET cache.

## Real-Life: Building an Inexpensive Web Farm

Problem: Startups often don't have enough money to buy expensive servers.

Solution: Load balance your servers to ensure some redundancy.

When we first went live with Pageflakes in 2005, most of us did not have any experience running a high-volume, mass-consumer web application on the Internet. We went through all types of problems, but have grown from a thousand users to a million users. We have discovered some of ASP.NET 2.0's under-the-hood secrets that solve many scalability and maintainability problems, and gained enough experience in choosing the right hardware and Internet infrastructure that can make or break a high-volume web application.

When Pageflakes started, we had to save every penny in hosting. When you have a small hosting requirement, Windows is quite expensive compared to PHP hosting. So, we came up with a solution to use only two servers and run the site in a load-balanced mode. This ensured redundancy on both the web application and on SQL Server, and there was no single point of failure. If one server went down completely, the other server could serve the whole web site. The configuration is shown in Figure 10-2.

We had two windows servers, both with IIS 6.0 and SQL Server 2005, so for this example, let's call them Web Server and DB Server.

Web Server got 60 percent web traffic configured via NLB. We used Windows NLB to avoid buying a separate load balancer and Windows Firewall instead of an external firewall. SQL Server 2005 on this server was used as a log shipping standby database, so we didn't have to pay a licensing fee for the standby server.

DB Server got 40 percent of the web traffic and hosted the database in its SQL Server 2005. We started with SQL Server 2005 Workgroup Edition because it was the only version we could afford ($99 per month). However, we couldn't use the new database mirroring feature—instead, we had to use good old transaction log shipping.

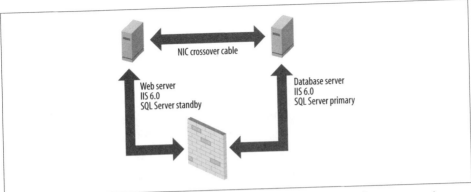

*Figure 10-2. A two-server web farm where both servers acts as a web server but one server is primary database server and the other is a standby database server*

Both servers were directly connected to each other via a network adapter using crossover cable. Because we had only two servers, we didn't have to buy a separate switch. An important lesson here is that you don't have to pay for a SQL server license if the server is only hosting standby databases.

So, we had two servers running the web site in NLB, and the web servers were properly load balanced and failsafe. If the DB Server went down, we could divert all traffic to the Web Server, bring up its standby database, and run the site solely from there. When the DB Server would come back online, we configured log shipping the opposite way and diverted most of the traffic to the DB Server. Thus, if needed, the database server could become the web server and the web server could become the database server. It required some manual work and is not fully automated. But it was the cheapest solution ($600 to $1,000 a month) for a reliable configuration, and it ensured 90 percent uptime.

## Transaction Log Shipping

SQL Server has a built-in transaction log shipping ability where it records each and every change made to a database and ships the changes periodically (say every five minutes) to another standby server. The standby server maintains a copy of the production database, it applies the changes (transaction logs), and keeps the database in synch with the main database. If the main database server fails or the database becomes unavailable for some reason, you can immediately bring in the standby database as active and run it as a production database.

# Real-Life: Adding Backup and Reporting Servers

Problem: When running a production server with a large database, you will soon run into storage issues.

Solution: Add another server as a backup store.

We ran a daily, full database backup and needed a lot of space to store seven days worth of backup. So, we added another server that acted as a backup store; it had very poor hardware configuration but enormous hard drives.

We also had to generate weekly reports from the IIS logs. Every day we used to generate 3 to 5 GB of web logs on each server, and they had to be moved off the web server to a reporting server so we could analyze them and generate weekly reports. Such analysis takes a lot of CPU and time and is not suitable for running directly on the web servers. Moreover, we need to combine logs from both web servers into one place. We had no choice but to go for a separate reporting server. After adding a backup storage server and a reporting server, the configuration looked like Figure 10-3.

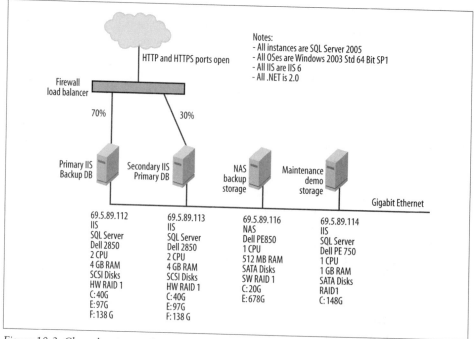

*Figure 10-3. Cheap hosting configuration with storage and reporting servers*

The web and database servers had SCSI drives with 15,000 RPM. But the storage and reporting servers had cheap SATA drives because those servers didn't need faster drives.

The web and database servers had an *F:* drive dedicated for storing SQL Server 2005 database's large MDF file. This *F:* drive was a physically separate disk, but the other physical disk had two logical partitions—*C:* and *E:*. The *E:* drive contained the LDF file and the web application.

If you put the MDF and LDF files on the same physical drive, the database transactions will become slow. So, you must put MDF and LDF on two separate physical disks and preferably under two separate disk controllers. If both physical disks are in the same disk controller, you will still suffer from disk I/O bottleneck when the database performs large jobs like full database backup.

## Designing a Reasonable Hosting Configuration

A reasonable web-hosting configuration should include two web servers, two database servers, a load balancer, and a firewall. It is the minimum needed to guarantee 95 percent uptime. Figure 10-4 shows a reasonable configuration for a medium-scale web application.

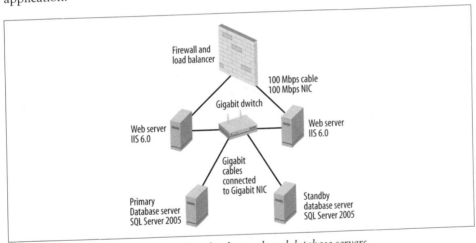

*Figure 10-4. A standard web farm with redundant web and database servers*

In this configuration, there's redundancy in both the web and database servers. You might wonder if the cheapest configuration has the same level of redundancy. This configuration gives you a dedicated box for running web applications and a database server, but the cheaper configuration had database and web applications running on the same box. We learned that IIS 6.0 and SQL Server 2005 do not run well in the same box and sometimes SQL Server 2005 hangs until the service is restarted. This was the main reason why we separated the web and database servers. However, adding more than two servers requires a switch. So, we added a gigabit switch that was connected to each server's gigabit Ethernet card via gigabit Ethernet cable. You could use optical fiber cables for faster and more reliable connectivity, but gigabit cables are also quite good. Both web servers have an additional 100 mbps Ethernet card that is connected to the firewall and load balancer. We used the hosting provider's shared firewall and had to buy two ports from the firewall. Luckily, that firewall had load-balancing capability built into it. If your hosting provider does not have a firewall like this, you will have to lease a load balancer in addition to the firewall. This configuration will cost about $4,000 to $6,000 per month.

# Thirteen Production Disasters That Could Happen at Anytime

Startups don't always have adequate resources in necessary areas like system administration, database administration, tech support, QA, and so on. In a startup environment, developers sometimes end up having multiple roles and may not be prepared for production challenges. At Pageflakes, we had several downtime and data loss problems in our first year of operation due to production disasters. However, all of these major problems taught us how to build a secure reliable production environment that can run a medium scale web site with 99 percent uptime.

## The Hard Drive Crashes, Overheats

We experienced hard drive crashes frequently with cheap hosting providers. There were several times when a hard drive would get overheated and turn itself off, and some were permanently damaged. Hosting providers used cheap SATA drives that were not reliable. If you can spend the money, go for SCSI drives. HP has a variety to choose from and it's always better to go for SCSI drives on web and database servers. They are costly, but will save you from frequent disasters.

Figure 10-5 shows the benchmarks for a good hard drive.

Pay attention to disk speed rather than CPU speed. Generally, the processor and bus are standard, and their performances don't vary. Disk I/O is generally the main bottleneck for production systems. For a database server, the only thing you should look at is disk speed. Unless you have some very CPU-intensive slow queries, the CPU will never peak. Disk I/O will always be the bottleneck for database servers. So, for databases, you need to choose the fastest storage solution. A SCSI drive at 15,000 RPM is a good solution—anything less than that is too slow.

## The Controller Malfunctions

This happens when the servers aren't properly tested and are handed over to you in a hurry. Before you accept any server, make sure you get a written guarantee that it has passed all sorts of exhaustive hardware tests. Dell's server BIOS contains test suites

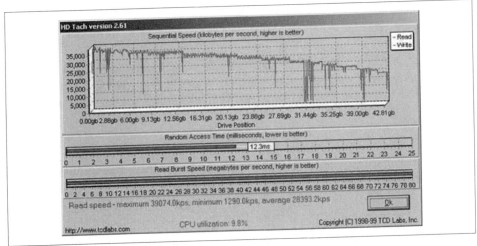

*Figure 10-5. HD Tach testing hard disk speed*

for testing controller, disks, CPU, etc. You can also use BurnInTest from PassMark (*www.passmark.com*) to test your server's capability under high disk and CPU load. Just run the benchmark test for four to eight hours and see how your server is doing. Keep an eye on the CPU's temperature meters and hard drives to make sure they don't overheat.

## The RAID Malfunctions

A RAID (Redundant Array of Inexpensive Disks) combines physical hard disks into a single logical unit by using either special hardware or software. Often, hardware solutions are designed to present themselves to the attached system as a single hard drive, and the *operating system* remains unaware of the technical workings. Software solutions are typically implemented in the operating system and are also presented to the RAID drive as a single drive.

At Pageflakes, we had a RAID malfunction that resulted in disks corrupting data. We used Windows 2003's built-in RAID controller, but we have learned not to depend on the software RAID and now pay extra for a hardware RAID. Make sure when you purchase a server that it has a hardware RAID controller.

Once you have chosen the right disks, the next step is to choose the right RAID configuration. RAID 1 takes two identical physical disks and presents them as one single disk to the operation system. Thus, every disk write goes to both disks simultaneously. If one disk fails, the other disk can take over and continue to serve the logical disk. Nowadays, servers support "hot swap"-enabled disks where you can take a disk out of the server while the server is running. The controller immediately diverts all requests to the other disk. The controller synchronizes both disks once the new disk is put into the controller. RAID 1 is suitable for web servers.

## Pros and cons of RAID 1

Pros:

- Mirroring provides 100 percent duplication of data.
- Read performance is faster than a single disk, if the array controller can perform simultaneous reads from both devices on a mirrored pair. You should make sure your RAID controller has this ability. Otherwise, the disk read will become slower than having a single disk.
- Delivers the best performance of any redundant array type during a rebuild. As soon as you insert a repaired replacement disk, it quickly synchronizes with the operational disk.
- No re-construction of data is needed. If a disk fails, all you have to do is copy to a new disk on block-by-block basis.
- There's no performance hit when a disk fails; storage appears to function normally to outside world.

Cons:

- Writes the information twice. Because of this, there is a minor performance penalty when compared to writing to a single disk.
- The I/O performance in a mixed read-write environment is essentially no better than the performance of a single disk storage system.
- Requires two disks for 100 percent redundancy, doubling the cost. However, disks are now cheap.
- The size of the drive will be the same size as the disk that has the lowest.

For database servers, RAID 5 is a better choice because it is faster than RAID 1. RAID 5 is more expensive than RAID 1 because it requires a minimum of three drives. But one drive can fail without affecting the availability of data. In the event of a failure, the controller regenerates the failed drive's lost data from the other surviving drives.

## Pros and cons of RAID 5

Pros:

- Best suited for heavy read applications, such as database servers, where the SELECT operation is used more than the INSERT/UPDATE/DELETE operations.
- The amount of useable space is the number of physical drives in the virtual drive minus 1.

Cons:

- A single disk failure reduces the array to RAID 0, which has no redundancy at all.
- Performance is slower than RAID 1 when rebuilding.
- Write performance is slower than read (write penalty).

## The CPU Overheats and Burns Out

One time our server's CPU burnt out due to overheating. We were partially responsible because a bad query made the SQL Server spike to 100 percent CPU. So, the poor server ran for four hours on 100 percent CPU and then died.

Servers should never burn out because of high CPU usage. Usually, servers have monitoring systems, and the server turns itself off when the CPU is about to burn out. This means the defective server did not have the monitoring system working properly. To avoid this, you should run tools that push your servers to 100 percent CPU for 8 hours to ensure they can withstand it. In the event of overheating, the monitoring systems should turn the servers off and save the hardware. However, if the server has a good cooling system, then the CPU will not overheat in eight hours.

Whenever we move to a new hosting provider, we run stress test tools to simulate 100 percent CPU load on all our servers for 8 to 12 hours. Figure 10-6 shows 7 of our servers running at 100 percent CPU for hours without any problem. None of the servers became overheated or turned themselves off, which means we also invested in a good cooling system.

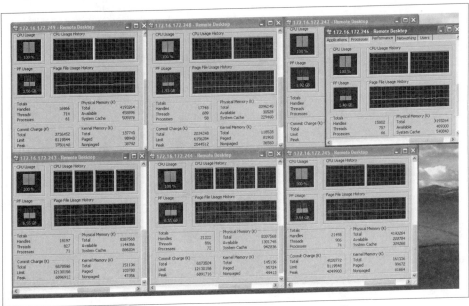

Figure 10-6. Stress testing the CPU at 100 percent load for 8 hours on all our servers

## The Firewall Goes Down

Our hosting provider's firewall once malfunctioned and exposed our web servers to the public Internet unprotected. We soon found out the servers became infected and started to automatically shut down, so we had to format and patch them, and turn on Windows Firewall. Nowadays, as best practice, we always turn on Windows Firewall on the external network card, which is connected to the hardware firewall. In fact, we also installed a redundant firewall just to be on the safe side.

You should turn off File and Printer Sharing on the external network card (see Figure 10-7). And unless you have a redundant firewall, you should turn on Windows Firewall as well. Some might argue that this will affect performance, but we have seen that Windows Firewall has almost no impact on performance.

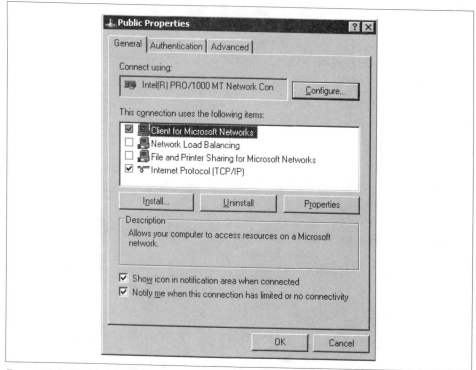

Figure 10-7. Disable File and Printer Sharing from the public network card. You should never copy files via Windows File Sharing over the Internet.

You should also disable the NetBIOS protocol because you should never need it from an external network (see Figure 10-8). You server should be completely invisible to the public network, besides having ports HTTP 80 and 3389 (for remote desktop) open.

## The Remote Desktop Stops Working After a Patch Installation

Several times after installing the latest patches from Windows Update, the remote desktop stopped working. Sometimes restarting the server fixed it, but other times we had to uninstall the patch. If this happens, you can only get into your server by using KVM over IP or calling a support technician.

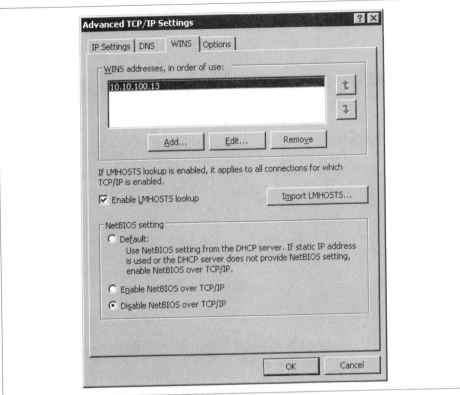

*Figure 10-8. Disable NetBIOS from the public network card. NetBIOS has security vulnerabilities.*

KVM over IP (keyboard, video, mouse over IP) is a special hardware that connects to servers and transmits the server's screen output to you. It also takes the keyboard and mouse input and simulates it on the server. KVM works as if a monitor, keyboard, and mouse were all directly connected to the server. You can use regular remote desktop to connect to KVM and work on the server as if you are physically there. Benefits of KVM include:

- Access to all server platforms and all server types.
- A "Direct Connect Real Time" solution with no mouse delays due to conversion of signals. Software has to convert signals, which causes delays.
- Full use of GUIs.
- Full BIOS level access even when the network is down.
- The ability to get to the command line and rebuild servers remotely.
- Visibility into server boot errors and the ability to take action, e.g., "Non-system disk error, please replace system disk and press any key to continue" or "Power supply failure, press F1 to continue."
- Complete security prevents hacking from the KVM; a physical connection is required to access the system.

If remote desktop is not working, your firewall is down, or your server's external network card is not working, you can easily get into the server using KVM. Make sure your hosting provider has KVM support.

## Remote Desktop Exceeds Connection Limit and Login Fails

This happens when users don't log off properly from the remote desktop by closing just the remote desktop client. The proper way to log off from a remote desktop is to go to the Start Menu and select "Log off." If you don't, you leave a session open and it will remain as a disconnected session. When disconnected sessions exceed the maximum number of active sessions, it prevents new sessions, which means no one can get into the server. If this happens, go to Run and issue a `mstsc /console` command. This will launch the same old remote desktop client you use every day, but when you connect to remote desktops, it will connect you in console mode. *Console mode* is when you connect to the server as if you are right in front of it and using the server's keyboard and mouse. Only one person can be connected in console mode at a time. Once you get into it, it shows you the regular Windows GUI and there's nothing different about it. You can launch Terminal Service Manager, see the disconnected sessions, and boot them out.

## The Database Becomes Corrupted When Files Are Copied over the Network

Copying large files over the network is not safe; data can be corrupted at any time, especially over the Internet. So, always use WinRAR in Normal compression mode to compress large files and then copy the RAR file over the network. The RAR file maintains CRC and checks the accuracy of the original file while decompressing. If WinRAR can decompress a file properly, you can be sure that there's no corruption in the original file. One caution about WinRAR compression modes: do not use the Best compression mode. Always use Normal compression mode. We have seen large files get corrupted with the Best compression mode.

## The Production Database Was Accidentally Deleted

In early stages, we did not have professional sys admins taking care of our servers. We, the developers, used to take care of our servers ourselves. And it was disastrous when one of us accidentally deleted the production database thinking it was a backup database. It was his turn to clean up space from our backup server, so he went to the backup server using remote desktop and logged into SQL Server using the "sa" username and password. Because he needed to free up some space, he deleted the large "Pageflakes" database. SQL Server warned him that the database was in use, but he never reads alerts with an "OK" button and so clicked OK. We were doomed.

There are some critical lessons to learn from this:

- Don't become too comfortable with the servers. Take it seriously when working on remote desktop because it can be routine, monotonous work.
- Use a different password for every machine. All databases had the same "sa" password. If we had different password, at least while typing the password, you can see where you are connecting to.

  Although this guy connected to the remote desktop on a maintenance server, from SQL Server Management Studio he connected to the primary database server just as he did last time. SQL Server Management Studio remembered the last machine name and username. So, all he had to do was enter the password, hit Enter, and delete the database. Now that we learned our lesson, we put the server's name inside the password. So, while typing the password, we know consciously what server we are going to connect to.
- Don't ignore confirmation dialogs on remote desktops as you do on your local machine. Nowadays, we consider ourselves to be super experts on everything and never read any confirmation dialog. I myself don't remember when the last time I took a confirmation dialog seriously. This attitude must change when working on servers. SQL Server tried its best to inform him that the database was being used, but, as he does a hundred times a day on his laptop, he clicked OK without reading the confirmation dialog.
- Don't put the same administrator password on all servers. Although this makes life easier when copying files from one server to another, don't do it. You will accidentally delete a file on another server (just like we used to do).
- *Do not* use the administrator user account to do your day-to-day work. We started using a power user account for daily operations, which limits access to a couple of folders only. Using the administrator account on the remote desktop opens doors to all sorts of accidents. If you use a restricted account, there's limited possibility of such accidents.
- Always have someone beside you when you work on the production server and are doing something important like cleaning up free space or running scripts, restoring, database, etc. And make sure the other person is not taking a nap!

## The Hosting Service Formatted the Running Production Server

We told the support technician to format Server A, but he formatted Server B. Unfortunately, Server B was our production database server that ran the whole site.

Fortunately, we had log shipping and there was a standby database server. We brought it online immediately, changed the connection string in all *web.configs*, and went live in 10 minutes. We lost about 10 minutes worth of data because the last log ship from the production to the standby database did not happen.

From now on, when we ask support crew to do something on a server, we remotely log in to that server and eject the CD-ROM drive. We then ask the support crew to go to that box and see whether there is an open CD-ROM drive. This way we could be sure the support crew is on the right server. Another idea is to leave a file named *FormatThisServer.txt* on a drive and inform the support crew to look for that file to identify the right server.

## Windows Was Corrupted Until It Was Reinstalled

The web server's Windows 2003 64 bit got corrupted several times. Interestingly, the database servers never got corrupted. The corruption happened mostly on servers when we had no firewall device and used the Windows firewall only. So, this must have had something to do with external attacks. The corruption also happened when we were not installing patches regularly. Those security patches from Microsoft are really important—if you don't install them in a timely fashion, your OS will get corrupted for sure. Nowadays, we can't run Windows 2003 64 bit without SP2.

When the OS gets corrupted, it behaves abnormally. Sometimes you will see that it's not accepting inbound connections and this error will appear, "An operation on a socket could not be performed because the system lacked sufficient buffer space or because a queue was full." Other times it takes a long time to log in and log off, remote desktop stops working randomly, or *Explorer.exe* and IIS process *w3wp.exe* frequently crashes. These are all good signs that the OS is getting corrupted and it's time for a patch installation.

We found that once the OS was corrupted, there's no way to install the latest patches and bring it back. At least for us, rarely did installing a patch fix the problem; 80 percent of the time we had to format and reinstall Windows and install the latest service pack and patches immediately. This always fixed these OS issues.

Patch management is something you don't consider a high priority unless you start suffering from these problems frequently. First of all, you cannot turn on "Automatic Update and Install" on production servers. If you do, Windows will download patches, install them, and then restart itself. This means your site will go down unexpectedly. So, you always have to manually install patches by taking out a server from the load balancer, restart it, and put it back in the load balancer.

## The DNS Goes Down

DNS providers sometimes do not have a reliable DNS server. GoDaddy was our host and DNS provider. Its hosting was fine, but the DNS hosting was really poor both in terms of DNS resolution time and availability—it went down seven times in two years. When the DNS dies, your site goes down for all new users and for a majority of the existing users who do not have the DNS result cached in a local browser or the ISP's DNS server.

When visitors visit *www.pageflakes.com*, the request first goes to DNS server to get the IP of the domain. So, when the DNS server is down, the IP is unavailable and the site becomes unreachable.

Some DNS hosting companies only do DNS hosting, e.g., NeuStar (*http://www.neustarultraservices.biz*), DNS Park (*www.dnspark.com*), and GoDaddy (*www.godaddy.com*). You should use commercial DNS hosting instead of relying on a domain registration company for a complete package. However, NeuStar was given a negative review in a DNSstuff (*http://www.dnsstuff.com*) test. Apparently, NeuStar's DNS hosting has a single point of failure that means both the primary and secondary DNS was actually the same server. If that's true, then it's very risky. Sometimes this report is given when the DNS server is behind a load balancer, and the load balancer's IP only is available from the public Internet. This is not a bad thing; in fact, it's better to have a load balancer distributing traffic to DNS servers. So, when you consider a DNS hosting service, test its DNS servers using DNSstuff and ensure you get positive report on all aspects. However, if the DNS servers are under load balancers, which means multiple DNS servers are serving a shared IP, then DNSstuff will report negative. It will see the same IP for both the primary and secondary DNS even if they are on different boxes.

When choosing a DNS provider, make sure:

- The IPs of the primary and secondary DNS server each resolve a different IP. If you get the same IP, make sure it's a load balancer's IP.
- The different IPs are actually different physical computers. The only way to do it is to check with the service provider.
- DNS resolution takes less than 300 ms outside the U.S. and about 100 ms inside the U.S., if your DNS provider is in the U.S. You can use external tools like DNSstuff to test it.

## The Internet Backbone Goes Down in Different Parts of the World

Internet backbones connect different countries' Internet together. They are the information superhighway that spans the oceans connecting continents and countries. For example, UUNET is an Internet backbone that covers U.S. and connects with other countries (see Figure 10-9).

There are some other Internet backbone companies, including BT, AT&T, Sprint Nextel, France Télécom, Reliance Communications, VSNL, BSNL, Teleglobe (now a division of VSNL International), FLAG Telecom (now a division of Reliance Communications), TeliaSonera, Qwest, Level 3 Communications, AOL, and SAVVIS.

All hosting companies are either directly or indirectly connected to an Internet backbone. Some hosting providers have connectivity to multiple Internet backbones.

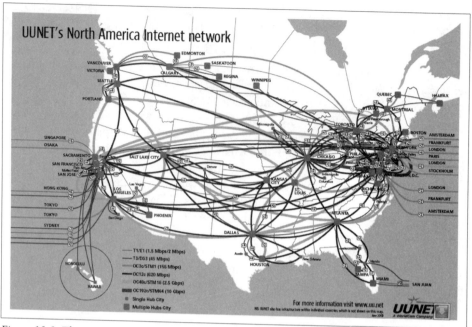

*Figure 10-9. The UUNET Internet backbone covers the U.S. and connects with other countries (source: http://www.nthelp.com/images/uunet.pdf)*

At an early stage, we used an inexpensive hosting provider that had connectivity with one Internet backbone only. One day, the connectivity between the U.S. and London went down on a part of the backbone. London was the entry point to the whole of Europe. So, all of Europe and a part of Asia could not reach our server in the U.S. This was a very rare sort of bad luck. Our hosting provider happened to be on the segment of the backbone that was defective. As a result, all web sites hosted by that hosting provider were unavailable for one day to Europe and some parts of Asia.

So, when you choose a hosting provider, make sure it has connectivity with multiple backbones, does not share bandwidth with telecom companies, and does not host online gaming servers. Both telecom companies and gaming servers have a very high bandwidth requirement. Generally, hosting providers provide you a quota of 1,000 GB per month, but not all companies require that much bandwidth, so multiple companies share a connection to the Internet backbone. Thus, if you and a gaming server are on the same pipe, the gaming server will occupy so much of the shared connection that your site's bandwidth will be limited and you will suffer from network congestion.

The *tracert* can reveal important information about a hosting provider's Internet backbone. Figure 10-10 shows very good connectivity between a hosting provider and the Internet backbone.

```
Tracing route to pageflakes.com [69.5.89.127]
over a maximum of 30 hops:

  1     9 ms      8 ms      9 ms  203.83.162.23
  2    14 ms     10 ms     11 ms  surma.citechco.net [203.191.33.23]
  3    11 ms     11 ms     11 ms  203.112.207.237
  4   203 ms    205 ms    189 ms  pos6-3.ar03.ldn01.pccwbtn.net [63.218.52.105]
  5   331 ms    291 ms    291 ms  pos5-1.br02.ash01.pccwbtn.net [63.218.44.70]
  6   300 ms    351 ms    293 ms  carpathia.ge12-1.br02.ash01.pccwbtn.net [63.218.
94.166]
  7   293 ms    266 ms    265 ms  xe-3-3.e4.iad1.cirn.net [209.222.130.29]
  8   265 ms    266 ms    266 ms  66.117.32.94
  9   265 ms    284 ms    266 ms  hosted.by.cirn.net [69.5.89.127]
```

*Figure 10-10. Tracert to the Pageflakes server from Bangladesh*

The tracert is taken from Bangladesh connecting to a server in Washington D.C. Some good characteristics about this tracert are:

- Bangladesh and the U.S. are in two different parts of the world, but there are only nine hops, which is very good. This means the hosting provider has chosen a very good Internet backbone and has intelligent routing capability to decide the best hops between different countries.

- There is only three hops from *pccwbtn.net* to the firewall. Also, the delay between these hops is 1 ms or less. This proves PCCW Global has a very good connectivity with the Internet backbone.

- There's only one backbone company, which is PCCW Global, so it has a direct connection with the backbone and there's no intermediate connectivity.

Figure 10-11 shows a bad hosting company with bad Internet connectivity.

```
Tracing route to Somebadhosting.com [69.41.160.66]
over a maximum of 30 hops:

  1    35 ms      9 ms      9 ms  203.83.162.23
  2    11 ms     10 ms      8 ms  surma.citechco.net [203.191.33.23]
  3    10 ms     11 ms     10 ms  203.112.207.237
  4   189 ms    189 ms    189 ms  pos6-3.ar03.ldn01.pccwbtn.net [63.218.52.105]
  5   189 ms    191 ms    190 ms  pos11-1.br02.ldn01.pccwbtn.net [63.218.12.182]
  6   292 ms    294 ms    302 ms  g2-0-230.core01.lon01.atlas.cogentco.com [130.117.0.13]
  7   314 ms    315 ms    313 ms  t2-1.mpd02.lon01.atlas.cogentco.com [130.117.2.18]
  8   314 ms    313 ms    314 ms  t4-3.mpd03.jfk02.atlas.cogentco.com [130.117.1.105]
  9   296 ms    308 ms    295 ms  g13-0-0.core02.jfk02.atlas.cogentco.com [154.54.5.233]
 10   320 ms    319 ms    318 ms  p12-0.core01.mci01.atlas.cogentco.com [154.54.3.202]
 11   295 ms    307 ms    295 ms  p14-0.core01.dfw01.atlas.cogentco.com [154.54.3.69]
 12   319 ms    347 ms    319 ms  v3568.na22.b010621-0.dfw01.atlas.cogentco.com [38.20.36.82]
 13   307 ms    305 ms    307 ms  cogent-1.j7r-1.dfw02.Somebadhosting.com [38.104.XX.XX]
 14   306 ms    308 ms    306 ms  v22.c6r-1.dfw02.Somebadhosting.com [XX.41.191.38]
 15   296 ms    308 ms    294 ms  v103.g3k-2.dfw02.Somebadhosting.com [XX.41.191.49]
 16   315 ms    316 ms    305 ms  www.Somebadhosting.com [XX.41.160.66]
```

*Figure 10-11. Example of a tracert showing bad connectivity*

Some interesting characteristics about this tracert include:

- A total of 16 hops and 305 ms latency compared to 266 ms. Therefore, the hosting provider's network connectivity is bad.

- There are two providers: PCCW Global and Cogent. This means the hosting provider does not have connectivity with tier-1 providers like PCCW Global. It goes via another provider to save money and introduce an additional latency and point of failure.

- Two hosting providers were connected to Cogent and both of them had latency and intermittent connectivity problems.

- There are four hops from the backbone to the web server. This means there are multiple gateways or firewalls. Both are a sign of poor network design.

- There are too many hops on *cogentco.com* itself, which is an indication of poor backbone connectivity because traffic is going between several networks to reach the destination web server.

- Traffic goes through five different network segments: 63.218.x.x, 130.117.x.x, 154.54.x.x, 38.20.x.x, and XX.41.191.x. This is sign of poor routing capability within the backbone.

# Choosing the Right Hosting Provider

Our experience with several bad hosting companies provided valuable lessons about choosing the right hosting company. Pageflakes started with very inexpensive hosting providers and gradually went to one of the most expensive hosting providers in the U.S.—Rackspace. They solved SQL Server 2005- and IIS-related problems that we frequently had to solve ourselves. So, when you choose a hosting provider, make sure it has Windows 2003 and IIS 6.0 experts, as well as SQL Server 2005 experts. While running production systems, there's always a possibility that you will have trouble that is beyond your capability. Onsite, skilled technicians are the only way to survive a disaster like that.

However, the problem with such a top-tier hosting provider is the high cost. The reasonable web hosting configuration in Figure 10-1 would cost about $30,000 per month. Be sure to provision your IT budget before you sign with a top-tier hosting company. You don't want to get into a situation where you need the space but don't have the funds to pay for it.

## Checklist for Choosing the Right Hosting Provider

There are a number of issues to be aware of when finding the right hosting provider:

- Test the ping time of a server in the same data center where you will be putting the server. Ping time should be less than 40 ms within the U.S. and around 250 ms from several other world-wide locations including London, Singapore, Brazil, and Germany.

- Ensure there is multiple backbone connectivity and intelligent routing capability that chooses the best hops from different countries. Do tracert from different countries and ensure the server is available to get anywhere in the world within 10 to 14 hops. If your hosting provider is in the U.S., the server should be available within five to eight hops from anywhere else in the U.S.

- Ensure there are only three hops from the Internet backbone to your server. You can verify this by checking the last three entries in tracert. The last entry should be your server IP and two entries back should be the Internet backbone provider. This guarantees there's only one gateway between your server and the Internet backbone. If there are more hops, that means the provider has a complex network and you will waste latency.

- 24×7 phone support to expert technicians. Call them on a weekend night and give them a complex technical problem. If the technician says she is only filling in for the real experts until they get back to the office on Monday, discard the provider immediately. A good hosting provider will have expert technicians available at 3 a.m. on Saturday night. You will usually need technicians late night on Saturday and Sunday to do maintenance work and upgrades.

- Live chat support. This helps immensely when you are travelling and cannot make a phone call.

- Ability to customize your dedicated servers as you want. You do not want to be limited to a predefined package. This will provide an indication of whether they have an in-house technician who can build and customize servers.

- It can provide you all kinds of software, including SQL Server Enterprise edition, Microsoft Exchange 2007, Windows 2003 R2, and Windows Server 2008, once it releases in 2008. If it can't, it probably doesn't have a good software vendor.

- It must be able to provide you with 15,000 RPM SCSI drives and storage area network. If it can't, don't consider this provider. You won't be able to grow your business with a provider if it doesn't have these capabilities.

- Before you set up a whole data center with a hosting provider, make sure you get a server and make it something that you will need in two years. See how fast and reliably they can hand over a server like this to you. It will be an expensive experiment, but if you ever get in involved with a bad hosting provider without doing this, the time and money spent to get out of the contract is much more than the cost of this experiment.

- Make sure the service-level agreement (SLA) guarantees the following:
  — 99.99 percent network uptime. Deduction in monthly rent if there is an outage in the amount of specified time and number of occurrences.
  — Maximum two-hour delay with hardware replacement for defective hard drives, network cards, mother board equipment, controllers, and other input devices.
  — Full cooperation if you want to get out of its service and go somewhere else. Make sure the hosting provider doesn't put you in a lifetime contract.
  — If there is service cancellation, you will be able to delete all data stored in any storage and backup storages.
  — Maximum two-hour delay in responding to support tickets.

This is not an exhaustive list—there are many other scenarios in which things go wrong with a hosting provider. But these are some of the common killer issues that you must try to prevent.

## Choosing a Web Site Monitoring Tool

There are many online web site monitoring tools that ping your servers from different locations and ensure the servers and network are performing well. These monitoring solutions have servers all around the world and in many different cities in the U.S. They scan your web site or do a transaction to ensure the site is fully operational and critical functionalities are running fine.

At Pageflakes, we used WebSitePulse (*www.websitepulse.com*), which was a perfect solution for our needs. We had set up a monitoring system that completes a brand new user visit every five minutes. It called web services with proper parameters and ensures the returned content is valid. This way we can ensure our site is running correctly. We also installed a very expensive web service call in the monitoring system to ensure the site performance is fine. This also gave us an indication whether the site has slowed down or not.

Figure 10-12 shows the response time of the site for a whole day. You can see that around 2:00 p.m. the site was down because it was timing out. Also, from 11:00 a.m. to 3:00 p.m., there's high response time, which means the site is getting a big hit.

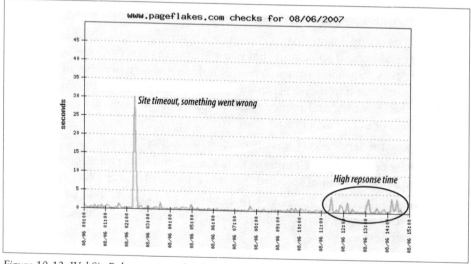

*Figure 10-12. WebSitePulse monitors the site response time and shows high response times*

All these settings give you valuable indications:

- There might be a job running at 2:00 p.m. that produces a very high response time, possibly a full database backup.

- There is a job running at 11:30 a.m. that is causing a high response time or a traffic surge that is causing a site-wide slowdown.

A detailed view (see Figure 10-13) shows the total response time from each test, the number of bytes downloaded, and the number of links checked. This monitor is configured to hit the homepage, find all links in it, and hit those links. It basically visits a majority of the site in one visit on every test and ensures the most important pages are functional.

| Check start | Check end | Status | Total Response time (sec.) | Total Size (b.) | Refs | Failed | Inline | | | External | | Details |
|---|---|---|---|---|---|---|---|---|---|---|---|---|
| | | | | | | | Images | Frames | Other | Links | Other | |
| 08/06/2007 00:02 | 08/06/2007 00:02 | OK | 0.927 | 21,646 | 20 | 0 | 0 | 0 | 0 | 20 | 0 | Details |
| 08/06/2007 00:06 | 08/06/2007 00:07 | OK | 0.260 | 21,646 | 20 | 0 | 0 | 0 | 0 | 20 | 0 | Details |
| 08/06/2007 00:11 | 08/06/2007 00:11 | OK | 0.410 | 21,642 | 20 | 0 | 0 | 0 | 0 | 20 | 0 | Details |
| 08/06/2007 00:16 | 08/06/2007 00:16 | OK | 0.489 | 21,646 | 20 | 0 | 0 | 0 | 0 | 20 | 0 | Details |
| 08/06/2007 00:20 | 08/06/2007 00:21 | OK | 0.585 | 21,646 | 20 | 0 | 0 | 0 | 0 | 20 | 0 | Details |
| 08/06/2007 00:25 | 08/06/2007 00:25 | OK | 0.220 | 21,646 | 20 | 0 | 0 | 0 | 0 | 20 | 0 | Details |
| 08/06/2007 00:30 | 08/06/2007 00:30 | OK | 1.001 | 21,646 | 20 | 0 | 0 | 0 | 0 | 20 | 0 | Details |
| 08/06/2007 00:34 | 08/06/2007 00:35 | OK | 0.227 | 21,646 | 20 | 0 | 0 | 0 | 0 | 20 | 0 | Details |
| 08/06/2007 00:39 | 08/06/2007 00:39 | OK | 0.817 | 21,642 | 20 | 0 | 0 | 0 | 0 | 20 | 0 | Details |

*Figure 10-13. A detailed view shows total response time and details of the check*

Testing the individual page performance is important to find resource-hungry pages. Figure 10-14 shows some slow performing pages.

| URL | Start Time | Total Time | DNS | Connect | First | Last | Status | Size (b.) |
|---|---|---|---|---|---|---|---|---|
| http://www.pageflakes.com/default.aspx | 00:02:15 | 0.9270 | 0.1710 | 0.0470 | 0.4400 | 0.2690 | UP | 21,646 |
| http://www.pageflakes.com/rss/blog.ashx | 00:02:20 | 0.0620 | 0.0000 | 0.0000 | 0.0620 | 0.0000 | UP | 0 |
| http://www.getfirefox.com/ | 00:02:21 | 1.0730 | 0.0000 | 0.1370 | 0.1370 | 0.8000 | UP | 0 |
| http://www.opera.com/ | 00:02:21 | 0.9330 | 0.2090 | 0.1440 | 0.2260 | 0.3530 | UP | 0 |
| http://www.pageflakes.com/PageflakesRegistration.aspx | 00:02:21 | 0.1700 | 0.0000 | 0.0000 | 0.0620 | 0.1080 | UP | 0 |
| http://www.pageflakes.com/Community/Help/Faq.aspx | 00:02:22 | 0.2350 | 0.0000 | 0.0460 | 0.1370 | 0.0520 | UP | 0 |
| http://www.pageflakes.com/Login.aspx | 00:02:22 | 0.2020 | 0.0000 | 0.0470 | 0.1070 | 0.0480 | UP | 0 |
| http://www.pageflakes.com/Community/Pages/Page.aspx | 00:02:24 | 1.8010 | 0.0000 | 0.0470 | 1.6940 | 0.0600 | UP | 0 |
| http://www.pageflakes.com/Community/Content/Flakes.aspx | 00:02:26 | 1.7740 | 0.0000 | 0.0460 | 1.6680 | 0.0600 | UP | 0 |
| http://www.pageflakes.com/Community/Help/Forum.aspx | 00:02:29 | 0.2260 | 0.0000 | 0.0470 | 0.1300 | 0.0490 | UP | 0 |
| http://www.pageflakes.com/Community/ProfileDirectory.aspx | 00:02:29 | 3.6780 | 0.0000 | 0.0470 | 3.5800 | 0.0510 | UP | 0 |
| http://www.pageflakes.com/Community/Help/Blog.aspx | 00:02:30 | 0.2190 | 0.0000 | 0.0450 | 0.1180 | 0.0550 | UP | 0 |
| http://www.pageflakes.com/Community/Help/Support.aspx | 00:02:30 | 0.2310 | 0.0000 | 0.0500 | 0.1250 | 0.0550 | UP | 0 |
| http://www.pageflakes.com/Community/Developers/Documentation.aspx | 00:02:30 | 0.2930 | 0.0000 | 0.0460 | 0.1990 | 0.0480 | UP | 0 |
| http://www.pageflakes.com/Community/Developers/Forum.aspx | 00:02:30 | 0.2500 | 0.0000 | 0.0000 | 0.1400 | 0.1100 | UP | 0 |
| http://www.pageflakes.com/pages/jobs.aspx | 00:02:31 | 0.1580 | 0.0000 | 0.0470 | 0.0610 | 0.0500 | UP | 0 |
| http://www.pageflakes.com/Community/About.aspx | 00:02:31 | 0.4750 | 0.0000 | 0.0470 | 0.3790 | 0.0500 | UP | 0 |
| http://www.pageflakes.com/Pages/webmaster.aspx | 00:02:31 | 0.1600 | 0.0000 | 0.0470 | 0.0620 | 0.0510 | UP | 0 |
| http://www.pageflakes.com/Community/Terms.aspx | 00:02:32 | 0.3340 | 0.0000 | 0.0470 | 0.2360 | 0.0510 | UP | 0 |
| http://www.pageflakes.com/Community/Privacy.aspx | 00:02:32 | 0.1560 | 0.0000 | 0.0510 | 0.0520 | 0.0530 | UP | 0 |
| http://www.pageflakes.com/Pages/press.aspx | 00:02:32 | 0.1670 | 0.0000 | 0.0500 | 0.0610 | 0.0560 | UP | 0 |
| Total: | - | 13.5240 | 0.3800 | 1.0380 | 9.6760 | 2.4290 | - | 21,646 |

*Figure 10-14. Hit individual pages and see their response time. This helps diagnose slow loading pages. The most important factor is the First column, which shows time to first byte (TTFB).*

The "First" column shows the delay between establishing the connection and getting the first byte of response. The time you see there is the time it takes for the ASP. NET page to execute on the server. So, when you see 3.38 seconds, it means the server took 3.38 seconds to execute the page on the server, which is very bad performance. Every hit to this page makes the server have a high CPU and disk I/O; in other words, this page needs to be improved immediately.

By using such monitoring tools, you can keep an eye on your sites 24×7 and look in on your site's performance at different times to see which pages are performing poorly.

# Configuring Proper Performance Counters

You need to keep a close eye on your production servers and monitor their performance all the time. The Windows Performance Monitor tool is a great way to keep an eye on important factors that tell you how well your servers are doing.

Web and database servers require a different set of performance counters. For example, on a web server you need to monitor Request/Sec, Requests in Application Queue, and Request Execution time carefully. These counters tell you how well the web application is doing. On a database server, you need to keep an eye on Transactions/Sec, Lock Wait, Disk Read/Write time, etc.

## Monitoring Web Server Performance Counters

Figure 10-15 shows some common counters that monitor a web server. All these counters give us valuable indications about how well the server is doing.

*Anonymous Requests/Sec*
> Number of requests coming in to the server from anonymous users/sec. Tells you how many users are anonymously browsing the site.

*Cache API Hit Ratio*
> If you are using ASP.NET Cache to store data, it shows the ratio of successful hits to the cache—the higher the value, the better the caching. If it's too low, then you have too many unique things in the cache, and cached data is not being used well, or you are running low in memory and cache cannot store much more data.

*Errors During Compilation*
> If you have more than zero, you have a page on the site that is not compiling— must be a deployment problem.

*Errors During Execution*
> Number of exceptions thrown. A nonzero value indicates a problem in the code.

*Output Cache Hit Ratio*
> If you are using an output cache on page or user controls, it shows how well the output cache is working. The higher it is, the better the output caching.

```
\\SRV224
  ASP.NET Apps v2.0.50727          __Total__
    Anonymous Requests/Sec           48.001
    Cache API Hit Ratio              98.721
    Errors During Compilation             0
    Errors During Execution               4
    Output Cache Hit Ratio           65.789
    Requests In Application Queue         0
    Requests/Sec                    112.002

  ASP.NET v2.0.50727
    Request Execution Time            1343
    Request Wait Time                    0
    Requests Current                    26
    Requests Queued                      1

  Memory
    Pages/sec                        0.000

  PhysicalDisk                     _Total        0 C: E:        1 F:
    % Disk Read Time                 0.000         0.000        0.000
    % Disk Time                      0.285         0.190        0.380
    % Disk Write Time                0.285         0.190        0.380
    Avg. Disk Queue Length           0.006          ----         ----

  Processor                        _Total
    % Processor Time                67.578

  TCPv4
    Connections Established           3230

  Web Service                      _Total
    Anonymous Users/sec            107.002
    Bytes Received/sec           53015.867
    Bytes Sent/sec              244603.000
```

*Figure 10-15. Web server performance monitor configuration*

### Requests in Application Queue

Shows the number of requests waiting in the application queue to be executed. This means users are waiting for requests to execute on the server before they can see anything on the page.

If this is nonzero, then it means:

- You have slow performing pages that are taking too long so the request queue is getting stuck.
- Your server has reached its limit. It cannot execute requests as fast as they come in.
- You have requests that fetch external data and are getting stuck frequently and eating up valuable worker threads.

### Request Execution Time

The time it takes to execute a request in milliseconds, so the higher the value, the worse the performance. If requests are spending more than 300 ms on the server, the delay is going to be visible to the user. If it's higher, then there are some slow performing pages.

*Request Wait Time*

Millisecond requests have to wait before they get executed. Ideally it should be zero.

*Requests Current*

Shows requests currently being executed.

*Requests Queued*

Number of request waiting in the queue. If it's nonzero, then it means the server is choked up and the ASP.NET Request Queue is full.

*Memory: Pages/Sec*

Number of paging the OS is performing from RAM to the Paging file. It should be zero. If nonzero, then it means server needs more RAM or there's too much memory allocation happening. It could be that the server is running too many applications or services.

*Physical Disk*

> *Percent Disk Read Time*
>
> Shows the disk reads happening. If it's 100 percent, it means the disk is working at full capacity. If you have a RAID controller where multiple disks are working, this will show incorrectly and sometimes you will see 300 percent. However, the higher the value it is, the higher the disk activity. If you have high disk activity and your application is not supposed to read that much data from the disk, then you have some problem in your code or there's a program running on the server that is occupying too much disk I/O.
>
> *Percent Disk Write Time*
>
> Same as Disk Read time but it's for disk writes.
>
> *Avg Disk Queue Length*
>
> Number of read/write requests waiting in the controller queue before the controller can perform on the disk. If it's high, then it means the controller cannot handle that much disk activity. Either the controller is bad or you just have too much disk activity due to some problem in your application, or some other application in the server is doing too much disk activity. The solution is to get faster disks or re-engineer the application code to reduce dependency on the disk I/O.

*Percent Processor Time*

Shows how much of the CPU is being used. If it's near 80 percent, it's time for you to get more hardware or tune your application.

*TCPv4 Connections Established*

Number of TCP connections open to your server. If it's too high, then it means too many users are connected to your server at that moment and you might want to load balance the server. You might also want to decrease the value of HTTP Persisted Connection Timeout from IIS Configuration. Persisted connections keep connections open. So, if you see too many open TCP connections, decrease the timeout value. An Ajax application will always benefit from a high timeout value because the more browsers can keep connections open with the server, the less it has to close and reconnect. Remember, Ajax applications are quite chatty. So, the higher timeout value helps browsers keep connections open for a longer period. However, the higher value creates scalability issues because the operating system has a limited number of connections.

### Web Service

#### Anonymous Users/Sec
Shows the number of calls being made to the web services.

#### Bytes Received/Sec
Bytes per second sent to the server from the browser.

#### Bytes Sent/Sec
Bytes per second sent from server to the browsers on web service calls.

## Monitoring Database Server Performance Counters

SQL Server has many performance counters available that can give you a valuable indication about how the database is performing, as shown in Figure 10-16.

| | _Total | 1 C: | 2 D: | 3 E: | 4 I: |
|---|---|---|---|---|---|
| **Memory** | | | | | |
| Pages/sec | 0.000 | | | | |
| **PhysicalDisk** | _Total | 1 C: | 2 D: | 3 E: | 4 I: |
| % Disk Read Time | 2.170 | 0.060 | 6.450 | 0.000 | --- |
| % Disk Write Time | 0.397 | 0.040 | 0.000 | 1.150 | --- |
| Avg. Disk Queue Length | 0.077 | --- | --- | --- | --- |
| Disk Read Bytes/sec | --- | 8193.013 | 73737.113 | 0.000 | --- |
| Disk Write Bytes/sec | --- | 41989.189 | 0.000 | 52742.518 | --- |
| **Processor** | _Total | 0 | 1 | 2 | 3 |
| % Processor Time | 17.578 | 15.625 | 18.750 | 7.813 | 28.125 |
| **SQLAgent:Jobs** | _Total | | | | |
| Active jobs | 0 | | | | |
| Failed jobs | 661 | | | | |
| Job success rate | 96.914 | | | | |
| **SQLServer:Access Methods** | | | | | |
| Full Scans/sec | 87.011 | | | | |
| Page Splits/sec | 0.000 | | | | |
| Table Lock Escalations/sec | 4.000 | | | | |
| **SQLServer:Buffer Manager** | | | | | |
| Buffer cache hit ratio | 99.871 | | | | |
| Page life expectancy | 9336 | | | | |
| **SQLServer:Databases** | PageFlakes117 | | | | |
| Log Bytes Flushed/sec | 52742.518 | | | | |
| Transactions/sec | 39.005 | | | | |
| **SQLServer:Locks** | _Total | | | | |
| Lock Wait Time (ms) | 0.000 | | | | |
| Lock Waits/sec | 0.000 | | | | |
| **SQLServer:Memory Manager** | | | | | |
| Target Server Memory (KB) | 11804128 | | | | |
| Total Server Memory (KB) | 11804128 | | | | |

*Figure 10-16. Performance counters for the database server*

*Memory*

> *Pages/Sec*
>
> > Ideally, it should be zero indicating that there is no paging between the RAM and page file. This means the server had adequate RAM. If it's nonzero for a long period, then you need to add more RAM to server or remove applications or services that consumes RAM.

*Physical disk*

> Just like the web server, the physical disk counters are more important for database servers because the database requires much higher disk activity than web applications. If the Disk Read/Write is too high, then it means you have slow-running queries or a table scan going on. Avg Disk Queue Length indicates how well the controller can handle the load. If it's too high, then you need to get better hard drives or controllers.

*Processor*

> Measures CPU utilization. If it is too high, then there is a slow-running query.

*SQLAgent*

> The SQL Agent comprises:
>
> *Active jobs*
>
> > Number of jobs currently running. If nonzero, then a job is running and if you see high CPU or disk activity, then it means the job is responsible for the slowdown of the server.
>
> *Failed jobs*
>
> > How many jobs failed to execute since SQL Server started. If it's nonzero, a jobs running in the SQL Server Agent is failing. Check each job's log and see what's wrong.
>
> *Job success rate*
>
> > Shows a job's success rate. If not 100 percent, then a job is failing to execute properly.

*SQL Server: Access Methods*

> *Full Scans/sec*
>
> > Number of table scans being performed. If it's nonzero, then you need to optimize your database design by implementing a better index and queries that use a better query plan. However, if you have small lookup tables, SQL Server won't use an index, but instead just scan the whole table. If that happens, do not be alarmed if you see a nonzero value here.
>
> *Page Splits/sec*
>
> > Number of page splits per second that occur as a result of overflowing index pages.

*Table lock escalation/sec*

Number of times the table lock was escalated, which means queries locking the whole table. This is related to the table scan also: the higher the value, the worse the database performance. You need to check your queries and database design to make sure they don't try to lock the whole table. Generally, when you have a query that updates a large number of rows, it's better for SQL Server to lock the whole table instead of locking so many rows one after another.

*SQL Server: Buffer Manager*

*Buffer cache hit ratio*

The percentage of pages found in the buffer pool without incurring a read from disk. The higher the value it is, the faster SQL Server performs. Add more RAM to the server if it's not more than 80 percent.

*Page life expectancy*

Number of seconds a page will stay in the buffer pool without references. The higher the value, the better SQL Server will perform. Increase RAM on the server to increase page life expectancy.

*SQL Server: Databases*

*Log Bytes Flushed/sec*

How much data is being flushed to the disk from logs. The higher it is, the more disk write it requires, which gives an indication to how much INSERT/UPDATE/DELETE activity is going on that makes SQL Server flush logs to disk. It should not be high unless you have a high volume OLTP application. If you suddenly get a large number of new users coming to the site, this counter will show a high value.

*Transactions/sec*

Number of transactions running per second on database. If this value is too high, then you have a chatty web application that talks too much to the database. Your goal would be to minimize it as much as possible because this has direct influence on database server's performance. Better middle-tier caching and reading multiple record sets in one call are two effective ways to reduce database transactions.

*SQL Server: Locks*

*Lock Wait Time(ms)*

Ideally it should be zero, meaning there's no lock that is preventing SQL Server from reading or writing data on tables. If it's nonzero then you have some poor queries that hold a lock on the table and prevent other queries from working on those tables. You might also have too many INSERT/UPDATE/DELETE actions going on, which requires SQL Server to lock rows and forces other queries trying to read/write rows to the same table to wait.

The easiest way to decrease lock wait time is to use "SET TRANSACTION ISOLATION LEVEL READ UNCOMMITTED" on your queries. This will not hold a lock on tables. However, it's a calculated risk because queries will then work on uncommitted transactions that might rollback. For noncritical data, like RSS feeds or a Flick photo XML feed, stored in a database, you can use this isolation level because you don't have to have 100 percent accurate data all the time. Moreover, you can use this on the aspnet_users table because it's unlikely you will have simultaneous parallel updates on the same user's data or that you will have to read a user that was deleted by some other request. Try to use this transaction isolation level as much as possible because it mitigates lock time significantly.

Lock Waits/Sec

Number of operations waiting for locks. If it's nonzero, then queries are waiting because of a bad query holding a lock on tables.

SQL Server: Memory Manager

Target Server Memory (KB)

Shows how much RAM SQL Server would like to allocate. If it's higher than the Total Server Memory, then it means SQL Server needs more RAM.

Total Server Memory (KB)

Shows how much RAM SQL Server is currently using. If it's less than the Target Server Memory, then you have more than enough RAM.

# Summary

In this chapter, you learned about best practices for deploying a high volume web site and how to monitor and maintain the site effectively. You also learned about some real-life challenges that are common to web applications running on dedicated hosting. Finally, you learned how to address some common scalability challenges that are essential to growing your web site from thousands to millions of users.

# Index

## Symbols

@OutputCache directive, 211, 249
_findChildByClass function, 67
_maxAge, 164

## A

ACT (Ajax Control Toolkit), 32
    DragDropManager, 34
    DragPanel extender, 61
    ExtenderControlBase class, 65
Activities, 9, 14
activity model, 113
Add Stuff area, 46–49
AddContentPanel, 47
AddNewTabWorkflow, 123
AddWidget function, 128
Ajax Control Toolkit (see ACT)
Ajax web portals, xii, 1, 3, 4, 10
    inactive user data cleanup, 109–112
AJAXASMXHandler project, 177
AnimationExtender, 48
ApplicationId, 105
applicationname attribute, 200
ASMX handlers, 172–175
    ASP.NET and ASP.NET AJAX handlers,
        compared, 175
ASMXHttpHandler.cs, 177
ASP.NET
    cookie authentication, 219
    fixed IDs for dynamically created
        controls, 54
    key generation, 220

membership tables, queries to, 201–203
    widgets as controls, 13
ASP.NET 2.0 optimization, 200
ASP.NET 2.0 Profile provider, 203–219
    aspnet_Profile_GetProperties, 206–209
    email, using for usernames, 209
    rendering page parts as
        JavaScript, 211–219
    using HttpModule, 216–219
ASP.NET AJAX, 8–9, 10
    extenders, 60–74
        event subscription support, 71
    Framework modification for handling web
        service calls, 175–177
    logout handler implementation, 98
    optimization (see ASP.NET AJAX
        optimization)
    performance, improving, 31–36
        debug mode and release mode,
            compared, 36
        reducing extenders and
            UpdatePanels, 35
        runtime size analysis, 32
        server-side versus client-side
            rendering, 31
ASP.NET AJAX optimization, 152–168
    Ajax server calls, timing and
        ordering, 154–165
    browser stuck with calls in
        queue, 158–161
    caching web service responses on
        browsers, 161–165
    impact of bad calls, 154

## About the Author

**Omar AL Zabir** is the CTO and co-founder of Pageflakes, a Microsoft MVP, the author of a popular .NET blog (*http://msmvps.com/omar*), and a frequent contributor to Code Project (*www.codeproject.com*). In 2006, Pageflakes out-ranked iGoogle, Live.com, Netvibes, and Protopage in a review conducted by Seattle-based SEOmoz.org.

## Colophon

The animal on the cover of *Building a Web 2.0 Portal with ASP.NET 3.5* is a giant green sea anemone (*Anthopleura xanthogrammica*). These anemones are found on rocks in tidal pools, rocky outcroppings, and concrete pilings from Alaska to Panama in intertidal and subtidal zones. The giant green sea anemone varies in size but can reach heights of 30 cm, have a 17 cm base, and a crown or head of 25 cm.

The giant green sea anemone gets its color from green pigment in its epidermis, so the more sunlight it is exposed to, the more green it becomes. This anemone is a solitary and mostly stationary invertebrate from the Cnidaria phylum, which also includes jellyfish. Like a jellyfish, the giant green sea anemone stings its prey with poison tentacles and then draws the food to its mouth. These anemones enjoy a carnivorous diet of mussels, sea urchins, and small fish, and have been known to eat a giant crab in 15 minutes. Clownfish are immune to its stings and often have symbiotic relationships with anemones. Scientists are experimenting with the poison as a cardiotonic to help ailing human hearts.

The enemies of the giant green anemone include starfish, snails, and sea slugs. However, development in coastal areas, pollution, human foot traffic, and harvesting for home aquariums also pose significant threats.

The cover image is from *The Riverside Natural History*. The cover font is Adobe ITC Garamond. The text font is Linotype Birka; the heading font is Adobe Myriad Condensed; and the code font is LucasFont's TheSans Mono Condensed.

# Related Titles from O'Reilly

## .NET and C#

ADO.NET Cookbook

ADO.NET 3.5 Cookbook, *2nd Edition*

ASP.NET 2.0 Cookbook, *2nd Edition*

ASP.NET 2.0: A Developer's Notebook

Building an ASP.NET Web 2.0 Portal

C# 3.0 in a Nutshell, *3rd Edition*

C# Cookbook, *2nd Edition*

C# Design Patterns

C# in a Nutshell, *2nd Edition*

C# Language Pocket Reference

Exchange Server 2007 Administration: The Definitive Guide

Head First C#

Learning ASP.NET 2.0 with AJAX

Learning C# 2005, *2nd Edition*

Learning WCF

MCSE Core Elective Exams in a Nutshell

.NET and XML

.NET Gotchas

Programming Atlas

Programming ASP.NET, *3rd Edition*

Programming ASP.NET AJAX

Programming C#, *4th Edition*

Programming MapPoint in .NET

Programming .NET 3.5

Programming .NET Components, *2nd Edition*

Programming .NET Security

Programming .NET Web Services

Programming Visual Basic 2005

Programming WCF Services

Programming WPF, *2nd Edition*

Programming Windows Presentation Foundation

Programming the .NET Compact Framework

Visual Basic 2005: A Developer's Notebook

Visual Basic 2005 Cookbook

Visual Basic 2005 in a Nutshell, *3rd Edition*

Visual Basic 2005 Jumpstart

Visual C# 2005: A Developer's Notebook

Visual Studio Hacks

Windows Developer Power Tools

XAML in a Nutshell

Our books are available at most retail and online bookstores.

To order direct: 1-800-998-9938 • *order@oreilly.com* • *www.oreilly.com*

Online editions of most O'Reilly titles are available by subscription at *safari.oreilly.com*

# The O'Reilly Advantage

## Stay Current and Save Money